For Race and Country

For Race and Country

*The Life and Career of Colonel
Charles Young*

DAVID P. KILROY

Westport, Connecticut
London

Library of Congress Cataloging-in-Publication Data

Kilroy, David P.
   For race and country : the life and career of Colonel Charles Young / David P.
Kilroy.
      p. cm.
   Includes bibliographical references and index.
   ISBN 0–275–98005–7 (alk. paper)
   1. Young, Charles, 1864–1922. 2. United States. Army—Officers—Biography. 3.
African American soldiers–Biography. I. Title.
U53.Y69K55 2003
355′.0092—dc21   2003046314

British Library Cataloguing in Publication Data is available.

Library of Congress Catalog Card Number: 2003046314
ISBN: 0–275–98005–7

First published in 2003

Praeger Publishers, 88 Post Road West, Westport, CT 06881
An imprint of Greenwood Publishing Group, Inc.
www.praeger.com

Printed in the United States of America

The paper used in this book complies with the
Permanent Paper Standard issued by the National
Information Standards Organization (Z39.48–1984).

10 9 8 7 6 5 4 3 2 1

For Jennette, Ciara, and Liam

Contents

Photo essay follows chapter 5

Introduction

On June 1, 1923, a large military cortege made its way through the heart of Washington, D.C., on its way to Arlington National Cemetery. Thousands of African American citizens, many of them children excused from school for the day to observe the event, lined the streets of the nation's capital to catch a glimpse of the procession. Inside the coffin, draped in the stars and stripes and drawn on an open carriage by four mounted cavalrymen, lay the body of Colonel Charles Young. Young had died one year earlier in Lagos, Nigeria, while visiting from his post as U.S. military attaché in nearby Liberia. His body was exhumed and returned to the United States at the government's expense following concerted pressure from the Black community. By compelling the government and the army to recognize Young's military service in the most elaborate way, his supporters paid fitting tribute to a man who was unquestionably the greatest African American military figure of his generation.[1]

Born to slave parents in Kentucky in 1864, Young was the last of only three African Americans to graduate from West Point in the Reconstruction era. He served his entire military career with the all-Black Ninth and 10th Cavalry regiments, the "Buffalo Soldiers," attaining the rank of colonel by the time of his retirement from active duty in 1917. During his career he served on the western frontier, saw combat in the Philippines, and rode with "Black Jack" Pershing during the "punitive expedition" in Mexico in 1916. He was the first African American to serve as a United States military attaché, first accredited to Haiti and later to Liberia. Young's diverse career included a posting to the Sequoia and General Grant National Parks in California to serve as superintendent and to

Wilberforce University to serve as a professor of tactics and military science.

Young proved himself to be an accomplished officer leading troops in combat in the Philippines, Liberia, and Mexico, while in Haiti and Liberia his intelligence work included mapping both countries for the first time. In the case of Haiti, his work made possible the occupation of the island nation by U.S. Marines in 1915. While in Haiti, he also compiled a French-English-Creole dictionary and added a working knowledge of Creole to his previously acquired proficiency in Latin, French, German, and Spanish. In Liberia, he conducted complex negotiations with the Liberian government and rebel factions in the country's interior, and his reorganization of the Liberian Frontier Force proved instrumental in restoring a degree of stability to the embattled West African republic. At Wilberforce University, he taught French and mathematics, in addition to his duties as professor of military science. On top of his skills as a spy, cartographer, diplomat, and teacher, Young was an accomplished musician and composer, published author, and active member of the Black intelligentsia. He counted among his friends African American notables such as W.E.B. Du Bois and Paul Laurence Dunbar, and corresponded with numerous other figures of national prominence such as Booker T. Washington, Theodore Roosevelt, and John J. Pershing.

While his exemplary professional record and extraordinary personal attributes were widely touted in the Black press, the majority of those people who lined the streets of Washington, D.C., that warm June day to see the colonel's body pass en route to Arlington Cemetery probably remembered him most for the controversy surrounding his retirement in 1917. With American entry into World War I and the mobilization of the American expeditionary force offering the probability of accelerated promotion, Lieutenant Colonel Young, fresh from notable service in Mexico, looked set to earn a general's star. However, when medical examiners found him physically unfit for promotion and recommended his retirement, a maelstrom of controversy erupted.

Charges of racism were levied against the army and the White House by those who felt that the medical board's findings were a ruse to avoid the eventuality of an African American officer attaining the rank of general and thus challenging the racial dogma of the incapacity of Blacks for leadership. To the Black community the army's decision to remove Young from active service was an act of grave injustice. In the eyes of his supporters Young had dispelled any doubt about his physical fitness by completing a well-publicized 497-mile horseback ride from his home in Wilberforce, Ohio, to Washington, D.C. It was this final act of bravery in a career characterized by dogged persistence in the face of racism and prejudice that leant a heroic air to Young's funeral. Fittingly, and no doubt by design, the procession came to a halt at the tomb of the Unknown Soldier in Arlington National Cemetery. Here the body was lowered from the catafalque and laid to rest with full military honors in the American military's most hallowed ground. The United States government, albeit in the face of consistent lobbying of the Republican administration by the Black constituency, honored Charles Young in death in a manner that it had deemed impossible in life.

The history of Young's life transcends the fields of military, diplomatic, and African American history and offers a guided tour through one of the most important epochs in the American experience, from the end of the Civil War to the emergence of the United States as a world power during the First World War. It is a story that highlights the African American struggle to make the quantum leap from slavery to citizenship. Like all Black Americans of his generation, Young had to live with the reality that Reconstruction had failed to meet the expectations it had aroused. Indeed, Young's lifetime saw a marked decline in the fortunes of African Americans as the promise of emancipation was swept away at the end of the nineteenth century by Jim Crow in the South and a deep-rooted racism that permeated most aspects of American society. Few institutions better illustrate the prevalence of racism in turn-of-the-century America than the United States Army.

Charles Young's career from beginning to end was shaped by the color of his skin. His assignments were always carefully chosen to deal with what his superiors saw as an anomaly, a Black officer in a White man's army. Young, along with the only other Black commissioned officers in the army at the time, John Alexander, John E. Green, and Benjamin O. Davis, was shuffled between the Ninth and 10th Cavalry, in Haiti, Liberia, and Wilberforce. Just as the army was always careful to station its four Black regiments in isolated posts, so too was it anxious, wherever possible, to keep its Black officers segregated from their White counterparts. When given the opportunity to serve in the field, however, Young was able to strike a few blows at the notion that Black men were incapable of providing effective leadership, an idea that was prevalent in the U.S. Army at the time.

Young saw his career as an opportunity to demonstrate to society at large that African Americans were deserving of the rights granted them under the 14th and 15th Amendments. As a soldier, he was utterly diligent in his observance of duty and loyal to the core to the United States. As a citizen, he was committed to the cause of Black civil rights. He clearly saw himself as part of what his good friend and confidant W. E. B. Du Bois dubbed the "Talented Tenth," the African American elite whose charge it was to demonstrate to White America the capabilities of Blacks if given a level playing field. At times Young found that maintaining a dual commitment to race and country was a strain, but for much of his career he

was able to compartmentalize his beliefs and loyalties. The bitter experience of his retirement and the Black experience during World War I, however, convinced him of the need to be more proactive in the cause of civil
rights. He carried the burden of his race with him throughout his career.
For Charles Young, success was more than a personal desire; it was his
obligation to the African American people. In his mind, personal failure
had equally widespread implications. Young's ultimate goal was to attain
the rank of general. Thus, his forced retirement on medical grounds in
1917 was a crushing blow.

    This book represents a modest beginning at resurrecting Charles Young
from the margins of American history. The Library of Congress contains
three works dealing with the life of Charles Young. Abraham Chew's
deceivingly titled *A Biography of Colonel Charles Young* is essentially an
obituary published as a pamphlet in 1923. Robert E. Greene's *The Early Life
of Colonel Charles Young* is a 1973 master's thesis from Howard University
published by the university in its original form. Expanding on his thesis,
Greene, himself a retired army officer, published at his own expense
Colonel Charles Young: Soldier and Diplomat in 1985. Based largely on
Young's military records, *Soldier and Diplomat* presents a detailed
overview of Young's life and career, but what it offers in terms of factual
narrative it lacks in contextual analysis and critical perspective. Another
important shortcoming of Greene's biography is his sources. While
Greene made extensive use of military records, neither the Young Collection at the National Afro-American Museum and Cultural Center in
Wilberforce, Ohio, nor the Young Papers in the private Coleman Collection were then available. Furthermore, Greene overlooked some important manuscript collections, such as the papers of W. E. B. Du Bois and Joel
E. Spingarn, that contain significant materials on Young. While there are a
number of monographs and articles on the role of African Americans in
the military in general that offer valuable insight into Young's historical
significance, this study offers the most comprehensive critical overview of
his life and career to date.[2]

To a large extent, Young's place on the margins of history reflects the relative lack of attention given by historians to the African American military
experience in this country. There are of course notable exceptions, but for
the most part the history of the Black soldier and officer has been confined
to the realms of popular history. Lacking a detailed critical study of his life
and career, Young's record has become infused with inaccuracies. This is in
large measure due to the fact that Young's image was steeped in legend
from early in his career. From accounts placing him in the thick of the
action on San Juan Hill in 1898 to the facts surrounding his retirement in
1917, it is often difficult to separate fable from fact in the story of Charles
Young. It is, nonetheless, a story worth telling when stripped of the myths.[3]

This books aims to provide a comprehensive biography of Charles Young, based on extensive archival research, and promises to fill a significant void in African American, and for that matter American, history. One possible reason that Young has received so little attention from scholars, while Black military contemporaries such Benjamin O. Davis, Sr. and Henry Osian Flipper have been the subjects of considerable study, is the nature of the sources. The Charles Young Papers at the National Afro-American Museum and Cultural Center in Wilberforce, Ohio, contain only a smattering of his correspondence, and the collection is largely confined to materials from 1917 to his death in 1922. Materials in the W. E. B. Du Bois papers, the Ripley Museum, the United States Military Academy Archives, Wilberforce University, the Moorland-Spingarn Research Center at Howard University, and the Fort Huachaca Museum help fill in some of the gaps in the evidence, but there are still many important questions left unanswered. In addition to tracking down all the above sources, I had the great fortune to discover during the course of my research a private collection that constitutes a veritable treasure trove of Charles Young material. The Coleman family collection was acquired when Young's grandchildren auctioned off the contents of the family home in Wilberforce before selling the house in 1981. The collection, which to this point has not been accessible to scholars, contains a large volume of Charles Young's personal and official correspondence, diaries, memorabilia, original verse and music, and a wealth of material pertaining to his life and career gathered by his wife and son after his death. It represents the richest single source of any I have encountered and has proved to be a critical asset in the task of divorcing fact from fiction in the life of Charles Young.[4]

Young's legendary stature among Black Americans in the early twentieth century has too long been overlooked. He was awarded the Spingarn Medal for service to his race by the NAACP in 1915, an organization on whose board of directors he would serve after 1918. African Americans openly mourned his death across the country, and his funeral had all the trappings of a presidential burial. From Colonel Young Park in Harlem to Colonel Charles Young Square in Cleveland, there are numerous elementary schools, American Legion Posts, city parks, private clubs, and city streets throughout the United States named in his honor. They are small but significant memorials to Young's importance as an early pioneer in the struggle for civil rights.

In recent years Charles Young has been the focus of renewed public attention. The Internet has provided an outlet for this resurgence of interest in Young, carrying with it, however, all the flaws of the medium. A lobbying group composed largely of Black officers and veterans has been formed to secure Young's posthumous promotion to general, while another group is campaigning to build a memorial for him in Cleveland. The Atlanta Buffalo Soldiers reenacted his famous ride from Wilberforce to Washington in 1994, and the Omega Psi Phi fraternity, of which Young was a member, is working with the Afro-American Museum and Cultural Center in Wilberforce to convert his house into an African American military history museum. He has been the subject of numerous recent newspaper articles from Maysville, Kentucky, to Cleveland. In 1999 he was inducted into the Military Intelligence Hall of Fame and, perhaps most notably, on May 25, 2001, Senator Mike Dewine of Ohio introduced Senate Resolution 97 IS honoring the Buffalo Soldiers and, specifically, one of the all-Black regiments' "most distinguished heroes, Colonel Charles Young, for his lifetime achievements." The bill cites Young "as a shining example of the dedication, service, and commitment of the Buffalo Soldiers."[5]

The Dewine resolution, and the Young revival in general, must be seen as part of a larger recent trend aimed at restoring what has long been the tarnished image of African Americans in the military. This reevaluation process began in earnest with the elevation of General Colin Powell to the chairmanship of the Joint Chiefs of Staff and his emergence as a figure of national prominence during the Gulf War. During the Clinton administration a number of posthumous promotions, medals, and pardons were granted to African American soldiers whose careers and reputations had been sacrificed on the altar of race prejudice. The Dewine resolution is part of this ongoing process of recognizing the achievements of Black soldiers and officers who served in the era before desegregation of the armed forces.

I have many people to thank for assistance during the long investigative process, chasing down leads on the life and career of Charles Young. Much of the research for this book was made possible by grants from the West Virginia Humanities Council (1997), Appalachian College Association (1998), and Wheeling Jesuit University (1997, 1999, 2002). The following people were particularly helpful in tracing information at their institutions and offering suggestions on other avenues I might explore: Floyd Thomas, Sue Parker, and Isabel Jasper (National Afro-American Museum and Cultural Center), Jim Finley (Fort Huachaca Museum), Walter Hill (National Archives), and Susan Lintelman (United States Military Academy Archives). I would like to thank the staff at the following institutions for their assistance and expertise: the Library of Congress, National Archives I (Washington, D.C.), National Archives II (College Park, Md.), the United States Military History Institute, the Moorland-Spingarn Research Center at Howard University, Hillman Library at the University of Pittsburgh, Houghton Library at Harvard University, Wilberforce University Library, the Ohio State Historical Society, the Kentucky Historical Society, the Greene County (Ohio) Historical Society, the Mason County (Kentucky) Historical Society, and the Ripley (Ohio) Museum. I am grateful to Dave Loney for giving me permission to visit his property—the cabin where Young was born is still standing there—to Brian Shellum for sharing some of his research on Young, to John Motley for sending me copies of some Young material from his extensive African American military history collection, to Katie Cox for her technical expertise in formatting the pictures for this book, and to the staff at Wheeling Jesuit University Library for accommodating my many interlibrary loan requests. I owe a special debt of gratitude to Malina and Jill Coleman for contacting me with information about Young materials in their possession, welcoming me into their home for two memorable days spent sifting through their wonderful collection, and for the many hours Malina devoted to scanning documents and pictures for me during and after my visits. Finally, and most important, I would like to thank my family: my father and mother, Michael and Kathleen, for their prodding and encouragement and critical feedback on an early draft, and my wife, Jennette, for her support, encouragement, and endless patience.

NOTES

1. Abraham Chew, *A Biography of Colonel Charles Young* (Washington, D.C., 1923), 11.

2. Ibid.; Robert E. Greene, *The Early Life of Colonel Charles Young, 1866–1889* (Washington, D.C., 1973); Robert E. Greene, *Colonel Charles Young: Soldier and Diplomat* (Washington, D.C., 1985); Marvin E. Fletcher, *The Black Soldier and Officer in the United States Army, 1890–1917* (Columbia, Mo., 1974); Claude A. Clegg, "'A Splendid Type of Colored American': Charles Young and the Reorganization of the Liberian Frontier Force," *The International Journal of African Historical Studies* 29 (winter 1996): 47–70.

3. In addition to Fletcher, *Black Soldier and Officer,* for general history of the African American military experience, see for example Bernard Nalty, *Strength for the Fight: A History of Black Americans in the Military* (New York, 1986).

4. Davis and Flipper have both been the subjects of scholarly biographies. Marvin Fletcher, *America's First Black General: Benjamin O. Davis, Sr., 1880–1970* (Lawrence, Kans., 1989); Jane Eppinga, *Henry Ossian Flipper: West Point's First Black Graduate* (Plano, Tex., 1996).

5. U.S. Congress, Senate, *A Bill Honoring the Buffalo Soldiers and Colonel Charles Young,* S.R. 97 IS, 107th Congress, 1st Session, 2001.

CHAPTER 1

Up from Kentucky

SONG OF RESURGENCE

The footsteps of God in the garden
Of the sad Negro-heart were heard
As it crooned a De Profundis
And hearkened His wonderful word:

Yes! Come to me, oh my children,
My arms they are loving and strong,
I have heard your prayers and complaining
And the wail of your sorrow-song!

Because ye lived blameless, my children,
Were meek and were helpful and kind
In a world where ruled pride and oppression,
I have breathed in your foes a new mind!

Arouse ye! Arise, oh my children,
I have ransomed your prisoned soul
And broken your bonds of proscription
Turned to singing your grief and your dole!

And ye are now men and are brothers,
Upstanding and valiant free:
In a world for the weak ye shall battle
For Right against Might and for me!

Then come to me, oh my children,
My arms they are loving and strong,
I have heard your sighing and crying
And the plaint of your sorrow-song!

The Centuries' dark sons who have suffered
Broke forth in a rousing refrain,
All singing: Resurgam! Resurgam!
Dear God, we now rise again!

—Charles Young

The town of Ripley, Ohio, sits perched on the north bank of the mighty Ohio River 52 miles upstream from Cincinnati. The bluffs that rise behind the town provide an expansive view of the rolling hills of northern Kentucky to the south. In 1866 the family of Charles Young, then 14 months old, made the short trip north to Ripley from the little hamlet of Mayslick, Kentucky. Although it was a journey of just 20 miles, Gabriel and Arminta Young's decision to move north would have profound implications for their infant son's future. In 1866 Ripley and Mayslick were worlds apart. Although the advance of the railroad had already heralded the decline of Ripley's heyday as a thriving river town, it still offered a more urban and industrial alternative to the rural environs of Mayslick. More important for the Youngs, Ohio offered Blacks an opportunity to escape the legacy of slavery in post–Civil War Kentucky. That brief journey north was the first of many critical episodes in Charles Young's life, a life spent endeavoring to prove that the son of former slaves could and should be admitted into the full fellowship of U.S. citizenship.

Gabriel Young and Arminta Bruen were both born into slavery. They married on the large veranda of the home of James Willet, Arminta's owner, in Mason County, Kentucky, in June 1864 when Arminta was 25 and Gabriel was 23. Three months earlier, on March 12, Arminta had given birth to their only child, Charles, in their two-room log cabin just outside Mayslick, "where the vermin and the rain either ruined their few precious belongings or worried them to their wits end." Charles entered the world not only in poverty but also against the backdrop of enveloping war between the northern and southern states. He was among the first born of a new generation of African Americans that would come of age in a society in which slavery did not exist. The institution that had kept his forebears in bondage for generations was already disintegrating in the state of Kentucky when Charles drew his first breath.[1]

After flirting with neutrality in the initial stages of the Civil War, Kentucky remained firmly committed to the Union throughout the rest of the conflict. The conservative Unionist Coalition in control of Kentucky's state government, however, resisted all federal policies designed to undermine the institution of slavery in the state. The Lincoln administration, for its part, proved reluctant to upset the antebellum order in Kentucky. Instead, it was the process of enlisting Black men into the Union army that brought the institution of slavery to an end in the state. By 1864 Washington had overcome the objections of White Kentuckians and had begun to enlist slaves for military service on a widespread basis. Slaves who enlisted became freemen, and by 1865 the federal government had consented to emancipate their dependents also. With nearly 60 percent of all eligible Black males in Kentucky serving in the Union army, slavery had all but ceased to exist in the Bluegrass State well before it was officially ended by the ratification of the Thirteenth Amendment.[2]

According to Charles Young, his father was a "runaway slave." A family history prepared by Charles's son indicates that Gabriel's first attempt to join the ranks of Union troops stationed in Maysville was thwarted when his master rode into camp and demanded his return, but in 1865 he eventually achieved his goal and enlisted with the United States Colored Troops (U.S.C.T.). His motivation was clear, the prospect of freedom for himself and his family. Like most of the other 178,000 African American troops who served in the Civil War, 23,703 of whom were Kentuckians, Gabriel Young no doubt desired to strike a blow at the institution of slavery and earn the rights of citizenship through military service.[3]

In February 1865 Gabriel enlisted as a private in Company F, Fifth Regiment, United States Colored Heavy Artillery, commanded by Captain James H. Johnson. Throughout his one year of service, the Fifth U.S.C.T. Heavy Artillery served garrison duty at Vicksburg, Mississippi, assigned among other tasks the duty of clearing the battlefield of skeletons. In February 1866 Gabriel Young earned an honorable discharge and 17 years later he was awarded a disability pension on the basis of partial deafness resulting from a concussion sustained during target practice in the summer of 1865. Disability pensions were available largely because of the efforts of the Civil War veterans group the Grand Army of the Republic (GAR). GAR, one of the first groups to pioneer the modern art of lobbying, fought doggedly for federal spending on pensions in the last quarter of the nineteenth century. Gabriel Young, like thousands of other Union veterans, was an active member.[4]

Gabriel Young's status as a Civil War veteran was an integral part of his identity as a freeman. He maintained close ties with a number of the men he had served with in the war and developed a close bond with other veterans through GAR in Ohio. His year of service in the Union army proved to be of lasting significance for his son. Gabriel's discharge notice, signed by Lt. Colonel L.S. Long, recommended him to the public at large as faithful, reliable, trustworthy, and honest and noted that he was a thorough soldier and a gentleman. Late in his life, Charles revealed this document to be one of his "dearest treasures." He remembered his father proudly as a man "whose heart glowed with love of country, liberty, and civic duty…[who] taught me my patriotism, [which] with us…was no fair weather word." These values became hallmarks of Young's life as both a civilian and a soldier, principles forged in the relationship between father and son. Charles Young cherished his roots as the son of former slaves and of a man who made a sacrifice to ensure a future free of bondage for his family. As a soldier, he prized the "heritage of honor" he enjoyed as the son of a "Grand Army man," and he would strive throughout his career to uphold this legacy "as an officer, for my family and [for my] race."[5]

Buoyed with the hope of emancipation and the promise of Reconstruction, the Youngs left their slave cabin in Mayslick behind and journeyed north across the Ohio River to Ripley. So many slaves had made this journey under cover of darkness in the past, crossing the frozen river on foot in the winter or in the boats of northern abolitionists in the warmer months. Before the Civil War, Ripley had been an important stop on the Underground Railroad ferrying runaway slaves north to Canada. Ripley abolitionists such as John Rankin and John Parker assisted the escape of hundreds of slaves in the decades before the Civil War, including the celebrated Eliza featured in Harriet Beecher Stowe's *Uncle Tom's Cabin*.[6]

Although Gabriel and Arminta Young made the journey in June 1866 as free people, like the slaves who had traveled the Underground Railroad, they were escaping. For free Blacks, postwar northern Kentucky held little promise beyond a life of sharecropping on the tobacco farms of former slave owners. Ripley on the other hand still held the promise of a busy river town, a center of commerce and industry where upward mobility was possible for those willing to work for it. Ripley offered hope for a new beginning for the Youngs and their infant son that would have remained out of reach were they to stay in Mayslick. His parents' experience as emancipated slaves seeking to forge a new life in post–Civil War America would leave a lasting impression on Charles. One of his core convictions as an adult was that Blacks who had toiled so hard to escape the legacy of slavery should not be expected to settle for anything less that "full manhood rights" as free people in America. Charles devoted much of his life to fighting the handicap of slavery that prevented the free Black man from holding his head high lest he be "condemned for his pride." A family anecdote recorded after his death related how Charles had once met "the old family mistress of slave day times" on a train in Kentucky. When she asked why he had not stayed with them in Mayslick, Young bowed and responded "Madam, I am not always your obedient servant."[7]

As was the case with almost all former slaves, Gabriel Young was illiterate. Using what skills he had acquired as a slave, he was nonetheless able to provide successfully for his family. In Ripley he entered the livery business, a trade he would ply for the rest of his life. The Youngs lived in "a neatly kept little white home" with a small adjoining barn on 2nd Street and became active members of the First Baptist Church in Ripley. Young would later remember his childhood with fondness, recalling the good times he shared with his mother and father in the "old Ripley days" when they strove to ensure that he had an education and the opportunity to "be a boy." On Sundays Charles would attend church with his grandmother Julia, who taught him to read and write, and read him stories from the Bible. His evenings were filled with his father's stories of "brave deeds" and "devotion on the field of battle." He attended the colored elementary school two blocks from his home on 4th Street, where he was an excellent student and impressed his teachers as a child of considerable promise. His academic prowess was equally in evidence at Ripley's integrated high school where, at age 17, he earned the highest academic rank in the graduation class of 1881. Charles's forte was in the study of foreign languages, an interest he would pursue for the rest of his life.[8]

While best remembered for his military career, Charles Young always exhibited a strong tendency toward intellectual pursuits and would at various times in his life adopt the role of educator. Education was clearly valued by his parents. This may have been especially true of his mother's side of the family, as Julia Coleman Bruen, his maternal grandmother, is reputed to have been one of the first Black teachers in Kentucky and was Charles's first mentor. Upon completing high school, Young was hired to teach arithmetic, grammar, spelling, reading, history, geography, and American literature at the colored elementary school. For two years he taught the Black children of Ripley "with great credit to himself and to the entire satisfaction of his patrons." With his first paycheck he purchased a plain gold ring for his mother and thereafter his salary enabled her to give up her sideline as a seamstress. In addition to education, Charles's great passion in life was music. The first musical instrument he learned to play was a melodeon that his father had purchased using "the proceeds of compost hauling and garden plowing, a sideline in the livery business." Charles quickly mastered the instrument and was soon "playing for Sunday school at the A.M.E. church and for both Sunday school and church services at the Baptist church." He would later learn the violin, and his mother would teach him to play the piano, an instrument he brought with him to every post he traveled to in the latter stages of his military career.[9]

While teaching at the elementary school, Young continued his own education with the assistance of the renowned Ripley abolitionist John Percival Parker. Parker was a former slave who bought his own freedom and settled in Ripley in 1849. By the 1860s Parker had become a successful businessman, the owner of a thriving foundry and blacksmith's shop. By the early 1880s Parker's business ventures were flourishing and he was a comparatively wealthy man. Young was a regular visitor to Parker's com-

fortable home on Front Street and spent many hours reading in his extensive library. This relationship provides one of the earliest indications of the
charisma and charm that would endear Young to so many people through
the course of his life. Parker was notoriously suspicious of people and
admitted few strangers into his home. He clearly saw something in young
Charles that convinced him to become the boy's mentor.[10]

By taking Young under his wing, Parker was continuing his earlier
efforts to counteract the evil effects of slavery. Before the Civil War Parker
had been a leading member of the close-knit abolitionist community in
Ripley, opening his home on numerous occasions to fugitive slaves, at
great personal risk. Following emancipation, Parker remained conscious
of the difficulties faced by African Americans and the limitations placed
on them by the legacy of slavery and the prejudice of White society. He
deliberately sought out Black buyers for his products and was conscious
of his role as a racial pioneer by obtaining patents for machines such as a
soil pulverizer and a tobacco press. By opening his home and his library to
this son of former slaves, Parker was acting out a larger mission to
advance the cause of his race. Parker's influence on Young is probably best
illustrated by the fact that Young would later collect an extensive library of
his own and his home in Wilberforce would become a hive of intellectual
activity and artistic endeavor. Young also inherited from Parker a philosophy that held a Black intellectual elite to be essential to the cause of racial
uplift, a belief shared by many other educated Blacks in the Victorian era.
Anxious to do his part, Young eagerly took on the role of mentor to
numerous young Black men through the years, whether students at
Wilberforce or soldiers under his command.[11]

Young's education also benefited greatly from the interest of his former
elementary school principal, James T. Whitson. Not only did Whitson hire
his former pupil as a teacher, but he also encouraged him to take classes in
Latin and Greek at Xavier University in Cincinnati. It was Whitson who in
1883 called Young's attention to an advertisement in the local Ripley
newspaper concerning examinations for the United States Military Academy to be held in Hillsboro, Ohio. However, it was Young's father who
was most instrumental in convincing his son to take the exam. Successful
admission into West Point offered Young the chance to earn a college education at the government's expense and a professional career in the United
States Army. A person from Young's socioeconomic background did not
easily ignore such opportunities. After overcoming his mother's initial
reluctance to see him embark on a career in the military, Young traveled
with his father to Hillsboro to take the exam.[12]

Of the 12 young men who took the competitive exam for the 12th District of Ohio, Young received the second highest score. There are conflicting accounts concerning the fate of the candidate who received the highest
score. According to some versions, he failed the preliminary examinations

at West Point in December 1883 and was instructed to return to Ohio. This rendering of events has Young traveling to West Point as the first alternate and succeeding where the principal had failed. Another source, however, contends that the principal, one Oswin Wells Lowry, also of Ripley, chose to attend the Naval Academy, thus opening the door for Young. In either event, it was 20-year-old Charles Young who was named the official nominee for Ohio's 12th District by Congressman Alphonso Hart on April 29, 1884. He received his official acceptance in May and was ordered to report to West Point on June 10. Congressman Hart wrote, encouraging him not to delay his departure and allaying his fears that two bad teeth might imperil his chance of passing the physical exam, and so on June 4 he said goodbye to his parents and left the small river town that had been his home for 19 years. The *Ripley Bee* reported his departure, and on behalf of its readership wished "Charley success in his new undertaking."[13]

Charles Young became only the ninth African American to be admitted to the United States Military Academy. These young men were the advance guard of a generation set to test the commitment of the United States to uphold the principle of the Reconstruction amendments to the Constitution that ended slavery and granted the freed slaves the rights and privileges of citizenship. Gabriel and Arminta Young had done their part to ensure that their son enjoyed the opportunities afforded by emancipation. Charles's entry into West Point served to vindicate their decision to move north. Ripley provided him with an education sufficient to enable him to prevail in the academy's highly competitive entrance exam. As a member of the postslavery generation, however, Charles would face significant new challenges of his own. The first 20 years of his life encompassed a period of remarkable transformation for Blacks in the United States. However, by 1884 the apogee of Reconstruction optimism had long since passed, and racial discrimination was an increasingly prevalent factor in the lives of African Americans. Charles Young entered West Point at a time when the plight of Black Americans was about to enter a tragic, new phase.

NOTES

1. Charles Noel Young, "Biography of Charles Young," Coleman Collection, Akron, Ohio. Charles Noel began writing a biography of his father in the 1950s but completed only a rough manuscript of his early life. Material for the biography came from documents in the family's possession, observations written by Charles's wife, Ada, shortly after her husband's death in 1922, and recollections gathered through the years from relatives. Some of the material in this document is contradicted by other sources, such as Pension and Service Records, which I deem more reliable. Therefore, when in doubt, I have erred on the side of official records; Pension Records for Gabriel Young, Old Military and Civil Records, National Archives, Washington, D.C. [hereinafter Gabriel Young Pension Records]

2. Eric Foner, *Reconstruction: America's Unfinished Revolution, 1863–1877* (New York, 1988), 8, 36–37; Victor B. Howard, "The Civil War in Kentucky: The Slave Claims his Freedom," *Journal of Negro History* 67 (autumn 1982): 245–56.

3. Charles Young to Atlee Pomerene, 30 August 1918, Coleman Collection; Charles Noel Young, "Biography of Charles Young," Coleman Collection; of these 178,000 Black troops, 144,000 came from slave states. See Joseph T. Glatthaar, *Forged in Battle: The Civil War Alliance of Black Soldiers and White Officers* (New York, 1990) National Park Service, Civil War Soldier and Sailor System, http://www. itd.nps.gov/cwss/ [hereinafter NPS CWSS].

4. Gabriel Young Pension Records; Charles Noel Young, "Biography of Charles Young," Coleman Collection; NPS CWSS; Greene, Robert E. *Colonel Charles Young: Soldier and Diplomat.* (Washington, D.C., 1985); Nancy Gordon Heinl, "Charles Young," in *Dictionary of American Negro Biography,* ed. Rayford W. Logan and Michael R. Winston (New York, 1985), 677–79 [hereinafter DANB].

5. Charles Young to Atlee Pomerene, 20 August 1918, Coleman Collection.

6. Ibid.; John B. Parker, *His Promised Land: The Autobiography of John B. Parker, Former Slave and Conductor on the Underground Railroad,* ed. Stuart Seely Sprague (New York, 1996); Eliese Bambach Stivers, *Ripley, Ohio: Its History and Families* (Ripley, 1965).

7. Charles Young Diary, Part I, Coleman Collection; Miscellaneous notes on the life of Charles Young, Coleman Collection; Notes from a speech, n.d. [1919], Coleman Collection.

8. Charles Young to Atlee Pomerene, 20 August 1918, Coleman Collection; Charles Young to Arminta Young, 11 May 1919, Coleman Collection; Charles Noel Young, "Biography of Charles Young," Coleman Collection; "Cavalry Ride Commemorates Famous Ripley Military Officer," *Ripley Bee,* 28 April 1994; Clipping in Charles Young File, Ripley Museum, Ripley, Ohio; John H. Purnell, "Colonel Charles Young, U.S.A.: Soldier, Diplomat, Philanthropist, Man of Culture," *The Oracle* (winter 1979): 5–8. Purnell served under Young in the Ninth Ohio Battalion during the Spanish-American War and remained acquainted with him through the Omega Psi Phi fraternity.

9. M. A. Broadstone, ed., *History of Greene County, Ohio: Its People, Industries, and Institutions* (Indianapolis, 1918), 948; Greene, *Soldier and Diplomat;* Stivers, *Ripley,* 189; High School Grade Book, n.d., Uncataloged Boxes, Charles Young Papers, National Afro-American Museum and Cultural Center, Wilberforce, Ohio [hereinafter Young Papers Uncataloged]; Charles Noel Young, "Biography of Charles Young," Coleman Collection; "The Desert and the Solitary Place," Notes on the life of Charles Young by Ada Young, 1922, Coleman Collection.

10. Purnell, "Colonel Charles Young" 5; Parker, "Promised Land."

11. Parker, "Promised Land," 10, 79.

12. Robert E. Greene, *The Early Life of Colonel Charles Young, 1864–1889,* (Washington D.C., 1973), 8–9; Extracts from Colonel Charles Young's Military Record, Correspondence Regarding the Black Soldier, 27 August 1966–8 February 1977, Marvin Fletcher Collection, U.S. Military History Institute, Carlisle, Pa. [hereinafter Fletcher Collection]. Young's full military record was destroyed in the 1974 fire at the National Archives repository in St. Louis. Young's son, Charles Noel,

mailed the document in the Fletcher Collection to Marvin Fletcher during the latter's research on Black soldiers and officers in the Old Army.

13. Greene, *Early Life*, 9–10; *New York Times*, 1 September 1889, 6; Purnell, "Colonel Charles Young," 5; *Historic Homes of Ripley* (Ripley, n.d.); Alphonso Hart to Charles Young, 10 May 1884, Coleman Collection; *Ripley Bee*, 4 June 1884.

CHAPTER 2

Alone at West Point

Of the nine African Americans who entered the United States Military Academy after the end of the Civil War, Charles Young was the third and last to complete the program and receive his stripes. Young's graduation in 1889 ushered in a 47-year interregnum before the next African American graduated from West Point in 1936. These years mark the nadir of the experience of African Americans as free citizens of the United States. The promise and hope of Reconstruction gave way in the 1890s to a "Bourbon" reaction in the South that ushered in the era of Jim Crow segregation. Although the same kind of legal restrictions were not imposed on African Americans north of the Mason-Dixon Line, the North, by turning its back on the abrogation of civil rights in the South and the violent culture that upheld it, effectively acquiesced in the process. In fact, a pall of racism descended over the whole country in the last decade of the nineteenth century and the first decade of the twentieth, stifling the limited gains made by Black Americans after the end of the Civil War.

Against this backdrop of deepening prejudice, Young's status as one of only three Black graduates from West Point became a mark of distinction and a source of pride among the African American community in this era. His very survival at West Point was cause for admiration and became one of the defining events of his life and career. Although he was immensely proud of his achievement, Young remembered his years there as among the most difficult of his life. He would later advise a young Black man contemplating taking the West Point exam that "going through the Military Academy means a dog's life while you are there." At West Point, Young was ostracized by many of his peers and professors and subjected to constant racial slurs and hostility. That he endured this ordeal alone, bears testimony to the fortitude and dignity that would win him so much admiration through the years from all those, both Black and White, who knew him well. While at West Point he would develop the outward steely calm that served as his defense against prejudice for the rest of his life.[1]

The United States Military Academy at West Point was established in 1802 to train officers for the United States Army. From the beginning, it was seen by critics as a center of military aristocracy, unwarranted in a democratic republic. It became the focal point of further criticism during the Civil War because many of the officers of the Army of the Confederacy, including Robert E. Lee, were graduates of the United States Military Academy. West Point survived the ravages of sectionalism and emerged from the Civil War determined to uphold its tradition. However, a new issue arose during the Reconstruction era that would focus national attention on the academy and bring renewed charges of elitism. The controversy centered on the desire of young Black men, some of whom were former slaves, to enter the ranks of the all-White officer corps. For West Point, which was based on tradition and heritage, this was a monumental challenge.[2]

Like the other eight young Black men who preceded him at West Point, Charles Young was in the advance guard of Reconstruction. These men tested the limits to which White America was willing to accept the amended Constitution and the rights it granted African Americans. Passing through the gates of West Point, they entered the very heart of the old order and challenged its patrician administrators to demonstrate their commitment to the increasing inclusiveness of American democracy. With so much at stake, it is hardly surprising that both supporters and detractors monitored the education of the young Black cadets with great interest. As Young would often later acknowledge, from this point on, he carried with him, in addition to his own hopes and ambitions, the burden of his race.[3]

The first African American to graduate from West Point was Henry Osian Flipper. The four Blacks who had preceded him either failed the physical examination required of incoming cadets or had fallen prey to the system of demerits and continual examination designed to ensure that only those individuals best suited to army life survived the grueling four-year process. During Flipper's tenure at the academy, two other Black cadets, James Webster Smith and John Washington Williams, were dismissed. Williams, who entered in 1884, was found deficient on the semi-annual exam during his first year and sent home. Smith, whose case gained significant attention because of a physical altercation with White cadets who had been taunting him, was dismissed following his failure in one exam at the end of his third year at the academy. While the manner in which Smith and Williams were dismissed was wholly consistent with the traditional method of reducing numbers at the academy, to African American observers and critics of West Point it appeared that no Black cadet would ever be permitted to graduate from the institution.[4]

Flipper put to rest that fear in 1877 when he received his diploma and assumed the rank of second lieutenant in the United States Army. Despite Flipper's profession not to become a cause célèbre in the struggle for Black equality, his autobiographical account of life at West Point published in 1878 added much fuel to the fire of controversy surrounding the military academy's treatment of its Black cadets. Flipper was a firm believer in the strict code of conduct and the system of cadet hierarchy prevalent at West Point and he aspired, beyond everything else, to be accepted as a gentleman and an officer. Although Flipper closely identified with West Point's aristocratic culture, his book betrays a pattern of racism among the officers, professors, and cadets. Subjected to four years of ostracism in which his peers and superiors spoke to him only in the course of drill or instruction, he experienced bouts of depression and loneliness. Worse still for Flipper, were the racial slurs and slights his fellow cadets often subjected him to. Most galling of all was the commonly occurring instances in which he was denied the privileges due him as an upperclassmen just to satisfy the prejudice of a junior cadet. Flipper dismissed those cadets who refused to sit by him in chapel or to fall in beside him in formation as lacking in the qualities of proper gentlemen. Yet, despite his efforts to portray such episodes as exceptions to the rule, Flipper acknowledged a pattern of "ill-treatment of colored cadets" at West Point.[5]

Flipper joined the 10th Cavalry, one of four Black regiments in the U.S. Army, following his departure from the academy in 1878. Nicknamed the "Buffalo Soldiers" by the Native Americans whom they fought, the Black troopers and White officers of the Ninth and 10th Cavalry compiled a distinguished record of service in the American West during the Indian wars. Flipper, the first Black commissioned officer to serve with either regiment, quickly earned the recognition of his superior officers during the pursuit of Victorio and his Mescalero Apaches across Texas, New Mexico, and Arizona in 1879.[6]

Despite this promising beginning, Flipper's army career came to an ignoble and early end when he was court-martialed and dismissed from the service in 1882. The charges against Flipper stemmed from the fact that his accounts came up short while he served as post commissary, a problem not uncommon for young, inexperienced officers. Although cleared of the primary charge of embezzlement, Flipper was convicted of "conduct unbecoming an officer and a gentleman." The case caused outrage among African American leaders, who believed Flipper had been forced out to preserve the lily-White nature of the officer corps. Although he went on to have a successful career in engineering, Flipper would devote much of his life to the fruitless attempt to clear his name.[7]

The sense of injustice African Americans felt following Flipper's court-martial was intensified in 1880 by the experience of another Black cadet at West Point, Johnson C. Whittaker. Whittaker had been admitted to the academy in 1876, a year before Flipper's graduation. Like the Black cadets who had preceded him, he suffered through a lonely existence at West Point during which his fellow cadets made abundantly clear their antipathy toward his presence. Once Flipper graduated in 1887, Whittaker's only social interaction was with the Black servants on the post.[8]

One morning in the spring of 1880, Whittaker failed to appear for drill. A search of his room found the Black cadet lying unconscious, tied to his bed. The scene had all the appearances of a hazing incident, a practice that, despite the disapproval of successive superintendents, had become increasingly common in the years after the Civil War. Though their initial inclination was to accept Whittaker's claim that his fellow cadets had assaulted him, West Point authorities soon came to doubt his version of events. After a brief inquiry, Whittaker was charged with faking the incident and called before a court-martial. The trial, because of the widespread public attention it attracted, thrust the debate over the place of Black cadets at West Point onto a national stage. In June 1881 the court-martial returned a verdict of guilty against Whittaker and he was dismissed from the academy. The highly circumstantial nature of the evidence against the Black cadet offered ammunition to those who alleged that the military academy and the United States Army were bending the rules to avoid integration.[9]

With the dismissal of Johnson Whittaker, West Point was without a Black cadet for the first time in 10 years. All the Black cadets to this point had gained entry through the system of congressional appointment, beneficiaries of the efforts of Republican congressmen in the South and their Reconstruction agenda. In 1877, however, President Rutherford B. Hayes made his infamous compromise with the Democrats, which resulted in the Republican Party virtually abandoning the field in the South and turning its back on the more radical elements of Reconstruction, in particular, the promotion of racial equality. With admission to the military academy based increasingly on competitive examination, those hostile to the presence of African Americans at the institution rejoiced that West Point would never again have to accommodate a Black cadet. The *Army and Navy Journal* reprinted a letter to a southern newspaper in which the author gloated that West Point was secure as African Americans were distinctly lacking in the "qualifications to insure success" in the competitive exam, and just as Flipper "had no predecessor...so he will have no successor on the role of graduates."[10]

The hollow rhetoric of such triumphal racism was soon exposed, however, when, in 1883, a Black teenager named John Hanks Alexander, a student from integrated Oberlin College, beat out his White rivals to finish first in the competitive exam for Ohio's 14th Congressional District. Alexander was reduced to the rank of first alternate, however, on the grounds that he was physically unfit, and Congressman George W. Geddes offered the appointment instead to Morrison Waite, son of the chief justice of Ohio. This move aroused considerable suspicion, and Alexander's supporters determined to send him to West Point nonetheless to take the preliminary entrance exam. When he passed and Waite failed, the academy had little choice but to welcome another Black cadet.[11]

Alexander faced all the same prejudice and hostility experienced by his predecessors. He was nonetheless determined to graduate, and throughout his years at West Point he consistently performed in the top half of his class. Academic performance was only half the battle, however, as he was the target of consistent criticism from the cadet officers charged with maintaining order and discipline at the academy. These officers had the power to issue demerits to a cadet whose conduct was deemed deficient. A roll of merit was kept for each class, and if a cadet earned 200 or more demerits in a given year he could be found deficient in conduct and dismissed from the academy. The records for his class indicate that during his four years at the academy, Alexander consistently received more demerits than his classmates. His demerits were earned for offenses such as "smiling in ranks," answering "boisterously" or "inaudibly" to mess hall roll call, "marching unsteadily," and "not depressing his toes while marching" to the dining hall. Designed to promote rigid discipline, the demerit system was by its nature harsh and exacting, but in Alexander's case it appears to have been applied more strictly than usual.[12]

Alexander's graduation in 1887 meant the U.S. Army once again had a Black officer among its ranks. He was assigned to the Ninth Cavalry and served in various posts in the West before receiving orders to assume the role of military instructor at Wilberforce University, a Black college in Ohio. Wilberforce had been added to the list of schools in which U.S. Army officers on detached service conducted military training. Tragically, his life and career came to an abrupt end in 1894. At the age of 30, while sitting in a barber's chair in Springfield, Ohio, he died of apoplexy. Alexander's untimely death, together with Flipper's court-martial, meant that, until his death in 1922, Charles Young would maintain the unique status of being the only Black West Point graduate in the officer corps of the United States Army.[13]

The experience of Flipper, Whitaker, Alexander, and the others did nothing to soften the academy's hostility toward Black cadets. Major General John D. Schofield, the superintendent of West Point from 1876 to 1881, made clear his position on the matter in his annual report in 1880: "To send to West Point for four years competition a young man who was born in slavery is to assume that half a generation is sufficient to raise a colored man to the social, moral, and intellectual level which the average

White man has reached in several hundred years. As well might the common farm horse be entered in a four-mile race against the best blood inherited from a long line of English racers."[14] Schofield had initially been somewhat sympathetic to the plight of the Black cadets, but his views were tempered by the storm of public criticism he faced over his handling of the Whittaker affair. Nonetheless, such an opinion was hardly unique in late-nineteenth-century America. In fact, Schofield's perspective fairly accurately portrays the thinking of the majority of White Americans at the time on the issue of race relations. By exploding the myth of racial hierarchy, the success of Flipper, Alexander, and Young, challenged the comfortable assumptions of White society. However, the accomplishments of the young Black cadets appeared only to anger their detractors, who responded by burying their heads deeper in the sand.

Flipper, Whittaker, Alexander, and the other Black cadets had pioneered the course that Charles Young would now travel. Young no doubt was privy to their stories and would benefit from their experiences. He would be doubly fortunate in the fact that Alexander was at the academy when he arrived in 1884 and so as a plebe he could benefit from the third classman's advice. Young's experience, however, would be no less difficult than that of the men who had gone before him; if anything it would be more so. A third African American cadet at West Point at this time, W. A. Hare, who flunked out after one semester, observed that Alexander was more popular with the other cadets than Young. Hare noted that his own position was mitigated by the fact that he was fair complexioned. The fact that Young was darker than both Hare and Alexander might have contributed to his greater isolation.[15]

Young turned 20 during his first year at the United States Military Academy; lacking both the college experience of Alexander and the aristocratic temperament of Flipper, he appeared ill fitted for life at West Point. Most of the Black cadets who had gone before him were handpicked and groomed by radical Republican politicians and Black leaders according to their perceived abilities to meet the particular challenges of the academy. Young was arguably the first Black cadet to enter West Point without an influential patron or the backing of a constituency anxious to advance the cause of civil rights. Charles Rhodes, a classmate of Young's, formed an initial impression of the Black cadet as "a rather awkward, overgrown lad, large boned and robust in physique, and of a nervous, impulsive temperament." Although Young impressed his fellow cadets with his talent as a pianist and his proficiency in classical and modern languages, he was not fully prepared for the rigors of a West Point education, with its heavy emphasis on mathematics and engineering.[16]

Young first began to experience academic difficulty during his second semester at the academy. While he excelled in the humanities, finishing in the top third in his class in English and French, mathematics proved to be his Achilles' heel. Although he was studious, his instructor noted that he had "little aptitude" for the subject. His inability to pass mathematics brought his first year at West Point to a very disappointing close. In June 1885 he was declared deficient and turned back to repeat the year. He would now join the class of 1889. That first year took its toll on Young, and he wrote his parents that he was unhappy at the academy, but his father "refused to think of such weakness" and persuaded his son to see it through. Charles did not disappoint and in his second year he improved his scores in English and French, passed the dreaded mathematics, and ranked 17th overall in a class of 75 cadets. The decision not to quit West Point after the first year was a vital moment in Charles Young's life. Thereafter, he got stronger with each adversity he faced and was determined not to leave before graduation. Photographs of him in his cadet uniform portray an impressive figure whose countenance exudes confidence and self-assurance, and who shows no sign of being awkward or nervous, as Rhodes remembered him. He caught the attention of a young tactical officer named John J. Pershing, who noted that he was "an earnest, studious cadet." That first year at West Point was the last time in his life that he had serious doubts about his own ability and strength.[17]

Courage and equanimity were prerequisites for any Black cadet who wished to graduate from West Point. The practice of ostracism that the White cadets had begun with the admission of the first Black cadet continued unabated during Young's years at West Point. He was more fortunate perhaps than some who had gone before him in that a number of other African Americans attended the academy during his years there, thus mitigating the isolation that had been such a cause of torment for Flipper. However, the companionship of other Black cadets that Young enjoyed was short lived. Alexander's graduation in 1887 and the failure of the other Black cadets to survive their first years meant that Young endured long periods at West Point in virtual solitude.[18]

Unwelcome in the rooms of White cadets, unable to attend the hops that highlighted the social calendar, and excluded from the conversation that flowed freely in the mess hall, Young was compelled to find other outlets to lift the burden of his loneliness. His proficiency in foreign languages proved useful in that regard, as he was able to converse with the German-born shoeblacks who worked at the academy. He also spent many hours drawing, one of the courses required for third-year cadets, and produced, among other works, an excellent likeness of Prince Louis Napoleon of France, who visited the academy in 1886. Such visits helped to break the monotony of cadet life, and so must have been particularly welcomed by Young. In addition to receiving Napoleon, West Point played host during Young's time to other dignitaries such as Queen Liliuokalani of Hawaii,

Prince Kamatsu of Japan, and Crown Prince Wilhelm of Germany. Mark Twain, who resided in nearby Connecticut, was a regular visitor, delighting the cadets with his nonchalance as he sauntered around "smoking an old corn cob pipe."[19]

Young also used his creativity to fight back against the racism and hazing he endured at the hands of the other cadets. Although West Pointers liked to downplay the incidence of hazing at the academy, the abuse of plebes was widespread, verbally, physically, and psychologically. Servility toward upperclassmen was an established tradition, and verbal abuse and physical intimidation were accepted methods of instilling discipline. While the orchestrated ostracism of Black cadets ironically tended to spare them the worst excesses of West Point hazing, they were nonetheless subject to routine racial abuse. Young reportedly responded to such mistreatment by composing ballads in French or English. Whenever he was on the receiving end of an act "calculated to gall him," he would sing his composition "to the heavens at a time when its sharp wit would carry home."[20]

Such boldness on Young's part infuriated his tormentors. According to one account, a fellow cadet took umbrage at Young's defiance and responded by questioning, within earshot of Young, the chastity of the Black cadet's maternal forebears. Young's "suavity" in the face of such abuse had earned him the respect of some of the White cadets, one of whom now came to his defense. The cadet in question realized that Young could not take the risk of defending his honor in the traditional fashion and so he challenged the offender to a bare-knuckle duel himself. The fight took place in the predawn hours of a Sunday morning behind old Fort Clinton. Stripped to the waist, Young's defender beat his adversary into submission and forced an apology for the insult against the Black cadet. The story illustrates the depth of Young's dilemma; his only remedy for answering insults was by proxy.[21]

His classmate, Charles Rhodes, contended that through "his dog-like perseverance," Young slowly but surely won increasing admiration from his fellow cadets. Each year he "gained ground" with his peers and by his fifth year, "his own class began to acknowledge and respect his finer traits of character." As a result, many of the cadets began "to treat Young with the kindness and consideration which had long been his due." Young later confided in a classmate, "While West Point was pretty hard pulling...the roughness was relieved" by the kindness demonstrated by a few of the cadets. The "friendship and sympathy" he received from a small number of classmates left a lasting impression on Young. West Point convinced him of the value of mentorship, and through the course of his life Young took on this role, mentoring students at Wilberforce, troopers in the cavalry, volunteers in the Spanish-American War, and several young men he encountered in the Philippines, Haiti, and Liberia. In a letter to one of these sympathetic cadets written late in his career, Young confided that the occasional words of cheer he received at West Point had significantly reinforced his faith in the prospect of racial tolerance and shaped his sense of service to others. He came to see service as "the true test of leadership."[22]

While the incidence of harassment and abuse may have subsided somewhat toward the end of his years as a cadet, it did not disappear. Even in his final year he was subjected to petty insults arising from the racial prejudice of the other cadets. When Cadet Captain George Langhorne, one of the handful of cadets friendly to Young, assigned him a place at a dining hall table "to which his scholarship entitled him," enough cadets protested to compel Langhorne to relegate Young to a lower table. Here Cadet Morris Barrol protested in such vociferous terms that Langhorne took insult and challenged him to a fistfight. Unable to defend his own honor, Young had to swallow hard and stoically endure such painful episodes. Incidents like this left Young with bitter memories of the "heartaches" he endured at the academy.[23]

There would be one final bitter pill for Young to swallow before he earned his commission in the army. When, on June 9, 1889, to the air of "Auld Lang Syne," the class of '89 marched before a thousand spectators in front of the old library to receive their diplomas, Cadet Charles Young was not among them. He had been found deficient in engineering, and thus he was not allowed to graduate. He was, however, granted three months by the academic board to make up the deficiency. His plight won sympathy from some of his classmates. Rhodes, for one, made a diary note of his hope that Young would "get through...[as] it would be a terrible disappointment for him to the lose the coveted diploma, after five years of intensive work." Having "narrowly escaped being dropped from the rolls" on account of his failure in engineering, Young now worked doubly hard to secure his diploma. He was fortunate in that the instructor who had failed him, Lieutenant George W. Goethals, who would go on to earn distinction for his work on the Panama Canal, "sacrificed his vacation" and agreed to tutor him over the summer. Goethals would later recall that his "sympathies were aroused" by Young's plight. Young took full advantage of Goethal's "disinterested" concern and in August 1889 overcame his deficiency in engineering.[24]

There were no speeches and marching bands to celebrate Charles Young's graduation from West Point. He graduated alone and last in a class of 49 cadets. Nonetheless, this would prove to be one of the crowning achievements of his life. With the death of Alexander and the court-martial of Flipper, he became the "only Negro West Point graduate now in the army." With the door to West Point effectively closed to African Americans in the early twentieth century, this distinction took on increasing significance with each passing year. To Black Americans struggling to disprove theories of racial inferiority that confined them to the status of second-class citizens, Charles Young's achievement was one of the utmost significance. The importance of the event was noted in a *New York Times* story under the heading "Another Colored Officer." Young had entered the lion's den and emerged bloodied, but alive.[25]

Eulogizing his close friend, W. E. B. Du Bois wrote, "No one knew the truth about the Hell he went through at West Point. He seldom even mentioned it. The pain was too great." Du Bois attributed his friend's success at West Point to his self-discipline, giving as an example an instance in which a southern cadet refused to take food from a dish passed first to Young. Young calmly ignored this snub, let the White cadet serve himself first, and then took the dish. Such acts of self-discipline, Du Bois notes, were critical to Young's success in forging a career in an institution in which he faced constant "insult and intrigue."[26]

Young left West Point convinced that discipline held the key to the success of African American efforts to overcome prejudice and discrimination. Through the years, Young earned a reputation as a strict disciplinarian among the Black troops under his command. He believed that he was not just training them as soldiers; he was also preparing them for life. Young maintained that "Negro youth need discipline worse than anything else" to succeed in life. Men under his command occasionally resented Young's heavy emphasis on discipline, and some critics charged that he perpetuated the image of the "subservient Negro" by ingratiating himself to White officers. Young, however, believed that giving in to the temptation to strike back at his antagonists would do more harm than good to the cause of racial equality. A court-martial and a truncated career would provide fodder for those inside and outside the army who claimed that a Black man did not have the stuff to make a good officer. Only by enduring in the face of hostility could Young prove the fallacy of such opinions. His goal was not simply personal success; he was motivated by a certainty that his success would help advance the cause of his race.[27]

Fortitude in the face of adversity was only the most visible manifestation of the effect on Young of five years spent at the military academy. Despite the many "heart-aches" he endured, Young eagerly embraced the "many advantages" that the academy had to offer. The West Point motto "duty, honor, country" formed the bedrock of his worldview. While Young traced the roots of his patriotism to his father's service in the Civil War, at the United States Military Academy he developed a deep commitment to serve "the country that educated me." His deep sense of American nationalism and his unqualified support for American imperialism were both products of his military education. Young embraced the opportunities that West Point afforded him, and it was here that the intellectual parameters of his world were firmly established.[28]

NOTES

1. Charles Young to Clarence Smith, 15 January 1919, Charles Young Papers, National Afro-American Museum and Cultural Center, Wilberforce, OH [hereinafter Young Papers].

2. See Henry Osian Flipper, *The Colored Cadet at West Point: Autobiography of Lieutenant Henry Osian Flipper, U.S.A.*, ed. Quintard Taylor, Jr. (Lincoln, Neb., 1998), xiv; Sidney Forman, *West Point: A History of the United States Military Academy* (New York, 1950), 135; Stephen Ambrose, *Duty Honor Country: A History of West Point* (Baltimore, 1966), 231–38; George S. Pappas, *To the Point: The United States Military Academy, 1802–1902* (Westport, Conn., 1993), 353–419.

3. Charles Young to W.E.B. Du Bois, 20 June 1917, W.E.B. Du Bois Papers, University of Massachusetts, Amherst, Mass. [hereinafter Du Bois Papers].

4. Flipper, *Colored Cadet*, xv–xvi.

5. Ibid., 106–7, 135–36, 143–44, 216.

6. Ibid., xx–xliv.

7. Charles L. Kenner, *Buffalo Soldiers and Officers of the Ninth Cavalry, 1867–1898: Black and White Together* (Norman, Okla., 1995), 284; Flipper, *Colored Cadet*, xx–xliv. The campaign to clear Flipper's name continued long after his death and reached a successful conclusion in 1999 when the Clinton administration overturned the decision of the court-martial and awarded Flipper an honorable discharge.

8. John F. Marszalek, *Assault at West Point: The Court-Martial of Johnson Whittaker* (New York, 1984), 38–43.

9. Ambrose, *Duty, Honor, Country*, 219–231; Marszalek, *Assault at West Point*, 237–55.

10. *Army and Navy Journal* 26 (August 1882): 71.

11. Kenner, *Buffalo Soldiers and Officers*, 293–295; Willard B. Gatewood, "John Hanks Alexander of Arkansas: Second Black Graduate of West Point," *Arkansas Historical Quarterly* 41 (summer 1982): 117.

12. Ibid., 295–296; Forman, *West Point*, 54.

13. Kenner, *Buffalo Soldiers and Officers*, 297–298; Gatewood, "John Hanks Alexander," 126.

14. Quoted in Flipper, *Colored Cadet*, xv.

15. Gatewood, "John Hanks Alexander," 119–120.

16. Charles D. Rhodes, "Charles Young," *Fifty-Third Annual Report of the Association of Graduates of the United States Military Academy, 1922*, 152.

17. Merit and Conduct Rolls, United States Military Academy Archives, West Point, New York [hereinafter USMA]; "The Desert and the Solitary Place," Notes on the life of Charles Young by Ada Young, 1922, Coleman Collection; Rhodes, "Charles Young," 152; John J. Pershing, testimony collected on the life of Charles Young by Harry Atwood, Coleman Collection, Akron, Ohio.

18. Rhodes, "Charles Young," 152; Kenner, *Buffalo Soldiers and Officers*, 297.

19. Rhodes, "Charles Young," 153; Greene, Robert E. *The Early Life of Colonel Charles Young, 1864–1889.* (Washington, D.C.), 1973; Charles D. Rhodes, "Diary Notes of a Soldier," USMA.

20. E.H. Lawson, "One Out of Twelve Million: Unrevealed Facts in the Life Story of Col. Charles Young, West Pointer," *Washington Post*, 26 May 1929, 11.

21. Ibid.; Kenner, *Buffalo Soldiers and Officers,* 301–302.

22. Rhodes, "Charles Young," 153; Charles Young to Delamare Skerett, 26 July 1915, Charles Young File USMA; Charles Young to Captain Alexander Piper, 26 July 1915, reprinted in Patricia W. Romero, *I Too Am an American: Documents from 1619 to the Present* (New York, 1968), 190; Charles Young Diary, Part II, Coleman Collection.

23. *Cleveland Gazette,* 16 February 1889, 2; Charles Young to Colonel Delamare Skerett, 26 July 1915, Young File USMA.

24. Rhodes, "Diary," 23–25; Rhodes, "Charles Young," 154; Charles Young to Colonel Delamare Skerett, 25 July 1915, Young File USMA; George Goethals to Ada Young, 8 May 1922, reprinted in Romero, *I Too Am an American,* 190; Charles Noel Young, "Biography of Charles Young," Coleman Collection.

25. "Here Is a List of Colored Men Who have Studied at West Point," *Cleveland Gazette,* 8 April 1916, 1; *New York Times,* 1 September 1889, 6.

26. W. E. B. Du Bois, "Charles Young," *The Crisis* (February 1922).

27. Charles Young to Benjamin O. Davis, 5 May 1905, Benjamin O. Davis Papers, U.S. Military History Institute, Carlisle, Pa. [hereinafter Davis Papers]; Charles Young to Benjamin O. Davis, 28 August 1905, Davis Papers; Letters to the editor of the *Cleveland Gazette* from members of the Ohio Ninth Volunteer Battalion, reprinted in Willard B. Gatewood, *"Smoked Yankees" and the Struggle for Empire: Letters from Negro Soldiers, 1898–1902* (Urbana, Ill., 1971), 110–121.

28. Charles Young to Delamare Skerett, 26 July 1915, Young File USMA; Charles Young to Atlee Pomerene, 20 August 1918, Coleman Collection.

CHAPTER 3

Black Officer in a White Army

In 1889 when Charles Young graduated from West Point, the United States Army had approximately 28,000 men in uniform, roughly half the size of the Belgium army and one-twentieth the size of the army of France. After the Civil War the United States government had drastically decreased the size of its armed forces. During that war a million men had served in the Union army alone, but in 1866 Congress reduced the size of the peacetime army to 54,302 officers and men. Four years later, in 1870, with the country returning to stability and the prospect of renewed conflict increasingly unlikely, Congress once again reduced the size of the army, this time setting the limit at 30,000.[1]

French escapades into Mexican politics aside, the United States faced no serious military threat from its neighbors. The army's primary role after the Civil War was to police the expanding western frontier and crush the resistance of the Indian tribes west of the Mississippi. The Indian wars, 1865 to 1890, were characterized by an intermittent series of campaigns and isolated skirmishes, which, although at times stretched available forces to the limit, never posed a serious offensive threat to the United States. The modest size of the U.S. Army was thus determined by limited need. It was, however, also wholly consistent with the customary U.S. antipathy toward large standing armies in peacetime.

As part of its reorganization of the army in 1866, the U.S. Congress created six segregated regiments of Black soldiers, the Ninth and 10th Cavalries and the 38th, 39th, 40th, and 41st Infantries. Although close to two hundred thousand Blacks had served in the Union army, influential figures within the military and without were hesitant to accept a permanent role for Black troops in the peacetime army. The new Black regiments came into existence largely at the insistence of the radical Republicans in Congress, who pushed the measure as part of their overall strategy for postwar Reconstruction. In 1869 the four Black infantry regiments were consolidated into the 24th and 25th, leaving a total of four Black regiments in the streamlined army. With more than two thousand men in uniform, Blacks thus made up 10 percent of the strength of the army in the years leading up to the Spanish-American War of 1898.[2]

While the army had no official policy mandating different treatment for its Black and White troops, the pattern of evidence indicates the practice was otherwise. Prevailing opinions in army circles held that Black troops were less capable than their White counterparts, better suited to warmer climates, and effective soldiers only when under the supervision of White officers. An early indication of racial discrimination in the postwar army occurred in 1866, when Commanding General Ulysses S. Grant drew the line at adding a Black artillery regiment on the grounds that only Whites were capable of performing such highly technical duty. Evidently Grant was oblivious to the fact that many such Black artillery units, including Gabriel Young's regiment, had contributed to his success in leading the Union army to victory over the Confederacy. These Civil War veterans, together with the Black troops who served with distinction during the Indian wars, provide sufficient counterevidence to demonstrate the fallacy of the army's racial orthodoxy. Racial stereotyping in the military, however, did not abate. In fact, it became even more pronounced as the country fell prey to the heightened prejudice of the Jim Crow era in the 1890s.[3]

Given the fact that the inferiority of Black soldiers was a generally accepted principle among the army brass, the notion of a Black officer defied all reason. The army simply did not entertain such an idea before Henry Flipper's graduation in 1877. In all, there were eight Black commissioned officers in the army between 1866 and 1898, all of whom served with the four Black regiments. Five of these officers were chaplains, and so did not hold positions of command. The three officers of the line, Flipper, John Alexander, and Young, however, posed a serious threat to the White monopoly of the officer corps and the sanctity of the army's racial dogma.

Flipper's court-martial and Alexander's untimely death left Young alone to face the onerous responsibility of overcoming fellow officers' resistance to the presence of a Black man among their ranks. On top of the usual pressures faced by a green officer embarking on a career in the army, Young came face-to-face early on with the culture of prejudice that permeated every pore of the institution. Young was closely monitored by supporters and detractors alike, so the lessons of West Point were reinforced from the beginning of his career; success or failure would have more than purely personal consequences. Despite the considerable obstacles he faced, Young remained resolute in his desire to succeed and do his part to explode the myth of the inferiority of the Black soldier.

Having received his diploma from the military academy in August 1889, Charles Young returned to live with his parents and await orders. While he was away at West Point his mother and father had moved from Ripley to Zanesville, fifty miles east of Columbus. Perhaps compelled to move during the depression of the late 1880s, which hit burgeoning Black entrepreneurs particularly hard, his father endeavored to establish himself in the livery business in his new hometown. The family had been struggling even before Charles left for the academy, relying on his modest teacher's salary to repair and maintain their Ripley home, but the sale of this house was sufficient to purchase a modest home on Putman Avenue in Zanesville. When Charles began drawing his salary as an army officer he paid to have a barn constructed and to have the Zanesville house painted. In addition to the financial relief he was now able to provide them, his achievement at West Point must in all probability have come as a great source of pride for his parents, these former slaves from Kentucky. The proud father of a newly commissioned officer in the United States Army, Gabriel Young no doubt was not averse to singing his son's praises to his fellow Civil War veterans at regular meetings of the GAR chapter in Zanesville.[4]

For Charles, however, the exultation of receiving his diploma was quickly tempered by a controversy concerning his first assignment that highlighted the difficulty his presence would pose for the army command. Having grown up around horses and having survived the rigorous riding instruction at West Point, Young was keen to join the cavalry. Assigned initially as an additional second lieutenant to the 10th Cavalry, he bought his uniform and waited for a vacancy to open up. To his surprise, however, he received notice in October that he had been transferred to the 25th Infantry. A perturbed Young immediately contacted the Adjutant General's Office and earnestly requested a transfer to a cavalry regiment. Young protested that he had already incurred considerable personal expense outfitting himself for the cavalry and that "naturally having a knowledge of horses," he was called to this branch of the service where he believed he would "be able to do more real good."[5]

The difficulty in meeting Young's assignment request stemmed partly from the fact that there were not enough positions available to accommodate all West Point graduates in the late 1880s. Congress responded to this glut by authorizing the status of additional second lieutenant, and it was at this rank that Young, like many of his fellow graduates, entered the army. Young's case, however, was unique and posed a particularly vexatious dilemma for the Adjutant General's Office. Additional second lieutenants were appointed with the understanding that they would be transferred to the first unit in which a vacancy became available. By taking the unusual step of transferring Young from a cavalry to an infantry regiment, the army was endeavoring to avoid the prospect of "appointing him to a vacancy...in a White regiment."[6]

In late October 1889, to the relief of the adjutant general, a vacancy opened in the Ninth Cavalry and Young received his desired assignment as a second lieutenant. Major Guy Henry, in temporary command of the Ninth, however, was incensed at the decision to assign Young to his regiment. Henry noted that the Ninth already had a Black commissioned officer in the person of Lieutenant John Alexander, and the major complained that the addition of a second Black officer might discourage White officers from applying for assignment to his regiment. Indicative of the competitive jealousy then existing between regiments in the U.S. Army and hinting at a possible alternative assignment for Young, Henry bemoaned what he believed to be the advantage given to the 10th Cavalry by this move. Henry even went so far as to argue disingenuously that placing the two Black officers in the same regiment would damage their chances of advancement and thus do damage to the cause of their race. He claimed that he had been informed that Alexander did not want Young in the same regiment and that his protest was for "the benefit of the colored race." The insincerity of his concern barely masks his assumption that merit would not be the primary factor in shaping their careers.[7]

Despite Henry's vehement opposition to the assignment, the Adjutant General's Office and the War Department, which reviewed the matter, were anxious to put the affair to rest. The facts of the case were explained to Henry in a manner that left little doubt that the ultimate goal of keeping Black officers in Black regiments was to supersede any concerns of the regimental commander. The whole incident offers a blatant illustration of the unwillingness of the army to come to terms with the existence of Black officers and the barely disguised hostility these officers faced from their White counterparts. Although Henry was perhaps guilty of hyperbole in outlining the damage he perceived Young's appointment would cause, his claim that White officers would be more reluctant to join his regiment was not without foundation. Since the creation of the Black units, many White officers, including the infamous George Armstrong Custer, had refused to serve with the regiments for fear of damaging their careers. The exemplary record of the Buffalo Soldiers during the Indian wars had somewhat assuaged this fear, but for many White officers there was still a stigma attached to serving with a Black regiment. The implication behind Henry's stated concern was that White officers would be more likely than ever to refuse service with the Ninth Cavalry because racism precluded them from treating Black officers as their equals.[8]

Largely oblivious to the controversy surrounding his appointment, Young joined Troop B of the Ninth Cavalry at Fort Robinson, Nebraska, in

November 1889. Fort Robinson, located in northwestern Nebraska near the Wyoming and South Dakota borders, originated as an army camp during the Sioux Wars of the late 1870s. In 1878 it was designated a fort, one of the many garrisoned posts used by the army to subdue Native American resistance and secure the West for the increasing number of settlers making their way across the Mississippi. As the *Omaha Bee* noted in 1883, Fort Robinson was one of a number of forts in the Department of the Dakota intended to "hem in the great Sioux nation with a circle of bayonets." By the time Young arrived there, the resistance of the plains Indians was almost at an end. During the winter of 1890–91, troops from the Ninth Cavalry stationed at Fort Robinson were involved in putting an end to the millenarian Ghost Dance movement and the final stand of the Sioux that it inspired. The massacre of Sioux Indians by the Seventh Cavalry at Wounded Knee in December 1890 brought this dark chapter in American history to a close.[9]

Charles Young, therefore, was beginning his career in an army in transition. Many of the forts established to secure the western frontier would remain in operation well into the twentieth century, but throughout the 1890s the soldiers who garrisoned these posts were called on less to fight Indians and more to police the growing settler population. Troops at Fort Robinson, for example, were called on in the 1890s to intervene in a number of civil disputes such as railroad strikes and cattle wars, which pitted small ranchers against large growers. More often than not, the firepower of the U.S. Army was used to uphold the will of the large growers and the railroad owners as the rugged frontier of the individualistic homesteader and cowpoke gave way to the march of capital enterprise and big business.[10]

Young's career got off to an ominous start at Fort Robinson. During the spring of 1890, he was subject to constant criticism from his commanding officers. On April 5 Colonel Joseph Tilford noted among Young's "tactical errors" at guard mount, his failure to correctly inspect boxes, his failure to salute at the required distance from a commanding officer, and his failure to give a change of direction order before the troop reached the camp colors. In late April Major James Randlett cited him for his failure to appear for duty at stables during grooming. Apparently, in the eyes of his superiors, nothing short of perfection would do for Lieutenant Young.[11]

As he had done at West Point, Young resorted to measured methods of defense. In his required letter of response, Young answered Major Randlett's critique by promising in future to comply with the "spirit" of the regulation, which required an officer's presence during stable duty. Colonel Tilford, sensing insubordination in Young's rejoinder, warned him to correct his behavior or meet with "more severe official action." Further reports followed, citing Young's "habitual lateness" and indifference to duty. Once again, when required to respond, Young fought back. He found the reports "very painful...as I hold doing my duty as my sole purpose in life." He accepted that in his six months in the army he was perhaps guilty of errors or lapses in duty, but he contended that he had made every effort to correct his deficiencies and he insisted that he was never guilty of intentional neglect. Evincing equal measures of youthful bravado and a wounded sense of honor, Young offered to decline to draw pay if he ever willfully neglected his duty. More important, Young asked that the several reports that cited his indifference to duty be forwarded with his efficiency report to army headquarters so that "it may be plainly seen in what this 'indifference' consists as the statement alone is too vague and indifferent....That there may have been neglect and errors springing from inexperience and want of practice I do not attempt to deny, but willfully and knowingly I must say no."[12]

Clearly Young could tolerate petty criticism concerning his tactical performance, but he bridled at the charge of indifference to duty. His request to have the basis of this charge clarified in his efficiency report indicates his relative certainty that it could not be substantiated. Young was well aware that "inexperience" and "want of practice" were to be expected in green lieutenants straight out of the academy, but indifference to duty was a serious charge that could damage his career. Anxious to avoid the same fate as Lieutenant Flipper, Young was determined not to provide his superiors with grounds to force him out of the army. Carefully choosing his battles, Young adapted to his situation and quickly learned to tread the thin line between defiance and defense, preserving both his honor and his career.

Along with these more dramatic encounters, soldiering on the frontier posed some mundane, but no less real, challenges. The men at Fort Robinson endured brutally cold winters and stifling hot summers in Spartan living conditions and daily faced the most persistent enemy of the frontier soldier, boredom. Rarely comfortable for either soldiers or officers, life at Fort Robinson posed special difficulties for a Black officer of the most junior rank. In the summer of 1890, with officers quarters in short supply, Young was evicted from his residence to make way for a newly arrived senior officer. Only the transfer of Major Randlett and the division of his residence into quarters for two lieutenants saved Young from an indefinite period of homelessness. Meanwhile, although his existence was not quite as hermetic as it had been at West Point, Young was excluded from the active social circle of the other officers and their wives. There was no place for him in the officers club or at the dances, parties, and socials that kept his White colleagues entertained in the relative wilderness of northwest Nebraska. Blacks were not welcome in the exclusive world of the White officer. To challenge such social mores would amount to professional suicide for a Black officer. Black officers who accepted their isolation, such as John Alexander, won praise from their White counterparts for "appreciating the delicate distinctions of social intercourse."[13]

Young, following Alexander's example, did not challenge the social segregation of the officer corps. William Hay, who later served as an officer
with Young in the 10th Cavalry, noted that Young "did not push in where
he was not wanted...he only desired the dignity of his rank." To satisfy
protocol, Young developed the habit of inviting White officers to his home
only to cancel at the last minute due to an unavoidable conflict. He once
described this to a junior officer as "a game of solitaire"; he was willing to
receive anyone who wanted to see him but he did not want to alienate
those who did not. Despite opening himself up to charges of being an
Uncle Tom, in the deteriorating racial climate of the 1890s, Charles Young
continued to see professional equality as a more attainable goal than social
inclusion. He was willing to sacrifice the latter to attain the former. His
White counterparts made it clear that such behavior was expected for him
to be "accepted as an officer."[14]

Following his transfer to Fort Duchesne, Utah, in the fall of 1890, army
life improved somewhat for Charles Young. For a start, his efficiency
reports markedly improved. This may be due to a combination of his spirited resistance to the harassment he experienced at Fort Robinson and the
sharp contrast between the two posts in the degree of racial prejudice. Fort
Robinson's reputation for racism received national attention in the Black
press. The Cleveland *Gazette* in July 1894, drew attention to the fact that
while there were only two companies of the White 8th Infantry compared
with six companies of the Black Ninth Cavalry at Fort Robinson, all the
clerical, administrative, and skilled positions at the post were held by
White soldiers. The ostracism of Young and Alexander and the controversial 1894 court-martial of Henry Plummer, a Black chaplain with the
Ninth, added to Fort Robinson's notoriety and fueled charges of an
orchestrated policy of racism on the part of the post commanders.[15]

Fort Duchesne was largely free of such controversy. Built in 1886 in
northeastern Utah, Fort Duchesne functioned as a base from which the
army could monitor the activities of the Ute Indians who had been placed
on reservations in the area after being driven from their hunting grounds
in Colorado. During Young's four years at the post, his emerging skill as
an officer was reflected in assignments such as the officer in charge of post
exchange, post adjutant, quartermaster, and recruiting officer. One of his
Fort Robinson detractors, Major Randlett, completely revised his opinion
of Young at Fort Duchesne, opining after the Black lieutenant's departure
in 1894 that he was losing an officer who possessed "untiring zeal, fidelity,
and well directed energy" and who was deserving of every "confidence
and high esteem." The Ninth Cavalry's chaplain, William H. Scott, echoed
this assessment, noting that Young was an "active and efficient officer"
who had the "entire confidence of his fellow officers."[16]

One of the many duties Young held while at Fort Duchesne was teacher
at the post school. Post schools offered an elementary education for the
dependent children of officers and enlisted men, many of whose families

resided on the post, as well as classes for illiterate soldiers and noncommissioned officers. At most posts throughout the West, the schools were
run by chaplains. That Young held this position at Fort Duchesne speaks
both to his energy and his evolving skill as an educator. From his first job
teaching elementary school in Ripley to the final years of his life, Young
evinced a passion for education. He would soon have an opportunity to
further develop his pedagogical skill when Wilberforce University began
a search for a new professor of military science and tactics.[17]

Located three miles from Xenia, Ohio, on the former site of Tawawa
Springs, a favorite resort of southern aristocrats before the Civil War,
Wilberforce University was founded in 1856 by the Methodist Episcopal
Church to educate "youth of color." As David Levering Lewis notes,
Wilberforce "had come into being as the sylvan solution to the sins of
slaveholding fathers" anxious to educate their illegitimate children born
of slave mistresses. In 1863 it was taken over by the African Methodist
Episcopal Church and for much of the rest of the nineteenth century
Wilberforce was considered to be among the premier Black universities in
the country. In 1894 the United States Congress added Wilberforce University to the list of schools at which army officers on detached service
conducted military training.[18]

Lieutenant John Alexander was the first officer assigned to the post.
His sudden death only a few months after arriving at Wilberforce, however, sent the university's administration in search of a replacement. In
the interest of prestige the university was anxious that the new professor
of military science and tactics hold a commission in the army, so, immediately following Alexander's death, Wilberforce president, S. T. Mitchell,
began a letter-writing campaign to secure Young's appointment. Among
those receiving letters from Mitchell were President Grover Cleveland, an
Ohio native; Senator Calvin Bryce of Ohio; Secretary of War Daniel Lamont; and Adjutant General George Ruggles. Initially thwarted by regulations stipulating that any officer holding such a post must have
completed five years of service—Young was three months short of the
mark—Mitchell continued to lobby vigorously until eventually he prevailed.[19]

That regulations were waived to enable Young to take up this post man-
ifests the relative importance of Wilberforce University in the 1890s and
the ability of its president to pull political strings. However, there was
another, more sinister, dynamic involved. In the years before World War I,
the army's most consistent response to the anomaly of the Black officer
was to assign him to extended periods of detached service or send him on
special assignment away from his regiment. Wilberforce University represented one of the few places where Black officers could be assigned without causing friction among the White officer corps. The army was
therefore only too willing to meet Wilberforce's request to assign first

Alexander and then Young to its military department. They would be succeeded at Wilberforce in the years to come by two other Black commissioned officers, Benjamin Davis and John Green, both of whom earned
their commissions following their promotion from the ranks during the
army's expansion in the early twentieth century. A measure of the incon-
venience these Black officers caused to the army, and also one of the great
ironies of Young's career, was the decision to assign Young to the all-White
Seventh Cavalry following his promotion to first lieutenant in 1896. This
decision was likely made to avoid the kind of political fallout that had
greeted Young's first assignment and of course it was made in the full
knowledge that he was safely ensconced at Wilberforce and so would not
actively serve with the White regiment. Promotion to first lieutenant also
brought another painful reminder of racial prejudice that was to haunt
Young throughout his career. Ordered to report to Fort Leavenworth,
Kansas, for the exam, Young had been refused accommodation at a local
hotel and had been compelled to travel into Kansas City to find a place to
stay.[20]

While the Black officers sometimes resented being detached from their
regiments, they often welcomed the special opportunities that these
assignments offered. Wilberforce, above all else, offered a level of social
interaction denied to them in the army. Young, in particular, was to relish
this aspect of life at Wilberforce. From the beginning of his tenure at the
university, he immersed himself in the social opportunities afforded both
by the institution and by the Black community of southwestern Ohio. It
was here that he cultivated his most important and lasting friendships.
Although he would spend much of the rest of his career stationed overseas or in other parts of the United States, Wilberforce was to become his
permanent home.

In addition to the ties of friendship that bound him to the area, Young
had another reason for establishing his residence at Wilberforce. On June
16, 1894, the same year that Young was assigned to Wilberforce, his father
died in Zanesville. Gabriel Young was 53 years old at the time of his death.
According to his death certificate, he had been battling tuberculosis for
almost two years, and had been extremely ill in the last few months of his
life. Charles later attributed the cause of his illness to "complications
brought on by exposure" during his Civil War service. The last years of his
life had been difficult; Gabriel was unable to work and he and Arminta
had become increasingly dependent on their son, particularly to cover the
cost of medications and medical bills. He had little in the way of tangibles
to leave his son, but to Charles his most valuable bequest was "a heritage
of honor" born of his service in the Civil War. Charles returned to
Zanesville to organize and pay for his father's funeral, and once Gabriel
was laid to rest in Greenwood Cemetery in Zanesville he brought his
mother to live with him in Wilberforce.[21]

Young and his mother purchased a large house on the main road to Xenia, about a mile from the Wilberforce campus. The house had once served as a roadside inn catering to stage traffic on the Columbus Pike, the main road from Cincinnati to the Ohio state capital. A Mississippi planter later purchased it as a home for his slave concubine and their eight children, and the house purportedly once served as a station on Ohio's Underground Railroad. Young's new home was "very commodious, with large rooms on the first and second floors, wide halls and broad stairways." Young delighted in his "beautiful place" with its "bath heaters, grates, good stables, and health," and he was clearly conscious that it gave him a certain "prestige with both students and visitors."[22]

"Youngsholm," as Charles proudly christened his new residence, stands as material testimony to the Young family's rise from slavery to the ranks of the middle class. Arminta and Charles pooled their resources to pay for their new home. The Zanesville property was eventually sold for $1,400 and Charles estimated that during the next several years he invested $3,700 in the house and in purchasing and developing adjoining farmland. Although they sometimes struggled to make ends meet, his salary together with his mother's income, which consisted of her husband's military pension and revenue from the bit-work she did as a seamstress, and rent from students they took on as boarders in the new house enabled them to maintain their new lifestyle. Charles Young's parents had never been wealthy but their hard work and support had provided the means for their son to achieve sufficient financial and intellectual status to enter the ranks of the Black elite. It was a status that Young was anxious to maintain. Even in times of acute financial strain, he was loathe to make any cutbacks that might open him up to "nigger talk" or gossip in the Wilberforce community. For all that, Young was neither a snob nor a materialist. In his view equilibrium in life lay halfway between materialism and idealism, a balance that might not produce utopia but did promote peace and practical justice.[23]

Young's happiest days were spent in Wilberforce. Here he was able to relax in a way that was never possible while on duty with his regiment. In Wilberforce the full gamut of his abilities and the true nature of his character came to light. Youngsholm became renowned throughout southern Ohio as a venue for social and intellectual activity. Befitting the house's history as a roadside inn, Young would "turn no one away from our door that asks for the shelter of the roof." Young's friends remembered that the house "was open to everybody...and people far and wide made [it] a Mecca for pilgrimages." Needy students were regularly accommodated at the house, and students in crisis commonly made the short trip from campus to seek the lieutenant's prized counsel. As a result of all this traffic, Charles and his mother rarely ever ate a meal alone and the guest rooms in their home were seldom ever empty.[24]

Among the frequent visitors to Youngsholm was Paul Laurence Dunbar, the rising Black poet from nearby Dayton. Young and Dunbar spent many evenings sitting by the fireside while Dunbar composed poetry, which Young then put to music. Arminta Young, a self-taught pianist and composer, had taught her son to play when he was a child, and Youngsholm routinely resonated to the sound of music. Gifted with a natural ear, Young became an avid pianist and developed a passion for composing and performing in his adult years. Another participant in these musical evenings was W. E. B. Du Bois. Du Bois, who joined the faculty at Wilberforce as professor of classics in 1894, the same year as Young, was just embarking on an academic career that would see him emerge as the foremost Black intellectual of the twentieth century. He spent many hours at Youngsholm in the company of Young, Dunbar, and others, sharpening the wit that would later become such a powerful weapon in the struggle for Black civil rights.[25]

Fresh from earning a Ph.D. at Harvard and a year of study at the prestigious University of Berlin, the youthful Du Bois came to Wilberforce convinced that he could help transform it into a "great university" in the manner of those at which he had just completed his studies. Disillusionment set in early, however, as his inflated expectations fell well short of realization, and he departed after only two years. Chief among the disappointments he found with Wilberforce was the institution's emphasis on Christianity. Du Bois saw his dreams of helping to build a great academic institution buried beneath a shallow veneer of Christianity, which he characterized at Wilberforce as little more than "a childish belief in Biblical fairy tales, a word of mouth adherence to dogma, and a certain sectarian exclusiveness."[26]

Frustrated and disillusioned, Du Bois found solace in his friendship with Young. Although he had grown up the son of practicing Baptists, Young shared some of Du Bois's suspicion of organized religion and espoused instead a belief in universalism. Together, the two friends balked at the university's expectations for its faculty to embrace its Christian image, refusing, for example, to "attend 'revivals' which interrupted school work every year at Christmas time." The two years they spent together at Wilberforce laid the foundation for an "unswerving" friendship, which would see each man go to the mat for the other on numerous occasions in the years to come.[27]

Du Bois came to admire Young's patience, discipline, and humility in the face of constant adversity. As one of his closest friends, however, Du Bois also knew both the "hearty" and "genial" Young and the man who kept hidden "behind the Veil" the pain he felt as a result of the racism and prejudice he endured in the army. It was only among those with whom he was most familiar that Young allowed such anguish to show. Du Bois was one of the few to witness the bouts of melancholy to which Young was prone, and which he countered by turning to "his beloved music, which always poured from his quick, nervous fingers, to caress and bathe his soul."[28]

Following Du Bois's departure from Wilberforce in 1896, the two men maintained their friendship through regular correspondence and visits whenever they found themselves in the same part of the country. Du Bois left Wilberforce lamenting its serious limitations as an academic institution and a center of learning. Young, on the other hand, sharing neither the scholarly ambitions nor the restless spirit of his friend, was quite content to stay at Wilberforce. In fact, Wilberforce's Christian emphasis aside, Young became "a staunch friend of the University." In addition to his duties as professor of military science and tactics, Young, though not officially required to do so, agreed to teach classes in French, German, and mathematics, the subject that almost prevented him from graduating from West Point. He immersed himself in extracurricular activities too, coaching the glee club and drama group, and organizing the first marching band at Wilberforce. His energy and geniality endeared him to his students and fellow faculty, one of whom would later remember him as an "inspiration" to everyone who met him.[29]

Young did not, however, allow his cordial relations with students to cloud his determination to uphold his duty as an officer of the U.S. Army while at Wilberforce. Equipped with 100 rifles, one cannon, and uniforms for the students, the Department of Military Science and Tactics was one of a number of such programs at universities across the country that were designed to provide the United States with a degree of military preparedness in case the army were to expand in the event of war. The program was in essence a nineteenth-century precursor to the ROTC. Young ran a steady program of drill and exercise and applied rigid standards of deportment and behavior. He had no tolerance for "weak and whining men who are forever complaining of the things they may not enjoy and who forget the inestimable blessings they accept each day as a matter of course." In his mind the mission of imparting self-discipline was as important as the task of any other professor on campus, if not more so. In a society awash in racial prejudice, Young firmly believed that "the colored boy needs in actual life this thing worse than all others to make him stick things out." Building self esteem was critical to overcoming the sense of "innate inferiority" that so many young Black men felt in the face of "insidious and persistent" racial propaganda from a section of the White community. Only through "virile determination" could Black men prevent their people from being "perpetually bound down as a lower caste in our own country."[30]

While many of the recipients of this tough-love approach became ardent admirers of the West Point man, some going so far as to follow him into the service, there were others who resisted his efforts to instill military discipline. One student, John Hilton, alleged that Young had assaulted him following an altercation and he wrote to the Adjutant General's Office seeking action against the lieutenant. The university, however, conducted an investigation that cleared Young of any wrongdoing in the affair and charged Hilton, who was subsequently dismissed from Wilberforce, with provoking the incident. The university's conclusion that its professor of military and science and tactics was doing the job that was expected of him was given independent corroboration by the army's acting inspector general who, following a visit to Wilberforce, commended Young for his "enthusiastic and energetic" performance of duty.[31]

Young's efforts to prepare his students at Wilberforce for the hardships they would face in turn-of-the-century America reflects his developing philosophy of life and his own sense of mission. He viewed himself increasingly as a race warrior out to slay the dragon of racial inferiority. Self-discipline and inner strength were the key weapons in his arsenal. Rather than bristle at the army's efforts to avoid controversy by shunting him off to Wilberforce, Young embraced the opportunity to train other young men in the cause. The crystallization of this agenda explains Young's willingness to accept detached service so readily although other officers of the line would not. The impending crisis in Cuba would provide another case in point.

At West Point, Charles Young had swum in largely uncharted waters; in the U.S. Army there was even less precedent by which he could map his course. The essence of his success as an officer lay in the sincerity with which he viewed the motto of his alma mater, "duty, honor, country." Although his career got off to a rocky start, he would gradually establish his credentials and, as he had at West Point, win increasing admiration from his White peers. His career too would continue to attract the attention of the African American press and public, and by the outbreak of the Spanish-American War in 1898 his celebrity was already established. These early years also saw Young nourish his alter ego. In uniform, Young was a rigid disciplinarian who valued duty and country above all else, a "spit and polish officer" in the words of Du Bois. Off duty, however, Young was a congenial, sensitive, cultured, and intellectually curious individual whose life revolved around family and close friends. Youngsholm served as his sanctuary from army life, a place where he could remove the armor that shielded him from the blows he received in advancing his career and could nourish his soul in the company of those who knew him best.

NOTES

1. Edward M. Coffman, *The Old Army: A Portrait of the American Army in Peacetime, 1784–1898* (New York, 1986), 215–222.

2. Marvin E. Fletcher, *The Black Soldier and Officer in the United States Army, 1890–1917* (Columbia, Mo., 1974), 19–21; Coffman, *Old Army,* 365.

3. Fletcher, *Black Soldier and Officer,* 27, 77.

4. Charles Young to Arminta Young, 4 September 1906, Coleman Collection, Akron, Ohio; Robert E. Greene, *Colonel Charles Young: Soldier and Diplomat* (Washington D.C., 1985).

5. Charles Young to Adjutant General's Office, 6 October 1889, Letters Received by the Appointment, Commission, and Personal Branch, Adjutant General's Office, 1871–1917, Record Group 94, National Archives, Washington, D.C. [hereinafter ACP File]; Adjutant General's Office to Charles Young, 9 October 1889, ACP File; Adjutant General's Office to Charles Young, 29 October 1889, ACP File; Charles Young to Adjutant General's Office, 30 October 1889, ACP File.

6. Edward M. Coffman, *The Old Army: A Portrait of the American Army in Peacetime, 1784–1898.* New York, 1986, 224; Adjutant General, J.C. Kelton, to Major Guy Henry, 20 January 1890, ACP File.

7. Major Guy Henry to the Adjutant General's Office, 3 January 1890, ACP File.

8. U.S. Department of War, Memorandum, 18 January 1890, ACP File; Adjutant General, J.C. Kelton, to Major Guy Henry, 20 January 1890, ACP File; Fletcher, *Black Soldier and Officer,* 21; For an account of the role of the Black cavalry regiments in the Indian wars, see William H. Leckie, *The Buffalo Soldiers: A Narrative of the Negro Cavalry in the West* (Norman, Okla., 1967).

9. *Omaha Bee,* 19 September 1883, quoted in Frank N. Schubert, *Buffalo Soldiers, Braves and the Brass: The Story of Fort Robinson, Nebraska,* (Shippensburg, Pa., 1993), 22.

10. Ibid., 32–42.

11. Lt. Walter F. Finley to Charles Young, 5 April 1890, ACP File; Major James Randlett to Adjutant Ninth Cavalry, 24 April 1890, ACP File; Schubert, *Buffalo Soldiers, Braves and the Brass,* 54.

12. Charles Young to Adjutant Ninth Cavalry, 26 April 1890, ACP File; Charles Young to Adjutant Ninth Cavalry, 7 May 1890, ACP File; Kenner, Charles L. *Buffalo Soldiers and Officers of the Ninth Cavalry, 1867–1898: Black and White Together.* (Norman, Okla., 1995), 303–304.

13. Frank N. Schubert, *Buffalo Soldiers, Braves and the Brass: The Story of Fort Robinson, Nebraska,* (Shippensburg, Pa., 1993), 48, 54.

14. Notes on an interview with William H. Hay by Earl Stover, 17 February 1967, "Correspondence concerning the Black Soldier, August 26, 1967–February 8, 1977," Marvin E. Fletcher Collection, United States Military History Institute, Carlisle, Pa.; Copy of a letter by S.B. Pearson to the Editor, *The Crisis,* 15 February 1922, Coleman Collection; Fletcher, *Black Soldier and Officer,* 106–7.

15. *Cleveland Gazette,* 14 July 1894, cited in Schubert, *Buffalo Soldiers, Braves and the Brass,* 133.

16. Herbert M. Hart, *Old Forts of the Far West* (New York, 1965), 134; Fort Duchesne, United States Army Post Returns, Records of the Adjutant General's Office, 1780–1917, RG 94, National Archives, Washington, D.C. [hereinafter Post Returns]; Fort Duchesne, Post Order 20, 18 May 1894, ACP File; William H. Scott to S.T. Mitchell, 5 April 1894, ACP File.

17. Frank N. Schubert, *On the Trail of the Buffalo Soldier: Biographies of African-Americans in the U.S. Army, 1866–1917* (Wilmington, Del., 1995), 489; Fletcher, *Black Soldier and Officer*, 114–15.

18. Donald A. Hustlar and David A. Simmons, "Taking the Waters: Xenia Springs in 1853," *Timeline*, November/December, 1999, 39; David Levering Lewis, *W. E. B. Du Bois: Biography of a Race, 1868–1919* (New York, 1993), 151; Willard B. Gatewood, *Aristocrats of Color: The Black Elite, 1880–1920* (Fayetteville, AR, 2000), 259; Emma Castleman Bowles, "Concerning the Origin of Wilberforce," *Journal of Negro History* VIII (July, 1923), 335–7; William Sanders Scarborough, "A Tribute to Colonel Charles Young," (Philadelphia, 1922), 5, William Sanders Scarborough Papers, Wilberforce University, Wilberforce, Ohio [hereinafter Scarborough Papers]; Kenner, *Buffalo Soldiers and Officers*, 298.

19. See S. T. Mitchell to Daniel S. Lamont, 2 April 1894, ACP File; George D. Ruggles to S. T. Mitchell, 5 April 1894, ACP File; S. T. Mitchell to Grover Cleveland, 2 April 1894, ACP File; S. T. Mitchell to Calvin S. Bryce, 11 April 1894, ACP File.

20. "The Desert and the Solitary Place," Notes on the life of Charles Young by Ada Young, 1922, Coleman Collection; Office of the Adjutant General, Department of the Army, Statement of Military Service for Charles Young, Fort Huachaca Museum; *New York Times*, 14 September 1896, 1.

21. Greene, *Soldier and Diplomat*, 37; Charles Young to Atlee Pomerene, 20 August 1918, Coleman Collection; Charles Young to Arminta Young, 4 September 1906, Coleman Collection; Graves Registration Card, Gabriel Young, Ohio Historical Society, Columbus, Ohio; Gabriel Young Pension Records.

22. Hallie Q. Brown, *Pen Pictures of Pioneers of Wilberforce* (Xenia, 1937), 38; Bowles, "Concerning the Origin of Wilberforce," 336; Charles Young to Benjamin O. Davis, 5 May 1905, Benjamin O. Davis, Sr., Papers, U.S. Military History Institute, Carlisle, Pa. [hereinafter Davis Papers]; Charles Young to Benjamin O. Davis, 28 August 1905, Davis Papers.

23. Charles Young to Arminta Young, 4 September 1906, Coleman Collection; Gabriel Young Pension Records; Charles Young Diary, Part II, Coleman Collection.

24. Scarborough, "Tribute," 8, Scarborough Papers; Charles Young to Ada Young, 6 August 1916, Coleman Collection; Purnell, John H. "Colonel Charles Young, U.S.A.: Soldier, Diplomat, Philanthropist, Man of Culture." *Oracle* (winter 1979): 6.

25. Scarborough, "Tribute," 14, Scarborough Papers; Ada Young to Arminta Young, 27 March 1921, Young Papers Uncatalogued Charles Young Papers, National Afro-American Museum and Cultural Center, Wilberforce, OH [hereinafter Young Papers Uncatalogued]; Purnell, "Colonel Charles Young," 5; Lewis, *Biography of a Race*, 175–77.

26. W. E. B. Du Bois, "The Future of Wilberforce University," *Journal of Negro Education* 9 (October 1940): 564.

27. W. E. B. Du Bois quoted in Lewis, *Biography of a Race*, 176.

28. W. E. B. Du Bois, "Charles Young," *The Crisis* (February 1922).

29. Scarborough, "Tribute," 8, Scarborough Papers; Purnell, "Colonel Charles Young," 6.

30. Charles Young to Benjamin O. Davis, 28 August 1905, Davis Papers; "Attitude of the College Man Towards Citizenship in the Republic," Speech by Charles

Young, 27 May 1907, Coleman Collection; "Colored Young Men of America," Speech by Charles Young, n.d., Coleman Collection.

31. John Hilton to George D. Ruggles, 6 February 1895, ACP File; S.T. Mitchell to J.O. Gilmore, 7 March 1895, ACP File; Acting Inspector General to Daniel S. Lamont, 22 August 1895, ACP File.

Chapter 4

Wars of Expansion

The Spanish-American War of 1898 marked a new departure in U.S. foreign policy, away from the traditional defensive application of the Monroe Doctrine and toward an aggressive pursuit of American interests overseas. Intervention in the Cuban insurrection launched the United States on the path to becoming a world power. Victory over Spain and the resulting occupation of Cuba and acquisition of Puerto Rico, Guam, and the Philippines earned the United States membership in the elite club of imperial powers. The rise of the United States as a world power would have important implications for its military. Increasing international commitments in the early twentieth century brought about expansion and modernization of the army. These were exciting, and potentially rewarding, times for ambitious, young officers like Charles Young.

They were, however, also controversial times. While expansionists reveled in the annexation of new territories beyond the contiguous United States, anti-imperialists feared for the integrity of the country's republican institutions. American imperialism posed a particular dilemma for Black Americans. Consistent with the mood of the country at large, many African Americans were swept up in the initial patriotic fervor and martial spirit that followed the sinking of the U.S.S. *Maine* in Havana harbor in February 1898. However, the implications of U.S. territorial expansion overseas caused growing concern among many Black commentators once the war with Spain was over. For African Americans who had applauded the exploits of Afro-Cuban rebels and the efforts of their Black and Brown brothers in the Caribbean and the Pacific to throw off the yoke of European imperialism, the repressive nature of U.S. policies in the occupied territories, the Philippines in particular, was not easy to justify. Criticism was often muted, however, for fear that appearing unpatriotic would damage the greater cause of civil rights at home.[1]

Perhaps the most acutely exposed to this paradox were the Black soldiers who fought in the Philippine war, a brutal conflict all but expunged from the collective memory of the United States during the past one hundred years. They witnessed firsthand the brutality of the occupation and the bigotry that so often infected American interaction with the native population. For a small number of African American soldiers, such as the notorious David Fagen, the congruence of Jim Crow and American policy in the Philippines served as a catalyst for desertion. Conversely, an equally small number, such as George W. Prioleau, chaplain of the Ninth Cavalry, joined their White compatriots in railing against the "indolence" and "laziness" of the Filipinos and urged that they must not be allowed to "retard American progress."[2]

The overwhelming majority of African American soldiers who served in the Philippines, however, performed their duty without question. Charles Young epitomized that professionalism, placing duty and patriotism above all other concerns. Without sharing the extremism of Prioleau, who due to his rank and race became one of Young's closest friends in the Philippines, Young resolutely believed in the civilizing mission that served to justify American occupation of the Philippines. Like most members of the Talented Tenth, he viewed Western civilization, and specifically its American incarnation, as implicitly good. That African Americans were denied many of their rights as citizens was a blemish on an otherwise laudable system, whose underlying principles were worthy of exporting overseas. During the next 24 years Young would serve as a dedicated agent of American interests and values, from the Philippines and Haiti to Liberia and Mexico.[3]

Charles Young was still on detached service as professor of military science and tactics at Wilberforce University when the United States declared war on Spain in April 1898. His regiment, the Ninth Cavalry, was ordered to Chickamagua Park, Georgia, as part of the army's efforts to amass its forces in the South in preparation for a planned assault on the Spanish in Cuba. The Ninth Cavalry would indeed reach Cuba and play a pivotal role in the capture of San Juan Hill, one of the most celebrated actions in the regiment's history. Young, much to his regret, however, missed out on the fighting in Cuba. Instead, he was to spend the duration of the brief war with Spain serving with a Black volunteer unit on home soil.

Although the outbreak of the Spanish-American War was not unexpected (momentum toward conflict had been building for some months), the United States was nonetheless militarily unprepared. Because of the systematic reduction of the army's size since the end of the Civil War, President McKinley was authorized by Congress to issue a call for volunteers soon after the outbreak of hostilities. The War Department satisfied its immediate need for volunteers by mustering into service state militia units. Ohio was one of eight states that included a Black unit among its initial volunteers. Ohio's large Black population held considerable sway in the state's Republican Party, and both Senator Mark Hanna and Governor Asa Bushnell recognized the political dividends to be gained from pressuring the War Department to answer the call for a Black volunteer unit from Ohio. Hanna and Bushnell's lobbying resulted in the Ninth Ohio Battalion becoming one of the first Black volunteer units to be mustered into service in the Spanish-American War.[4]

Politics also played a role in determining who would command the unit. The War Department adopted the army's traditional policy regarding Black soldiers, which held that they were to remain in segregated units under the command of White officers. Black newspapers, however, spearheaded a national campaign for the appointment of Black officers to Black units. The *American Citizen* of Kansas City coined the motto "No officers, no soldiers." This sentiment was particularly pronounced in Ohio, the home state of the army's only Black commissioned officer. The state's Republican Party bosses concluded that the political advantage to be gained among Black voters by appointing Charles Young to command the Ninth Ohio was greater than the backlash it might cause among their White constituents. Governor Bushnell received Young at his office in Columbus on May 10 and three days later, with the permission of the War Department, designated him major of the Ninth Ohio Battalion (infantry), United States Volunteers.[5]

Young had mixed feelings about accepting this assignment. While the wartime rank of major was certainly a prestigious honor for a junior officer, Young had been on detached service since 1894 and only a month before his meeting with Bushnell he had written to the Adjutant General's Office asking that he be allowed to rejoin his regiment in the event of war. Expecting that his request would be granted and that he would see action in Cuba, he made arrangements with his friend William Broad to safeguard his growing body of musical compositions and verse and to take care of his mother in the event of being killed. Since his promotion to first lieutenant, Young's anxiety to resume his regular army career had been growing. He accepted the appointment with the Ninth Ohio and a further period of detached service for a mixture of personal and political reasons. By demonstrating his effectiveness as a commander he could boost his own reputation as an officer. At the same time he could advance the cause of racial equality by debunking the myth that only White officers could lead Black troops. It was a valuable stepping stone in advancing both his career and his sense of mission, but one on which he was determined not to be stranded. When asked in 1899 if he would accept a position as captain with a Black volunteer unit from Kentucky bound for the Philippines, Young rejected the offer in no uncertain terms. He demurred on the grounds that more time away from his regiment would retard his prospects for promotion and that he had an obligation to "the considera-tion of seven millions of a race of people" who expected to see him rise through the ranks of the regular army.[6]

The Kentucky assignment was made redundant by Young's earlier suc-cess with the Ninth Ohio. One of only two exclusively Black volunteer units to serve in the Spanish-American War, the Ninth Ohio, under the command of the regular army's only Black West Point graduate, was a source of considerable pride to the African American population of the state and, according to the governor, the state as a whole. The pride of Black Ohio was on full display on May 19, 1898, when Major Young and his troops readied to depart Columbus for Camp Alger near Falls Church, Virginia. The mood was festive as large crowds gathered on the state house lawn to hear speakers recount the notable history of Black partici-pation in America's previous wars. Young pledged to the assembled audi-ence that the Ninth Ohio would do its part to uphold this tradition. Following the presentation of a stand of colors to the regiment by a Grand Army of the Republic veteran and a sword and belt to the major by the cit-izens of Columbus, the Ninth Ohio paraded through the city to the rail-way station escorted by marching bands and representatives of several fraternal organizations. Unfortunately for the eager volunteers and their ambitious commander, that day in Columbus would arguably prove to be the high point of their experience during the brief war.[7]

At the time the battalion arrived in Camp Alger, the men still expected to see action and they were anxious to prove themselves on the field of battle. Their commander was determined to transform the four hundred volunteers under his command into an efficient, well-trained infantry unit. Major Young put his troops through a rigorous daily regimen of physical exercise and parade ground drill. Conscious that the army was undertaking an "experiment," Young was determined to prove that Black officers were fit to command. His application of rigid discipline and his expectations for proper military conduct earned him the nickname "Dynamite" from the men. With the prospect of combat looming large on the horizon, morale in the unit was high and the volunteers accepted the exacting routine of Dynamite's command.[8]

Conditions at Camp Alger were far from hospitable. In addition to intense heat, the soldiers complained the "yellow Virginia dust was ankle-deep." The volunteers bemoaned the prohibition against "pies and spiri-tuous liquor" on camp grounds, and dreaded the early-morning one-mile sprints and mandatory laundry days. It was only on rare occasions that men in the Ninth could secure a pass from Major Young to visit nearby Falls Church or Washington. Young's antipathy to alcohol and day passes was motivated by a desire to avoid racial antagonism with the local population rather than by a puritanical streak, as some of the men suspected. Black troops stationed in the South routinely found themselves subject to racial hostility from White citizens, and the tension arising from their presence occasionally erupted into violence. Right or wrong, Black troopers usually came off the worst in the public relations fallout from these affairs. Charles Young was firm in his resolve that White Virginians would not be able to levy any charges of unruliness against his men and that under his command the Ninth Ohio's record in the South would be untainted by controversy. Young dealt firmly with two officers of the Ninth who were accused of raping a young White woman. Although the two men protested that the woman in question had consented, he threatened to initiate court-martial proceedings, and the two officers subsequently tendered their resignations. Young was not prepared to allow anything to happen that might jeopardize his success in this "experiment."[9]

No amount of discretion and discipline could protect the Ninth Ohio from the prejudice of White units at Camp Alger. General M. C. Butler, formerly a senator from South Carolina famous for his unbridled racism, instructed Young that under no circumstances should any man from the Ninth Ohio cross the lines that bound his headquarters. The general's South Carolina volunteers had been the cause of considerable racial tension since arriving at Camp Alger and soon after Butler's warning, Young had a personal encounter with one of his men that exemplified the plight of the Black officer in a White-dominated army. A regular visitor to the camp later recounted the story of one of the South Carolinian soldiers who refused to salute Major Young when the two men's paths crossed. On hearing of the incident, the camp commander summoned Young and the offending soldier to his headquarters. Here the commander requested that Young take off his coat and hang it on the back of a chair. He then ordered the southern volunteer to salute the chair adorned with the major's jacket. It was a lesson in military color blindness worthy of Young's own devise.[10]

Aware that his restrictive policies were breeding tedium, Young encouraged the men to play baseball and swim and, ever the agent of cultural enrichment, he actively facilitated their participation in dramatic productions. When his good fried Paul Laurence Dunbar visited Camp Alger, Young assembled the men for a recital by the rising Dayton poet. The Ninth organized a night of Shakespearean entertainment in honor of the visiting Ohio congressional delegation to which all the officers in the camp were invited. The visiting Dunbar offered recitations, and Charles Burroughs, an aspiring actor and one of a number of Young's Wilberforce students serving with the battalion, performed soliloquies from Macbeth. Meanwhile, other distinguished guests such as Charles Douglas, son of the famous abolitionist Frederick Douglass, and General O. O. Howard, former head of the Freedman's Bureau, also visited the camp. Such visits, however, offered only a momentary distraction for the men, who were growing gradually more frustrated as the Ninth Ohio was repeatedly detached from divisions and brigades that were then sent to the front. As news reached Camp Alger of the heroic exploits of Black regulars at El Caney and San Juan Hill, the men's anxiety to participate in the action before it was all over became even more pronounced. Major Young's prediction that a summer of provost duty would be followed by participation in the anticipated siege of Havana proved less and less comforting as the summer months wore on.[11]

Young's emphasis on discipline and drill may not have endeared him to the volunteers under his command, but he succeeded nonetheless in earning a singular reputation for the Ninth Ohio. The Ninth won high praise from many of the other officers at Camp Alger, and the Ohio volunteers were singled out by local merchants as one of the few units, Black or White, that did not participate in looting and shoplifting. Their reputation preceded them on their arrival at Camp Meade, Pennsylvania, where they were transferred in August 1898. The soldiers were proud of the fact that "larger crowds than any other command" turned out to observe their march from the Harrisburg train station to the nearby camp. The Harrisburg *Commonwealth* lauded the Ninth Ohio as "the best drilled command at Camp Meade," and the camp commander, General W.H. Graham, thought particularly highly of Young's battalion.[12]

However, by this time the war with Spain was over and as one soldier in the Ninth attested "now that the hope of participating in battle is gone, our boys, in common with all volunteers, are eager to don the habiliments of civilian life." The honor of being chosen to participate in the Peace Jubilee celebration in Philadelphia in the fall of 1898, where the Ninth marched immediately behind General Graham and his staff, served as slight consolation for the disappointment of missing out on the fighting. Young did what he could to maintain morale—including ordering extra rations of food—but his unwillingness to relax the battalion's daily regimen did not sit well with the volunteers. From reveille at 5:30 A.M. to parade from 5:45 P.M. until dusk, the major continued to insist on a heavy daily schedule of drill and exercise. Most galling to the men, however, were the frequent "bayonet exercises, [and] hand, foot, and body exercises for the edification of the crowds of white people who come for the purposes of seeing the show."[13]

In letters home, some of the men vented their frustrations regarding the junior officers in the battalion whom they charged were anxious only to remain in uniform "since they have been drawing good salaries for the first time in their lives." Such self-interest, these soldiers charged, led officers to disregard procedure in the manner in which they rejected furlough applications and to censor outgoing mail to prevent the battalion's low morale from becoming public. Young for his part was accused of using his volunteer command to position himself for promotion in the regular army. One soldier lamented that Young, in his eagerness to impress, had allowed the Ninth Ohio to be pressed into service as the camp commander's private guard, and that this was a great source of humiliation as there was no honor in being "General Graham's Nigs."[14]

The growing tension between Young and the men of the Ninth Ohio reflected the conflicting priorities of the professional soldier and the volunteer. With the prospect of glory on the field of battle having passed, the volunteers were anxious to be free of the regimented routine of the army and to return to civilian life. Young, on the other hand, was committed to maintaining regular army standards in the battalion until the order to muster out was given. Till then, he was adamant that the volunteers remain subject to the same rules and expectations as soldiers in the regular army. Some of Ohio's Black newspapers reprinted letters from men in the battalion charging Young with cultivating his own ambition and ego and pandering to White visitors and officers at the expense of his own troops. Young was furious. "We are trying to make soldiers out of these boys, and the yellow journals are trying to turn them back into tin soldiers."[15]

Disillusionment among the men mounted as fall turned to winter and cool winds made life at Camp Meade "very disagreeable." Letters continued to filter out of the camp to newspapers back in Ohio charging Young with self promotion and drilling the men "to death" to please White guests. As he had done many times before, Young felt compelled to answer his critics. He wrote to the Adjutant General's Office denying that a "system of terrorism" existed in the battalion and asserting that accusations of such came primarily from "a few malcontents," mostly married men anxious to return to their wives. He vowed to remedy the battalion's sinking morale by discharging some of these men and replacing them with bachelors, among them some of his former students at Wilberforce. Young was determined not to tolerate "unsoldierly" behavior; the officers and men of the Ninth Ohio served at the will of the government and for the good of the country, and he instructed them in no uncertain terms that it was not their place to question either.[16]

Young's patience with his volunteer charges reached breaking point when one of his men, Corporal Robert Allen, wrote to Senator Hanna claiming that his requests to secure a discharge through the regular channels had been stymied by his commanding officers. When Senator Hanna took up the issue with the War Department, Young lobbied that Allen's request be denied "for the sake of discipline in the organization." Young charged that Allen had "persisted in giving trouble" and since joining the battalion had routinely resisted "the necessary requirements of military service." The crux of Young's objection, however, stemmed from his belief that Allen's recourse to outside agents to secure his discharge struck "at the very root of military discipline and should not be tolerated if the best interests of the army are to be preserved." Young pledged that he would have given Allen's application his seal of approval had it been presented to him in "respectful and soldierly terms." The major's spirited stand to preserve the integrity of his military authority failed to counteract the weighty influence of Senator Hanna, and Allen received his discharge.[17]

Young was largely unaware of the political controversy that had followed his appointment to command the Ninth Ohio and that continued to excite the passions of Black Republicans in the state long after the battalion was mustered into service. Divisions between Hanna and Bushnell factions in Ohio's Republican Party had contributed to the governor's decision to replace Major Charles Fillmore as commander of the battalion. Young's appointment rankled Bushnell's Black detractors, and fueled charges that he had allowed himself "to be used by a white man to down another [black] man." Charges that Young was Bushnell's man and therefore particularly ruthless to those men under his command with anti-Bushnell connections, together with Hanna's intervention on behalf of Allen, kept the fires of political controversy stoked. Young's detractors accused him of being "a regular tyrant" and called for an investigation of his treatment of the troops, while his supporters responded that such accusations were slanderous and that Young was an officer and a gentleman beyond reproach. The political machinations that resulted in Allen's discharge made Young more anxious than ever to return to the regular army, where the links in the chain of command were stronger and the propensity for political intervention was less pronounced.[18]

Before that could take place, the Ninth Ohio Battalion was transferred once more. In November 1898 the battalion was sent to winter quarters at Camp Marion, South Carolina. According to one soldier, this "piney woods crossroads," 22 miles from Charleston, was "the worst place we have struck as yet." In addition to the poor water supply and the laborious task of clearing brush, the men had to endure the hostility their presence caused in this "southern backwoods." The same soldier noted unhappily that despite the overwhelming majority of African Americans in the region, "the Southern 'cracker' is seen at his best here." To the horror of the men, the local newspapers were filled with stories of "white supremacy" and the threat of "Negro domination." This atmosphere was confirmed by one of the officers who noted that the Ninth Ohio's reception in the South was "not cordial" and that "the white citizens were not at all favorably disposed towards colored soldiers." It was hardly the environment to improve the morale of an already dispirited battalion.[19]

Recognizing a potentially explosive situation, Young took steps to preempt the possibility of trouble. He instructed his company commanders to ensure that their men did nothing to reinforce the hostility of the local

Whites and that they "understand the necessity of dispelling this opinion by treating all whom they meet with respect and courtesy." A measure of his success in this regard was evident in one local newspaper. On the eve of the Ninth Ohio's departure the paper reported that "the people of Summerville are very much pleased with the record of Major Young whose battalion…has behaved in a most exemplary fashion." While Young's instructions to his men might be interpreted as evidence of his bowing to the pressure of Jim Crow, commendations from the local press and recognition for the Ninth Ohio from such military heavyweights as Major General S. B. M. Young, commander of the Second Army Corps, went a long way toward meeting both his political and his personal goals for his volunteer command. The excellence of the Ninth Ohio offered a strong case against those critics who questioned the viability of an all-Black unit and demonstrated for Young's superiors in the army his proficiency as a commander.[20]

Despite the vindication that such recognition entailed, the order to muster out, when it came through in January 1899, must have been as much a relief to Young as it undoubtedly was to his men. The volunteers were finally able to return home to their families and resume their lives as private citizens. In many instances the communities to which they returned welcomed them with almost as much fanfare as when they had departed. In the spirit of the moment the griping of the previous few months was forgotten, and the Cleveland *Gazette* noted that "the fine appearance of the men" proved beyond question the value of the major's leadership.[21]

Freed from his volunteer command, Young was ready to rejoin his regiment. But before that could happen he was destined to return home. Throughout much of 1898 the president of Wilberforce University had lobbied the Adjutant General's Office and even President McKinley to have Young resume his role as professor of military science and tactics. Anxious to keep Young on detached service, the secretary of war instructed his aides to "keep this in mind" and bring it to his attention "when the 9th is mus[tered] out." For his part, Young was eager to see his mother and friends at Wilberforce and so accepted the permission of the Adjutant General's Office to temporarily return to his teaching position while awaiting orders for reassignment.[22]

Young had briefly toyed with the idea of taking up a similar position at Booker T. Washington's Tuskegee Institute in Alabama. However, when Washington balked at arming students on his campus, fearing the controversy it might cause throughout the White South, Young promptly withdrew his consideration. For Young, to contemplate military training without weapons was absurd and he informed Washington that such half-measures were a major cause of embarrassment when Blacks were called on for volunteer service. This was an early sign that Young was at the vanguard of a generation of African Americans who were about to challenge the gradualist approach of established Black leaders such as Washington. Young was content to return to Wilberforce where, with the requisite support and equipment, he could continue his mission of instilling "pride and manliness...self-respect and obedience, [and] the strong virtues of promptness, reverence, neatness, and command" in the students under his charge. However, even the comfort of Wilberforce could not temper his growing anxiety to rejoin the regular army. Between May and August 1899 he wrote five times to the adjutant general reminding him of the impermanent nature of his position and hinting at his desire to rejoin his regiment. Finally, in September, orders arrived for him to proceed to Fort Duchesne, Utah, to take up his duties once again as a first lieutenant with the Ninth U.S. Cavalry.[23]

It is somewhat fitting that Young would pass the turn of the century at Fort Duchesne. In addition to signaling a new direction in American foreign policy, the Spanish-American War marked the beginning of an era of transformation in the United States Army. The war and the resulting exigencies of colonial occupation prompted a threefold increase in the size of the army between 1897 and 1900, from 25,000 to 75,000 men. The old army of the Gatling gun and Krag carbine was slowly giving way to the modern army of the machine gun and the high-velocity, clip-loading rifle. In this new era of the modern military, the aging western forts that had played such a critical role in the Indian wars and westward expansion were becoming obsolete. The early-twentieth-century American soldier was destined to spend more time overseas than on the western frontier.[24]

Young's second tour of duty at Fort Duchesne exposed him to the residual problems that lingered on the frontier as dusk descended on the Wild West. The Ute Indian reserves that the fort was originally created to police were increasingly subject to encroachment by large sheep herds moving into the region. Soon after returning to Utah, Young was called into action to settle a land dispute between the Utes and the herders. During the next year and half at the post, Young led Troop I of the Ninth Cavalry on numerous such missions, sometimes traveling into Colorado in "the dead of winter [where] temperatures hovered around 32° below in camp and the snow was 12 to 18 inches deep." Within 11 years of his second tour at Fort Duchesne, however, White settlers had so largely overrun the area that the Utes had lost the ability even to raise such disputes and the army concluded that there was no reason for the fort to remain open. Fort Duchesne would be officially abandoned in 1912.[25]

The return of Charles Young to Fort Duchesne in the fall of 1900 caught the attention of a young corporal by the name of Benjamin O. Davis. Like many young Black NCOs, Davis was impressed by "the only colored line officer in the Regular Army." He served under Young in Troop I and was greatly impressed by Young's presence and his ability to inspire the men under his command. Struck by Young's acumen as a musician, Davis remembered the lieutenant teaching group singing and encouraging those with a flare for music to nurture their talent. It was not uncommon to see the men of Troop I marching to the sound of their own chorus. "Nothing at that time seemed to lift up their spirits as a song started by the Lieutenant at the head of the column." Young's presence in general helped to transform life at this desert outpost for the men of the Ninth Cavalry. In addition to his promotion of music, Young helped to organize football and baseball teams and spent extra time drilling the men in the art of horsemanship. Young recounted for his men stories of his hero Toussaint L'Ouverture, the liberator of Haiti, the inspiration for his ambition to one day become a "Black General." Among the men of Troop I, even the tough old veterans of the Indian wars, the ambitious young lieutenant became affectionately known as "Uncle Charley."[26]

Fresh out of high school, Davis had served in the Eighth United States Volunteer Infantry during the Spanish-American War. At the conclusion of the conflict, following his boyhood dream of becoming an army officer, he enlisted in the regular army with a view to earning a commission. Davis rapidly earned promotion to the noncommissioned rank of sergeant major and when Congress authorized an expansion of the officer corps in 1900, he determined to take the competitive exam. Such a move was unprecedented for a Black NCO, and the old soldiers of the Ninth Cavalry, resigned to White domination of the officer corps, told Davis that he was wasting his time. Charles Young, on the other hand, devoid of the fatalism that gripped so many of the enlisted men, embraced Davis and his ambition with the zeal of a crusader. Despite the fact that his regular duties often kept him "too busy to breathe," he became a mentor to the young NCO.[27]

With the unwavering support of Lieutenant Young, Davis disregarded the naysayers and submitted his application. In his letter of recommendation, Young stated that in the two years of their acquaintance he had come to know Davis as a "temperate, polite, intelligent, [and] trustworthy" officer, "faithful to his duties," and capable of filling "any position to which he may be appointed in the Army." Young spent many hours coaching Davis for the competitive examination, offering particular assistance in mathematics, the subject with which he himself had struggled so mightily at West Point. In the spring of 1901 Davis easily passed the exam at Fort Leavenworth, finishing third among the 12 candidates in his group who had received commissions. His highest score was in math, prompting the examiners to ask him what college he had attended![28]

Young was proud of his protégé, and he and "Ollie" remained "intimately" acquainted for years to come, their paths crossing on numerous occasions, most notably in Wilberforce and Liberia. Davis remained grateful for the "great deal of time" and "invaluable assistance" Young had given him in earning his commission, and participated in annual services honoring his friend for a number of years after his death. He never fully embraced the mission of his mentor, however. In an interview conducted late in his life, Davis categorized Young as his opposite, someone who harbored an agenda and who "was very sensitive of his color." He, on the other hand, professed to have no motive for his ambition but military professionalism. Whereas Young openly allied himself with the cause of civil rights as it gathered steam in the early twentieth century, Davis "regarded Du Bois and the NAACP with suspicion."[29]

It is ironic therefore that Davis was to become a pioneering agent of change in the army, the role Young had foreseen for him when he took him under his wing at Fort Duchesne. Young's mentoring of Davis represents in essence a baton change from the Old Army to the new, and from the Buffalo Soldiers and the pioneering Black officers of the Reconstruction era to those Black soldiers and officers who would live to see an integrated army. Davis ultimately achieved the one career goal that would so sorely elude Young, rising to the rank of brigadier general in 1941. Consciously or not, Davis became a successful agent of Young's agenda. In a final ironic twist to their relationship, in 1936 Davis's son, Benjamin, Jr., became the first African American to graduate from West Point since 1889, the year Charles Young received his diploma.[30]

The expansion of the army that had opened the door of opportunity for Benjamin Davis was engendered by the growing overseas commitments of the United States, and most immediately by efforts to crush an anti-America insurrection in the Philippines. The capture of Manila Bay by Admiral George Dewey in May 1898 contributed to America's speedy victory in the Spanish-American War. The decision of the McKinley administration to ignore Filipino pleas for independence and impose the U.S. mission of "benevolent assimilation" on the archipelago had more lasting consequences. Emilio Aguinaldo's resistance to American control led to wholesale military intervention in 1899. Although the conventional phase of the conflict lasted only a few short months, U.S. forces became embroiled thereafter in a guerrilla struggle that persisted until 1903.

It was during the guerrilla phase of the Philippine war that Charles Young first experienced combat as an officer in the United States Army. The order for the Ninth Cavalry to proceed to the Philippines came just two months after Young's promotion to captain in February 1901. He set sail for the Philippines in April as commander of Troop I. In his thirty-seventh year, Young had reached an important stage in his career. No Black officer in the regular army had ever achieved the rank of captain. Having struck a blow at the fallacy that Black men were unfit to command through his service with the Ninth Ohio Volunteers, Young now would have an opportunity in the regular army, under combat conditions, to prove his ability as a leader of men.[31]

All four Black regiments in the regular army served in the Philippine war. Contrary to stereotypes then prevalent in the army, African American soldiers were no better suited to service in tropical climates than their White counterparts. One veteran noted the propensity of the men to suffer from body sores while serving on Samar Island. They were, however, less prone to hostility toward the native population than their White compatriots. While White soldiers routinely referred to Filipinos as "niggers," "black devils," or "gugus," and White volunteer units earned a particular reputation for looting and pillaging, Black soldiers were for the most part empathetic toward the Filipinos and in many cases developed close relations with the local population. So cordial were these relations that William Howard Taft, then American governor of the Philippines, fretted that intimate liaisons between Black troopers and the local women might damage morale. Despite their misgivings and the parallels some men noted between Jim Crow and official American policy toward the Filipino population, the overwhelming majority of Black regulars nonetheless served in the Philippines with distinction. The qualms these soldiers may have had concerning the questionable tactics of lynching prisoners and carrying out reprisals against the civilian population for the transgressions of a guerrilla army were muted by their sense of duty.[32]

The Ninth Cavalry was stationed in southern Luzon, the most populous and perhaps strategically most important island in the Philippines because of the location there of Manila Bay. The regimental history of the Ninth Cavalry records the unit's service during the "arduous days of the insurrection" filled with "continuous escort and scouting duties, engaging the Filipino enemy and destroying supplies wherever they were found." The troops of the Ninth were routinely faced with the "heart breaking work...[of] pursuing insurrectors in the heart of the tropics, through rice-paddy and forest, over mountains and river; on foot, by banca and on horse." According to one of the men in Young's troop, for much of the Philippine campaign conditions were "extremely rough."[33]

Soon after arriving in the Philippines, Captain Young and Troop I were separated from the regiment and posted to the island of Samar. The third largest island in the archipelago after Luzon and Mindanao, Samar had a fearsome reputation among American troops. Samar's small population was confined to a smattering of coastal towns, but the dense jungle of its rugged interior provided ideal cover for guerrilla forces. In September 1901 Company C of the Ninth U.S. Infantry were attacked at Balalinga. The widespread press coverage afforded the brutal massacre would secure for the island a place of infamy in the mind of Americans. The event prompted an intensification of the American campaign on Samar, which included widespread reprisals and terror tactics. General Jacob Smith, who was given the task of pacifying Samar, ordered his subordinates to "take no prisoners," "kill and burn" at will, and reduce the interior of

Samar to a "howling wilderness." While Smith's tactics reportedly succeeded in putting "the fear of God" in the Filipinos on the island, they outraged anti-imperialist sentiment at home and led ultimately to his
court-martial.[34]

It was on Samar in the months leading up to Balalinga that Young led
his first combat missions. Young and his men were part of a campaign
against the forces of Filipino commander Vincente Lukban. Veterans of
Troop I later recounted numerous stories of Young leading the pursuit of
"insurrectos" in the interior of Samar. Traveling upriver on a chartered
English gunboat called the *Hercules*, Young on a number of occasions
stood and returned fire with his revolver and urged his men to action as a
hail of bullets descended from the heavy brush on both banks. When a
scouting party he was commanding came under attack, Young led the
defense firing his revolver so many times that "its sight was blown off and
its barrel blown to shreds." He grabbed the revolver of one of his officers
and continued to lead the fight until reinforcements arrived. Years after
his death his son recounted a story of Captain Young guiding his men,
weighed down with extra food rations and ammunition, through "a ter-
rific tropical storm" into the teeth of enemy fire. "Clothes tied in a bundle
on his head, cartridge belt and revolver held up, [Young] waded a river
with his men under fire from both banks where natives were in ambush."
Such exploits earned Young the nickname "Follow Me" from his men who
vowed that they "would have died for him."[35]

A struggle eerily reminiscent of the quagmire in Vietnam more than half
a century later, the guerrilla warfare in the Philippines had a psychologi-
cal impact that intensified the hostility harbored by many American soldiers toward the Filipino people and inspired numerous atrocities against
the civilian population. Young's participation in one of the bloodiest campaigns of the Philippine insurrection, however, appears not to have
robbed him of compassion for the native population. In a conflict in which
American troops earned a reputation among the local population for looting and terrorizing civilians, the men of Troop I enjoyed cordial relations
with the Filipinos they encountered. When the troop entered Blanca
Aurora on Samar they found the town burned and looted. Young put his
men to work in the rebuilding process and won the confidence of the
town's inhabitants and the commendation of General Robert B. Hughes,
who reportedly promised a choice post for Troop I on their return to the
United States. Despite his conviction that American rule would ultimately
benefit the Philippines by infusing the people with the habits of "civilized
living" and imposing "government according to western standards,"
Young did not share the deep-rooted racism toward the Filipinos that
guided the decisions of so many of his White counterparts. Young
believed that, far from being doomed to perpetual inferiority, the Filipinos
were gifted with "great natural intelligence" and, given the opportunity,

they could prove themselves the equal of their American overlords. Although Young often betrayed the paternalism so characteristic of Victorian philanthropists, his solution to the pacification of the Philippines mirrored his philosophy for "racial uplift" in the United States. According to an article published shortly after Young's death, "many a young Filipino educated in America came here at the instance of Young from the far interior, and has returned to his native land to apply the arts of peace."[36]

In August 1901 Young and his men returned to Luzon and, remounting for the first time since arriving in the Philippines, took over the horses of the Sixth Cavalry in the southern town of Darago. Here they participated in services marking the September 6 assassination of President McKinley and then moved on to Tobaco, where they would remain until the following spring. Young and his charges saw little military action in this period, yet these were probably their most difficult months in the Philippines. The horses were plagued by surra, a deadly disease similar to sleeping sickness, while the men battled a cholera epidemic then rampant throughout the islands. A series of typhoons and heavy rains compounded their discomfort and made Young's task of containing the spread of disease among his men more difficult. In June, after moving on to Rosario in the unsuccessful pursuit of a band of Aguinaldo supporters, Troop I was ordered to the island of Panay.[37]

More densely populated and fertile than Samar, Panay had witnessed little resistance to American occupation since early in the conflict. In any case the war was winding down and one month after Troop I arrived on Panay President Roosevelt declared the conflict over. As in Luzon, Young's primary task in Panay was preventing the spread of disease, which in addition to cholera now included smallpox and malaria. Young himself was briefly bedridden with a bout of fever, and at Panay Troop I suffered one of only two casualties of the campaign when a man died of beriberi. Young took each death very hard; he was heartbroken when during a training exercise he lost a man in an accidental drowning. His genuine concern for his men was returned, with interest. He stayed in touch with members of his "beloved rowdy gang" for years afterward. To one Troop I Philippine veteran "he was a father, brother, teacher, and a real true friend at all times under all circumstances...I really loved him." In the fall of 1902 the Ninth Cavalry was recalled to the United States. Young and his men traveled on the U.S.S. *Sumner* from Manila to Nagasaki, Japan, before returning to San Francisco aboard the U.S.S. *Sheridan* in October. According to a report in the Indianapolis *Freeman*, "the colored officer of the Ninth Cavalry...was a great favorite on the *Sheridan*," entertaining his fellow travelers on the piano and cementing his reputation as "a pianist of rare ability." Young had grown as an officer and leader of men during the Philippine campaign, and he radiated confidence in everything he did.[38]

For the next several months Troop I was stationed at the Presidio, the storied army base on the outskirts of San Francisco. Despite a drunken shooting incident that left one of his men in the post hospital, Captain Young's troop enjoyed "a splendid reputation for discipline and good behavior" while at the Presidio. The Presidio, with its urban setting and the Bay Area's large African American population, was regarded by the men as a much more desirable post than the remote forts of the West or the hostile towns of the South. The setting afforded the opportunity for numerous visitors such as Booker T. Washington, who in January 1903 accepted an invitation from Young to speak to the men. The event drew a large public audience, and afterward in his residence on officers' row Young hosted a lunch for Washington and some of the other guests. Other visitors to the Presidio that winter included the influential Black journalist T. Thomas Fortune, President Roosevelt, and Charles Young's mother, whose visit was more noteworthy in the minds of many of the men than the famous dignitaries. In the spring of 1903, however, Troop I was on the move again with orders to proceed to Sequoia and General Grant National Parks, three hundred miles southeast of San Francisco. Here Young was to take up the position of acting superintendent, another novel posting that would open a new chapter in an already eclectic career.[39]

The Spanish-American War and the subsequent occupation of the Philippines afforded unprecedented opportunities for junior officers in the United States Army. In an age when American society was infused with the martial spirit and war had not yet lost the veneer of glorious adventure, these young officers were eager to gain combat experience of their own to rival the exploits of their superiors during the Civil War and the Indian campaigns. Furthermore, the requirements of empire were welcomed by all officers because of the prospect of accelerated promotion arising from the army's enlargement.

America's wars of expansion, therefore, represented a critical juncture in the careers of Charles Young and his peers. Despite missing the action in Cuba, Young took full advantage of the opportunities afforded him during this period. Although his service with the Ninth Ohio Volunteer Battalion gave him some cause for regret, the experience served to solidify his reputation as an officer and dispel any doubts about his ability to command. If any did remain, they were put to rest by his tour of duty with Troop I of the Ninth Cavalry in the jungles of Samar.

When he returned to the United States in 1902, 2 years shy of 40, Young was a captain with combat experience under his belt. While his presence in an officer's uniform still drew resentment from many White soldiers, Young was gradually making inroads with some of his White colleagues. This is perhaps most clearly illustrated by a story that made headlines in 1903 concerning Young and Lieutenant B. R. Tillman, son of the infamous

South Carolina race baiter Benjamin "Pitchfork" Tillman. Young was an invited guest at a banquet thrown by the younger Tillman for some offi-cers stationed at the Presidio. When asked by incredulous reporters if the invitation of the Black officer had been an oversight, Lieutenant Tillman retorted, "No, he is a gentleman and a friend of mine."[40]

Rare as such invitations were, Young must have welcomed it as another small stride forward in his personal crusade. Far from being tempered by such breakthroughs, however, Young was committed to the larger strug-gle for racial equality and that commitment intensified with each advanc-ing year. At every opportunity he planted new seeds for his cause. He served as a mentor to prodigies in uniform such as Benjamin Davis at Fort Duchesne and Lieutenant Wilson Ballard of the Ninth Ohio, who would later serve with Young in Liberia. He provided educational opportunities to the Filipino students whose study he sponsored in the United States and to enlisted men at Fort Duchesne to whom he taught basic literacy. Imbued with boundless energy, Charles Young welcomed the new cen-tury filled with the optimism of a man who envisaged a new dawn for race relations in America.

NOTES

1. Willard B. Gatewood, "Black Americans and the Quest for Empire, 1898–1903," *Journal of Southern History* 38 (November 1972): 545–566.

2. Stuart Creighton Miller, *"Benevolent Assimilation:" The American Conquest of the Philippines, 1899–1903* (New Haven, Conn., 1982), 92; Michael C. Robinson and Frank N. Schubert, "David Fagen: An Afro-American Rebel in the Philippines, 1899–1901," *Pacific Historical Review* 44 (1975): 68–83; Scot Ngozi-Brown, "African-American Soldiers and Filipinos: Racial Imperialism, Jim Crow and Social Rela-tions," *The Journal of Negro History* 82 (winter 1997): 42–54; George W. Prioleau to the Editor, *The Freeman* (Indianapolis), reprinted in Willard B. Gatewood, *"Smoked Yankees," and the Struggle for Empire: Letters from Negro Soldiers, 1898–1902* (Urbana, Ill., 1971), 308.

3. Charles Young, *The Military Morale of Nations and Races* (St. Louis, 1912), 207–15, 251–54.

4. Willard B. Gatewood, "Ohio's Negro Battalion in the Spanish American War," *Northeast Ohio Quarterly* 45 (1973): 58; The other seven states to include a Black volunteer unit in their initial quota of volunteers were North Carolina, Alabama, Illinois, Kansas, Virginia, Indiana, and Massachusetts. See Marvin Fletcher, "The Black Volunteers and the Spanish American War," *Military Affairs* 38 (April 1974): 48–53; Gatewood, *"Smoked Yankees,"* 101; General James Marshall to General H.C. Corbin, 25 July 1898, Letters Received by the Appointment, Com-mission, and Personal Branch, Adjutant General's Office, 1871–1917, Record Group 94, National Archives, Washington, D.C. [hereinafter ACP File]; Asa Bush-nell to General H.C. Corbin, 10 May 1898, ACP File.

5. Asa Bushnell to Adjutant General's Office, 6 April 1898, ACP File; Gate-wood, "Ohio's Negro Battalion," 58.

6. Charles Young to Adjutant General's Office, 6 April 1898, ACP File; Charles Young to Charles Broad, 6 April 1898, Coleman Collection, Akron, Ohio; Adjutant General's Office to Charles Young, 28 August 1899, ACP File; Charles Young to Colonel William P. Duvall, 24 August 1899, ACP File; Charles Young to Adjutant General's Office, 26 August 1899, ACP File.

7. Gatewood, "Ohio's Negro Battalion," 59; Asa Bushnell to the Officers of the Ninth Ohio Battalion, 28 June 1898, Asa S. Bushnell Papers, Ohio Historical Society, Columbus, Ohio; "The Colored Troops," *Ohio State Journal*, 20 May 1898, 1; Fletcher, "Black Volunteers," 49.

8. Gatewood, "Ohio's Negro Battalion," 59–60; Charles Young to Assistant Adjutant General, 30 June 1898, Regimental Book Records of the Ninth Ohio Colored Battalion, Spanish-American War, Records of the Adjutant General's Office, RG 94, National Archives, Washington, D.C. [hereinafter Regimental Book]; *Cleveland Gazette*, 16 July 1898.

9. J. Madison Pierce to the Editor, *Cleveland Gazette*, 2 July 1898, reprinted in Gatewood, "*Smoked Yankees*," 111–112; Gatewood, "Ohio's Negro Battalion," 60; *Cleveland Gazette*, 13 August 1898.

10. *Cleveland Gazette*, 9 July 1898; Interview with William West, Vienna, Va., 24 June 1970, cited in Greene, Robert E. *Colonel Charles Young: Soldier and Diplomat* (Washington, D.C., 1985), 52.

11. *Ohio State Journal*, 9 and 12 June 1898; J. Madison Pierce to the Editor, *Cleveland Gazette*, 2 July 1898, and 30 July 1898, reprinted in Gatewood, "*Smoked Yankees*," 111–112; Gatewood, "Ohio's Negro Battalion," 60.

12. J. Madison Pierce to the Editor, *Cleveland Gazette*, 23 August 1898, reprinted in Gatewood, "*Smoked Yankees*," 114; *Harrisburg Commonwealth* cited in *Cleveland Gazette*, 19 November 1898; Wilson Ballard, "Outline History of the Ninth (Separate) Battalion, Ohio Volunteer Infantry," in T.G. Steward, *The Colored Regulars in the United States Army* (New York, 1969), 296.

13. J. Madison Pierce to the Editor, *Cleveland Gazette*, 23 August 1898, reprinted in Gatewood, "*Smoked Yankees*," 114; Major A.J. Steward to Charles Young, 18 October 1898, Regimental Book; Ballard, "Ninth Battalion," 296; T. Miles Dewey to the Editor, *Cleveland Gazette*, 8 October 1898, reprinted in Gatewood, "*Smoked Yankees*," 115–116.

14. T. Miles Dewey to the Editor, *Cleveland Gazette*, 8 October 1898, reprinted in Gatewood, "*Smoked Yankees*," 115–116; Winslow Hobson to the Editor, *Cleveland Gazette*, 15 October 1898, reprinted in Gatewood, "*Smoked Yankees*," 117–119.

15. Fletcher, "Black Volunteers," 50; Newspaper clipping, n.d. [1898], Coleman Collection.

16. T. Miles Dewey to Editor, *Cleveland Gazette*, 22 October 1898, reprinted in Gatewood, "*Smoked Yankees*," 119–120; Charles Young to Adjutant General's Office, 22 October 1898, Regimental Book; Charles Young to Adjutant General's Office, 2 November 1898, Regimental Book; Charles Young to Adjutant General's Office, 6 December 1898, Regimental Book.

17. Charles Young to Adjutant General's Office, 22 October 1898, Regimental Book; Adjutant General's Office to Charles Young, 25 October 1898, Regimental Book.

18. Gatewood, "Ohio's Negro Regulars," 57–58; Ralph Tyler to George Myers, 11 May 1898, George A. Myers Papers, Ohio Historical Society, Columbus, Ohio

[hereinafter Myers Papers]; Ralph Tyler to George Myers, 12 September 1898, Myers Papers; "Major Young Slandered," *Cleveland Gazette,* 19 November 1898, 1.

19. Unsigned letter to the Editor, *Cleveland Gazette,* 12 November 1898, reprinted in Gatewood, *"Smoked Yankees,"* 121; Ballard, "Ninth Battalion," 297.

20. Special Order No. 3, Camp Marion, 7 November 1898, Regimental Book; *The Chronicle* (Augusta, Ga.), 30 January 1898, quoted in Gatewood, "Ohio's Negro Regulars," 62–63; Ballard, "Ninth Battalion," 297.

21. *Cleveland Gazette,* 4 February 1899, quoted in Gatewood, "Ohio's Negro Regulars," 63.

22. S. T. Mitchell to General Russell A. Alger, 26 August 1898, ACP File; S. T. Mitchell to President William McKinley, 26 August 1898, ACP File; S. T. Mitchell to Secretary of War, with margin note, 28 August 1898, ACP File; Charles Young to Adjutant General's Office, 18 May 1899, ACP File.

23. Charles Young to Booker T. Washington, 9 March 1899, in Louis R. Harlan, ed., *The Papers of Booker T. Washington,* vol. 5 (Champaign, Ill., 1975), 53–54; Charles Young to Booker T. Washington, 31 May 1899, in Harlan, *Papers of Booker T. Washington,* 5, 69–70; Charles Young to Adjutant General's Office, 18 May, 1 June, 30 June, 1 August, and 31 August 1899, ACP File.

24. Fletcher, *Black Soldier and Officer,* 28; Office of the Chief of Military History, United States Army, *American Military History: Army Historical Series* (Washington, D.C., 1989), 345.

25. Charles Noel Young, "Biography of Charles Young," Coleman Collection; Ronald G. Coleman, "The Buffalo Soldiers: Guardians of the Uintah Frontier, 1886–1901," *Utah Historical Quarterly* 47 (fall 1979): 420–439; Robert Foster, "Buffalo Soldiers in the Utah Territory," *Wild West* 12 (February, 2000): 1–7; Sergeant Nichols, Troop I, Ninth Cavalry, testimony collected on the life of Charles Young by Harry Atwood, 1 January 1945, Coleman Collection.

26. "Family Tree and Early Life," Benjamin O'Davis, Sr., Papers, U.S. Military History Institute, Carlisle, Pa. [hereinafter Davis Papers] Sergeant Nichols, Troop I, Ninth Cavalry, testimony collected on the life of Charles Young by Harry Atwood, 1 January 1945, Coleman Collection; Charles Noel Young, "Biography of Charles Young," Coleman Collection.

27. Marvin E. Fletcher, *America's First Black General: Benjamin O. Davis Sr., 1880–1970* (Lawrence, Kans., 1989): 13–28; Charles Young to William Broad, 20 December 1899, Charles Young File, Moorland-Spingarn Research Center, Howard University, Washington, D.C. [hereinafter Young File MSRC].

28. Letter of Introduction by Charles Young, 26 January 1901, Davis Papers; Fletcher, *America's First Black General,* 27; Taped interview conducted with Benjamin O. Davis, Sr. by Marvin Fletcher and Edward Coffman, Chicago, Ill., 2 June 1968, Marvin Fletcher Collection, U.S. Military Institute, Carlisle, Pa. [hereinafter Fletcher Collection].

29. Charles Young to Benjamin O. Davis, 28 August 1905, Davis Papers; Benjamin Davis to Colonel Burt, 7 March 1925, Coleman Collection; Benjamin O. Davis interview with Marvin Fletcher, 2 June 1968, Fletcher Collection.

30. See Fletcher, *America's First Black General.*

31. Young had an average score of 91 percent on the promotion exam. This was a 2 percent improvement over his score in his promotion exam for first lieutenant in 1896. Promotion Examination Results, 30 January 1901, ACP File; Adjutant Gen-

eral's Office to Charles Young, 5 February 1901, ACP File; Entry under Charles Young, "Military History of Officers, 1898–1919," 58, Ninth Cavalry, 1866–1918, Regimental Records, Records of the U.S. Regular Army Mobile Units, RG 391, National Archives, Washington, D.C. [hereinafter Regimental Records].

32. Veteran questionnaires and correspondence in Spanish-American War, Philippine Insurrection, and Boxer Rebellion Veteran Research Project, U.S. Military History Institute, Carlisle, Penn. [hereinafter Spanish-American War Project]; Miller, "Benevolent Assimilation," 193; Robinson and Schubert, "David Fagen," 70–71; Ngozi-Brown, "African-American Soldiers and Filipinos," 42–45.

33. Lieutenant Colonel George B. Rodney, "History of the Ninth Cavalry," n.d., Regimental Records; Sergeant Nichols, Troop I, Ninth Cavalry, testimony collected on the life of Charles Young by Harry Atwood, 1 January 1945, Coleman Collection.

34. Rodney, "History of the Ninth Cavalry," Regimental Records; Miller, "Benevolent Assimilation," 199–232.

35. Sergeant Nichols, Troop I, Ninth Cavalry, testimony collected on the life of Charles Young by Harry Atwood, 1 January 1945, Coleman Collection; J. A. S. Blakeney, Troop I, Ninth Cavalry, testimony collected on the life of Charles Young by Harry Atwood, 18 April 1922, Coleman Collection; Charles Noel Young, "Biography of Charles Young," Coleman Collection; Extracts from Colonel Charles Young's Record, Fletcher Collection; "Military History of Officers, 1898–1919," 58, Regimental Records; Nancy Gordon Heinl, "Charles Young," in Dictionary of American Negro Biography, ed. Rayford W. Logan and Michael R. Winston (New York, 1985), 677.

36. Miller, "Benevolent Assimilation," 176–195; Charles Noel Young, "Biography of Charles Young," Coleman Collection; Sergeant Nichols, Troop I, Ninth Cavalry, testimony collected on the life of Charles Young by Harry Atwood, 1 January 1945, Coleman Collection; E. H. Lawson, "One Out of Twelve Million: Unrevealed Facts in the Life Story of Col. Charles Young, West Pointer," Washington Post, 26 May 1929, 11.

37. Charles Noel Young, "Biography of Charles Young," Coleman Collection; Sergeant Nichols, Troop I, Ninth Cavalry, testimony collected on the life of Charles Young by Harry Atwood, 1 January 1945, Coleman Collection; S. B. Pearson to Ada Young, 17 March 1922, Coleman Collection; "Military History of Officers, 1898–1919," 58, Regimental Records.

38. Charles Noel Young, "Biography of Charles Young," Coleman Collection; S. B. Pearson to Ada Young, 17 March 1922, Coleman Collection; Charles Young to Joseph Clark, 16 October 1916, Coleman Collection; Sergeant Nichols, Troop I, Ninth Cavalry, testimony collected on the life of Charles Young by Harry Atwood, 1 January 1945, Coleman Collection; "Military History of Officers, 1898–1919," 58, Regimental Records; Indianapolis Freeman, 27 December 1902, quoted in Schubert, On the Trail of the Buffalo Soldier, 490.

39. San Francisco Chronicle, 8 November 1902, quoted in Schubert, On the Trail of the Buffalo Soldier, 140; Account of Booker T. Washington's 1903 California Tour by Max Bennett Thrasher, 31 January 1903, in Harlan, Papers of Booker T. Washington, 7, 23–24; "Military History of Officers, 1898–1919," 58, Regimental Records.

40. Indianapolis Freeman, 31 January 1903, quoted in Schubert, On the Trail of the Buffalo Soldier, 490.

CHAPTER 5

Our Man in Hispaniola

The first president to serve a full term in the twentieth century, Theodore Roosevelt set the tone for American government in the modern era. Roosevelt redefined the constitutional role of the executive and set in motion the rise of what contemporary observers have dubbed the imperial presidency. Promising a square deal at home and carrying a big stick abroad, he inaugurated a new relationship between the president and Congress in both domestic and foreign policy. Roosevelt's progressive domestic agenda and aggressive pursuit of American interests overseas left an indelible imprint on the American republic.

The impact of Roosevelt's activist presidency was arguably most keenly felt in the areas of foreign policy and the environment. Charles Young's service in the early years of the twentieth century reflected the expanding role of the American government in these two fields. Young's appointment as acting superintendent of Sequoia and General Grant National Parks in 1903 came under a president who demonstrated a passion for environmentalism and preservation that no subsequent occupant of the White House has matched. It was a passion that Young shared, as he devoted himself to the tasks of making the parks accessible to the public and preserving the giant sequoia trees for future generations.[1]

In 1904 Young became the first United States military attaché ever posted to Haiti and the Dominican Republic. In 1889 the U.S. War Department began posting military attachés overseas under the supervision of the newly created Military Information Division (MID). The majority of initial postings were to the capitals of the major powers in Europe and Asia. It was only following the Spanish-American War that the United States began to consistently post military attachés to countries in Latin

America and the Caribbean. Much of the impetus for these new postings came from the Roosevelt corollary to the Monroe Doctrine, which unilaterally sanctioned U.S. intervention in the affairs of the Latin American nations to preserve the Western Hemisphere from European intervention.[2]

As opposed to the more traditional diplomatic function of those who served in Europe and Asia, military attachés in Latin America and the Caribbean were charged with gathering military intelligence and compiling geographic surveys. This intelligence was critical to the successful implementation of the practice of gunboat diplomacy, whereby the United States intervened regularly in the affairs of its southern neighbors to safeguard American interests. Military attachés thus played a pivotal role in the establishment of U.S. hegemony in the region in the first quarter of the twentieth century. For example, the Roosevelt administration relied heavily on information gathered by military attachés in Venezuela and Colombia to facilitate critical U.S. military intervention in Panama in 1903. Young's posting to Haiti and the Dominican Republic was similarly designed to gather relevant intelligence to be used in the event Washington determined that a U.S. invasion of either island nation was warranted.[3]

On May 20, 1903, Captain Charles Young rode out of the Presidio at the head of a column containing 3 officers and 93 enlisted men, Troops I and M of the Ninth Cavalry. With 4 escort wagons and 20 draft mules in its wake, the column marched southeast from San Francisco to the outskirts of the Sequoia and General Grant National Parks. With stops in San Jose and Fresno, among other places, it took Young and his men 16 days to traverse the rich farmland of central California before reaching the slopes of the Sierra Nevada. From his headquarters at Kaweah, just west of the entrance to Sequoia National Park, Young launched himself enthusiastically into his new role as acting superintendent.[4]

Before the establishment of the National Parks Service in 1916, the task of maintaining and improving America's national parks fell to the United States Army. Military officers, usually no higher than captains, were detailed by the Department of the Interior to serve for the summer months as acting superintendents. These assignments were rarely renewed, and so most parks, Sequoia and General Grant included, never had a superintendent who served more than two consecutive seasons. As a result, the army had a history of limited accomplishments in the parks, and expectations for major improvements were low.[5]

Sequoia National Park was established by the Department of the Interior in 1890 to preserve the natural wonder of the giant sequoias, the largest trees in the world, from encroachment by the growing settler population in Tulare County. This was one of many examples of the clashing interests of progress and preservation in late-nineteenth-century America.

The struggle was brought into sharper focus by the environmental wing of the progressive movement, which decried the damage already done by the unbridled post–Civil War expansion of commercial agriculture and industry in the lands west of the Mississippi. Although nationalization succeeded in protecting the giant sequoia trees from the lumber industry, there were other human dangers that threatened the pristine nature of the park. The first troop of U.S. cavalry, which arrived in the park in May 1891, discovered thousands of sheep grazing in the mountain meadows and numerous hunters and trappers preying on the deer, bear, and other wildlife. Enforcing federal law on the pioneer population of the region was not easy.[6]

The task was made that much more difficult by the fact that army units were detailed to the parks only in the summer months, leaving the land exposed for nine months of the year. Gradually, however, violation of the Sequoia and General Grant Parks by hunters and farmers was brought to an end, and by the turn of the century the acting superintendents were free to turn their attention to making the parks accessible to the growing number of tourists who were eager to visit. In 1900, following the authorization of an annual $10,000 appropriation by Congress, the army began the task of building a road to the Giant Forest, the chief attraction of the Sequoia National Park. Progress was fitful, however, as the work completed each summer was often undone during the long winter season. As a result, by the time Young and his men arrived at Kaweah in 1903, only five miles, roughly two-thirds, of the planned road was complete.[7]

After securing the park against "depredations" and inspecting the construction area in the company of the engineer, Young wasted little time in setting about the task of completing the road. He worked his men tirelessly for two months until finally the first wagons rolled into the Giant Forest. On August 15 Young organized a picnic beneath "the Big Trees" to reward the men for their labors and to celebrate the completion of the project. The men put together an elaborate feast that was attended by numerous local dignitaries and guest-of-honor Governor George Pardee. With the summer season not yet over, however, the acting superintendent was not content to rest on his laurels. Following a brief respite, he put the men back to work and extended the road another two miles from the Giant Forest to the base of Moro Rock, another of the park's premier attractions. Troop I also completed a road begun the previous season connecting the General Grant National Forest with the county road leading to the town of Visalia seven miles to the west. In addition to improving trails and building fire brakes, Young and his men constructed in one summer more road than their predecessors had built in three.[8]

Where previous acting superintendents perhaps saw this assignment as a temporary summer sojourn, Charles Young committed himself body and soul to the parks. In his final report to the secretary of the interior,

Young envisaged a future in which thousands of "overworked and weary citizens of the country can find rest, coolness, and quiet for a few weeks during the hot summer months," accessing both Sequoia and General Grant National Parks on a ring road "where wild scenic beauty cannot be surpassed." In keeping with his perspective of the parks as national treasures, Young recommended that "irresponsible parties" be prevented in future from naming the giant sequoia trees for personal reasons. The names of the trees, in his view, should "be acceptable to the entire nation." Building on the earlier tradition of naming trees for Civil War heroes such as Generals Grant and Sherman, Young permitted the christening of the G.A.R. Tree in honor of all the unheralded union veterans, like his father, who had fought in the war. In addition, to honor the toil of the Black troopers who had completed the Giant Forest Road, he named a tree after that "great and good American, Booker T. Washington."[9]

Committed to "the preservation of these mountains just as they are," Young urged the Department of the Interior to take note of the continuing danger of environmental degradation in the parks. If the United States government was to take seriously the need for "forest preservation," Young warned, it must learn from the mistakes of Europe, where the "wanton destruction of the forests" caused, in his view, inestimable damage. To prevent further destruction of the sequoias, he urged the Department of the Interior to purchase the roughly 4,000 acres of privately held land in the park. To facilitate the process Young obtained options from the owners on 3,877 acres of this land for the sum of $73,000, or $19 an acre. Congress, however, declined to appropriate the funds, in the process deferring to future taxpayers a larger bill. In 1916 Congress appropriated $70,000 toward the purchase of just 670 acres of this land, and between 1919 and 1927 the National Park Service paid a great deal more than Young's original asking price for a further 2,166 acres.[10]

Young's successor as acting superintendent was impressed by the excellent condition of the parks and the quality and quantity of the work done on the roads and trails. This he put down "to the strict personal supervision of the work given by Captain Young." Meanwhile, the Inspector General's Office commended Young for his work as acting superintendent and noted that his men were "without doubt the best instructed of any of the four troops" then serving in America's national parks. Young also earned the esteem of the local citizen population for his work in the parks. The Visalia Board of Trade, cognizant of the financial benefits that would follow the influx of tourists into the region, offered a unanimous vote of thanks to Captain Young for "his energy and enthusiasm" and "his interest shown in the discharge of his duties" as acting superintendent of Sequoia and General Grant National Parks. For one Visalia merchant however, prejudice proved to be a stronger force than gratitude. When Young stopped at his restaurant one evening for a meal, the proprietor refused under any circumstances to serve him.[11]

In November 1903, Young led his men back to their winter quarters at the Presidio. Any pangs of regret Young may have felt about leaving the beautiful Sierra Nevada were no doubt overshadowed by the prospect of returning to San Francisco where his fiancé, Ada Mills, was waiting for him. Ada was the 23-year-old daughter of a well-to-do mulatto family from Oakland, California. Charles, 16 years her senior, had begun dating his bride-to-be before being posted to Sequoia National Park. They would spend long hours together among the California poppies "in the meadows around the Presidio." It was Young's second serious romantic relationship; he had briefly been engaged to Delilah Beasley, another Oakland native, who would go on to enjoy considerable renown as a groundbreaking Black female journalist in California. Indeed Young, whose handsome features were enhanced by the pageant of uniform, had no shortage of female admirers. According to his friends, while Young loved people, he particularly liked women and gravitated toward their company in social settings. While at Fort Duchesne he felt compelled to write to a White woman he had met out East, asking her to stop sending him letters, books, and presents. He confided to his sergeant that he feared if he did not "stop this lady's attentions to me...the colored folk will hang me and whites will burn me." With Ada, however, there was never any doubt about his intentions. On February 4, 1904, following a Catholic ceremony in Oakland, Charlie and Ada Young began their new life together as a married couple.[12]

Charles Young's wedding day was "one of the most momentous and happy days of his life." Right up until his death in 1922 he remained deeply in love with Ada. For much of his career she accompanied him to posts throughout the United States and overseas, from the Philippines to Haiti and Liberia. Together they shared a passion for music and literature, and a penchant for foreign languages and culture, which drove their mutual ambition to live out their retirement years in Europe. She was his most important confidant and he regularly sought, and acted on, her advice on a range of issues, from the personal to the professional. "Only he and she knew of the sleepless night hours when life pressed too sorely upon him that she kept watch with him, of the difficult hours of the day made tolerable by the stay of her compassion and counsel." Ada's empathy for the burden of Young's position as ranking Black officer in the army was grounded in personal experience. Her marriage to Charles had caused uproar among the wives of the White officers in the Ninth Cavalry because protocol demanded that they call on her and invite her to all post functions.[13]

As he entered this new phase in his life, Young was beginning to refine his political views, and particularly his perspective on the civil rights struggle. For much of the post–Civil War era, Booker T. Washington was the most visible public figure in Black America, and there were few serious challengers to his accommodationist approach to race relations, as outlined in his "Atlanta Compromise" speech of 1895. However, in the early twentieth century a number of young Black intellectuals began to voice increasing misgivings about the leadership of the "Wizard of Tuskegee" and his gradualist agenda. This opposition would coalesce around the Niagra Movement after 1905 and ultimately find a leader to rival Washington in the person of Young's good friend, W. E. B. Du Bois. Although Young admired Washington, and would later answer his call to serve in Liberia, his own civil rights philosophy was taking shape along lines similar to the thinking of Du Bois.[14]

As a guest lecturer speaking before a group of students at Stanford University in December 1903, Young took issue with Washington's philosophy of promoting industrial and agricultural training as a necessary prerequisite to breaking the barriers that denied Blacks access to education and political power. Young told his listeners that such a plan would not succeed because once African Americans had conquered the industrial trades, when seeking employment they would still meet the refrain of no Black man need apply. For Young, and a growing number of other young African Americans, crumbs from the counter served only to impede the ultimate goal of earning a seat at the table. This seat was to be achieved by the advancement of the "Talented Tenth" through education and the ranks of the professions.[15]

The Stanford speech illustrates Young's increasingly sophisticated ideological perspective on race relations, but one that served only to reinforce his already deep-rooted conviction. Flush with confidence from his professional and personal triumphs, Charles Young had reached a point of stability in his life. He no longer feared for his future in the army, as he had early in his career. The pressure to prove his capabilities as an officer was a burden that now weighed less heavily on his shoulders. On the threshold of middle age, Young had found companionship, and he and Ada looked forward to returning home to Wilberforce and starting a family together. Before that could happen, however, Young received word in April 1904 that he was to be sent to Port-au-Prince to serve as United States military attaché to Haiti and the Dominican Republic. On May 12, Captain and Mrs. Young left San Francisco and, after taking leave of family and friends in the United States, they traveled to Haiti, arriving in Port-au-Prince on May 30.[16]

The need for a military attaché on the island of Hispaniola reflected the growing interest and influence of the United States in the Caribbean. Hispaniola was of strategic importance because of its proximity to U.S.-occupied Cuba, the U.S. territory of Puerto Rico, and, most important, Panama, where the United States had resolved to construct a transisthmian canal. The chronic instability of the two small republics that shared the island was a matter of grave concern for an American administration anxious to preempt conditions from arising that might invite European intervention in a region Washington regarded as its exclusive sphere of influence. In the words of the *Army and Navy Journal* "the chaotic conditions of political affairs [there]...may yet require the intervention of American influence to prevent...oppressive demands from foreign creditors." With insufficient intelligence to develop viable contingency plans for military action in Hispaniola, the army impressed on the War Department the necessity of dispatching an attaché to the island.[17]

Charles Young's appointment as military attaché to Haiti and the Dominican Republic was undoubtedly the highest singular honor of his career to that point. In addition to becoming the first African American to hold such a position, he was one of only 23 U.S. Army officers serving in that capacity overseas. His appointment reflected the War Department's confidence in his capabilities as an officer. His service in the Philippines and his knowledge of French and Spanish were no doubt significant factors in his selection. Above all else, however, he was chosen for this assignment because he was the most senior Black officer in the United States Army. The army hoped that, "being a member of the colored race," Young would "command the immediate confidence and good will" of the Haitians and Dominicans. Young's presence in Haiti, one of only two independent Black nations then in existence, and the Dominican Republic, with its mixed Black and Hispanic population, would be far less conspicuous than that of a White officer, an important consideration given the sensitivity of the mission.[18]

Young arrived in Port-au-Prince less than five months after the army had initially determined the need for a military attaché in Hispaniola. The rapidity of the implementation process, together with the dual nature of the position, presented some initial communications problems. By the time Young disembarked at Port-au-Prince, the American minister, William P. Powell, had not yet received instructions concerning the new attaché's duties. As it turned out, the War Department had mistakenly forwarded this information to the legation in Santo Domingo, the Dominican capital. Young himself appeared confused and requested clarification from Washington as to whether he should travel to Santo Domingo to present his credentials. Clearly the War Department had not sufficiently thought through the logistics of the position, and so, less than a month after Young first set foot on Hispaniola, the secretary of war cancelled his appointment to Santo Domingo citing the inexpediency of serving in the two capitals at the same time.[19]

Despite this inauspicious beginning, Young quickly demonstrated adeptness for his new post, wearing the twin hats of ambassador and intelligence officer with customary aplomb and requisite tact. In addition to settling into his new quarters and organizing his desk at the legation, Young spent his first week in Port-au-Prince meeting with various Haitian government officials. As the first military attaché to be appointed to Haiti from any country, his arrival caused quite an official stir in Port-au-Prince. In quick succession he met with Haiti's octogenarian president, General Pierre "Tonton" Nord Alexis, as well as the minister for foreign affairs and the minister for war and marine. The finale to this whirlwind week was a champagne reception in honor of the dashing "Capitaine Young" hosted by the president at the Palais National. To the strains of the palace band, Port-au-Prince's notables maneuvered for an audience with "the handsome Black" military attaché, who exhibited throughout a "distinguished bearing and charming manners."[20]

Young's immediate celebrity in Port-au-Prince provided a solid foundation for the work he was about to undertake. The goodwill of Haiti's powerful and influential people was a necessary prerequisite for Young to carry out his orders—compiling an original study of the two republics on Hispaniola. In late summer he was granted permission by Haitian officials to travel into the interior, and in September 1904 he undertook the first of many reconnaissance missions that would take him to places that no American had gone to before. During the next two years, traveling on horseback and accompanied only by an interpreter who also served as his guide, Young traversed the length and breadth of Haiti and made numerous excursions across the border into the Dominican Republic. Usually absent from the capital for two to three weeks at a time, Young would return to Port-au-Prince laden with information that he then compiled into detailed reports to be forwarded to the military information division in Washington.[21]

The results of Young's labors were manifold. In addition to composing numerous detailed reports on the topography, communications, fortifications, and military preparedness of Haiti and Santo Domingo, Young compiled a 294-page monograph on Haiti analyzing all aspects of the republic, from its government and laws to its culture and language. He drafted a series of detailed maps of the regions he had toured, many of which were previously uncharted, and in the process created the first systematic cartographic record of the island of Hispaniola. Young also found time to exercise his considerable skill as a linguist by compiling a meticulously detailed French-English-Creole dictionary and grammar. His indefatigable efforts more than rewarded his superiors for their faith in his ability.[22]

The extent of Young's accomplishments during his three years in Haiti won him the admiration of the American personnel with whom he served. Minister Powell commended Young to the secretary of state for his "careful and painstaking work." He praised the Haiti monograph as "a most interesting book," full of indispensable information on Haiti and its people. Powell informed his superiors that Young's maps were unequivocally the best of any ever made of Haiti and the Dominican Republic, very often containing information that was previously unavailable to the governments of the two island republics. Young, in the American minister's estimation, had exceeded the call of duty, diligently following "the instructions of his Department, even at times when he was unfit from sickness to travel, and even at times against the advice of his physician." Powell's successor highlighted one of the reasons for Young's success when he noted approvingly the military attaché's cordial relations with Haitian government officials, who willingly supplied him with information, wrote letters of introduction to officers in distant places, and granted him every facility to carry out his assignment.[23]

This genial relationship came under mounting strain, however, as Young's operations became increasingly covert in nature. From January 1905 Young had been authorized by the MID to begin traveling incognito. There was a limit to the scope and content of the information that Young's hosts were willing to share. Secrecy was required to gather information on leading Haitian individuals and their movements, photograph buildings and structures of military or political importance, and survey potential "landing places" and encampments for occupying troops. By the spring of 1906 Young's welcome in Haiti was beginning to wear thin, and he was finding it increasingly difficult to "obtain desired information." During the next 12 months word began to reach the American legation in Port-au-Prince about accusations of spying leveled against Young for sketching fortifications and gathering information on the government. There was even a rumor, which both Young and the American legation strongly denied, that he had been detained and mistreated by a contingent of Haitian soldiers following an exchange of abusive words with a senior Haitian official. The American minister noted that, true or not, such rumors had the potential to do serious damage to America's reputation in Port-au-Prince.[24]

In April 1907, while Young was away on a reconnaissance mission to Cape Haitien, an incident occurred that brought the mounting tension concerning his activities in Haiti to a head. Young's clerk, Charles Stephens, took advantage of the attaché's absence to break into his office and steal some confidential papers. Foremost among these was the only draft copy of the monograph on the Dominican Republic that Young had been preparing. This breach of security and the theft of classified documents not only jeopardized Young's personal safety, but also undermined his future effectiveness as an intelligence agent in Haiti and the Dominican Republic. W. H. Furniss, the new American minister in Port-au-Prince, informed the State Department that in his opinion the whole affair had been instigated by the Haitian government to embarrass Young and have him recalled. Despite Furniss's pleas that recalling Young now might serve to encourage the already widespread belief that the United States was planning an invasion of Haiti, the War Department concluded that it had little choice. In March 1907 Young received orders to return to the United States.[25]

On April 28 Charles Young left Port-au-Prince with bittersweet memories of Hispaniola. Among the many newfound friends he was leaving behind were the leading Haitian meteorologist Father Scherer, whom Young had come to know through his frequent research visits to the College of St. Martial, and historian J. F. Geffrard, who dedicated his 1915 monograph *Some Historical Points* to "My Friend Major Charles Young." On the other hand, his recall to the United States enabled Young to leave the scene of one the greatest personal tragedies of his life. In May 1905, a heartbroken Young wrote his friend Benjamin Davis, who had just been married and was considering renting Youngsholm, that he hoped he would be "more successful with children than I, as I have lost one before its time, due to the hot climate here doctors say." Clearly devastated, Young found comfort in the hope that "there are plenty more where that one came from." His hopes were soon fulfilled, and when it became clear the following spring that Ada was pregnant again, Charles insisted that she return to Wilberforce to live with his mother "to save her life and that of the child." On Christmas Day 1906, Ada gave birth to a healthy baby boy who, in honor of his father and the season of his birth, was christened Charles Noël. To mark his conception in Haiti the boy was nicknamed Tonton, an unofficial title meaning "big man" adopted by successive Haitian leaders. Four months after his son's birth, the proud father was finally on his way home to see his infant son.[26]

Young's service in Haiti had lasted a good deal longer than he had expected. As early as the summer of 1905 he had anticipated completing his assignment and eagerly looked forward to returning home, which he noted with emphasis "is nothing like this." This uncharacteristic bout of homesickness was no doubt closely related to the tragedy of Ada's miscarriage, and Young appears to have regained some enthusiasm for the Caribbean island as his melancholy retreated. Throughout the following year he attended numerous social functions and affairs of state and continued his extensive explorations of the island's interior.[27]

Young's posting to Haiti gave him both the inspiration and opportunity to begin researching a drama on the life of Toussaint L'Ouverture, a personal hero and, in his mind, the most important figure in modern Black history. Young contended that no man could surpass the leadership of L'Ouverture, "a pure Negro and a slave until after fifty years" who "routed the best troops of Napoleon Bonaparte." The L'Ouverture drama became a lifelong endeavor. He was dismayed on his arrival in Port-au-Prince at the lack of memorials and monuments to the man who had liberated the African slave population from their French overlords, and he became more determined than ever to tell his story. Young's exposure to the eclectic world of Haitian politics and the tragic history of the Black Republic sparked his increasing intellectual curiosity in the African Diaspora and the cultural legacy of the continent from which his forebears had been abducted. His travels in the interior of Haiti brought him into regular contact with the practice of voodoo, "a tenacious blend of West African beliefs and practices infused...with hedge Catholicism." To the uninitiated voodoo was something to be feared, and in Western minds it evoked negative images of ritual magic and blood sacrifice. Although its detractors dismissed it as sorcery, no serious study of Haiti could ignore the widespread influence of this "mystery religion." Young, recognizing the importance of voodoo in shaping the culture of Haiti's largely peasant population, devoted a whole section of his monograph to the subject.[28]

Young's interest in voodoo was anthropological. Few people of African descent in the Western Hemisphere were as closely linked to the culture of the continent of their ancestors as those of the Haitian interior. The horde of spirits, or loa, who controlled the natural forces that shaped these people's world constituted one of the most direct links to Africa in the Americas that Young would ever encounter. On one of his many excursions into the interior, Young reportedly became "an initiate by request" in the voodoo cult. New initiates underwent a ceremony that began in the early afternoon and concluded in the early morning hours when "the African spirits leap the broad Atlantic and possess the candidate...and to him all of the secrets of the island become an open book."[29]

Young does indeed appear to have left Hispaniola imbued with the spirit of Africa. From this point forward much of his thinking on the status and condition of African American and Afro-Caribbean people was informed by his awakening interest in the history of slavery and the heritage of Africa. For example, during an official visit to Jamaica in 1906 in the company of Minister William Furniss, Young noted the strong sexual appetite of Black Jamaicans, a phenomenon he attributed to a slave culture in which masters forced sex on their slaves and the slaves themselves were encouraged toward prolific breeding. In this instance and others, Young believed that "200 years of slavery" had upset the equilibrium of the people who were its victims and that not enough time had elapsed since emancipation to restore a sense of balance.[30]

Young's overseas experience exposed him to a broad range of issues of race and ethnicity. From the capacity of Filipinos for self-rule to the legacy of slavery and Western paternalism in the Caribbean, he struggled to find meaning in a world in which people of color appeared always to be subject to White rule or to be laboring under the legacy of that rule. It was part "love for a true a patriot" and part "race pride" in the "enlightenment, magnanimity, statesmanship, and military prowess of the full blooded African slave" that fueled his admiration for L'Ouverture. His L'Ouverture drama was more than simply an effort to resurrect a neglected historical figure; it was part of a larger endeavor to challenge the White dogma of racial superiority that buttressed colonialism and segregation around the world. Taking his cue from the increasing popularity of the social sciences in Western intellectual circles at the turn of the century, Young also completed a monograph in Haiti in which he sought to explain the relative strengths and weakness of disparate ethnic and racial groups spanning the globe.[31]

Young began work on *The Military Morale of Nations and Races* following his return from the Philippines in 1903 and completed the manuscript in Haiti in 1906. He spent a number of years thereafter refining the text before the book was published in 1912. In *Military Morale,* Young employed what he called "ethno-psychology" to gauge the military capabilities of the various peoples of the world. Largely on the basis of the writings of European sociologists and anthropologists, Young attempted in *Military Morale* to establish a causal relationship between culture and environment on the one hand and military and political strength on the other. He examined in the process everything, from diet to dress, that might contribute to a uniform national or racial characteristic.[32]

Military Morale, with its emphasis on the primacy of the nation state and its propensity to engage in racial stereotypes, is in many respects conventionally Victorian. It would be easy to dismiss it along with the thousands of other pseudoscientific studies that littered the intellectual landscape of the early twentieth century but for the fact that its author was anything but conventional. *Military Morale* offers a rare, if veiled, insight into the mind of a man who was at once both a staunch American patriot and a vocal critic of racial discrimination in the United States. Young was proud of the emerging power of the United States, which he attributed in the book to its democratic traditions and advanced industrial economy. While offering no overt commentary on race in the United States, he hints at its existence as the one major weakness in the American system. Young warns that "no wise rulers...will countenance the systematic debasement of one class of their country's citizens by the other; for the most important asset of a country must be the number of its good, happy, and intelligent individuals taking part in the...work of its government and having an interest in its perpetuation." He concludes with emphasis that "in a perfect nation there is no place for...hate."[33]

Young echoed in his book contemporary themes in the Western worldview that held human history to be an ongoing march from savagery to civilization, with different peoples around the world in various stages of the process. Young clearly believed in the merits of Western civilization, with its advanced technology and complex system of governance, but he stopped short of endorsing the notion that Western dominance proved the inferiority of non-Western peoples. He rejected Social Darwinist theories that divided the world into five racial categories, White, Brown, Yellow, Red, and Black, each in a different stage of the evolutionary process. Young dismissed such notions of innate racial characteristics, and instead held that the unequal relationship between Western and non-Western peoples was a product of environment. Whether in the Philippines or Haiti, Young believed American imperialism was therefore justified because of the disinterested role it could play in bridging that gap. This emphasis on environment, however, also led him to conclude that, with the burden of slavery lifted, African Americans were every bit as capable and worthy of their full rights as citizens of the United States as were their White counterparts.[34]

Although the publication of *Military Morale* in 1912 went largely unnoticed, Young did win one very important admirer for his work. In 1911, as part of his efforts to secure a publisher for his manuscript, Young enlisted the aid of former President Teddy Roosevelt. The hero of San Juan Hill became an admirer of Young following his service in Haiti, praising him as "a most excellent officer, a man fit to uphold the traditions of the American Army as only our best officers uphold them." Displaying typical ambiguity on the subject of race, Roosevelt sympathized with Young for having to "contend not only with race prejudice, but against the fact that more than once in the past colored men whom it was sought to make officers of the Army have turned out badly." The former president agreed to forward Young's manuscript to his friend, Harry Pratt Judson, the president of the University of Chicago, with a strong note requesting that the University of Chicago Press publish it. Roosevelt claimed that it had been a number of years since any book impressed him to the extent that *Military Morale* did. Judson evidently did not share the former president's enthusiasm and passed on the project. The Francis Hudson Press in Kansas City eventually published *Military Morale*.[35]

Teddy Roosevelt may have been moved by flattery to endorse Young's book. Young identifies him in *Military Morale* as a shining example of one of those rare "great men" who can enhance a country's feeling of national consciousness by developing a "rapport with the thought and intent of the people." The Bull Moose's enthusiasm for the book was nonetheless genuine, as was his admiration for its author and his ideas. Young and Roosevelt were very similar in many respects. They were both filled with a strong sense of machismo, equating manliness with war and physical pursuits and decrying weakness and luxury as effeminate characteristics. Yet behind the machismo exterior they were both capable of great sensitivity, evident in their opinions on a host of issues ranging from the environment to social inequality. It is hardly surprising therefore that Young viewed T. R. as one of the greatest men of his age, while Roosevelt, in turn, saw Young as the epitome of Black manhood.[36]

Consistent with his hands-on approach to foreign policy issues while in the White House, Roosevelt had taken a personal interest in Young's work in Hispaniola. He read many of Young's reports and heaped praise on the military attaché for "the admirable character" of his work. Haiti was one of the countries Roosevelt had in mind when he issued his corollary to the Monroe Doctrine in 1904 citing the dangers of "chronic-wrong doing" and "impotence" on the part of America's neighbors to the south. Such persistent wrongdoing, Roosevelt warned, might "force the United States...to the exercise of an international police power." When American military intervention in Haiti finally took place in 1915, the surprise was that it had taken so long.[37]

The ease with which the United States took possession of Haiti in 1915, as well as its ability to occupy the republic for 19 years thereafter, was due in no small measure to the maps, reports, and monographs so painstakingly compiled by Charles Young. In 1907 Young's immediate superiors in MID had noted with satisfaction the extremely detailed nature of his monograph and the valuable information it afforded the U.S. military. One of the key players in the occupation, Marine major Smedley Butler, reportedly relied heavily on Young's maps and reports to carry out his operations in the interior. Although many Black leaders and newspapers levied charges of racism and imperialism against the U.S. government following its intervention in Haiti, Young never expressed any misgivings about his role in the affair. Young believed that Haiti's continued instability was damaging to Black people the world over because it "left room for argument as to the capacity of Negro race for establishing and maintaining a decent independent government." In his view "civilization seems to spring from contact with superior people," and Haiti could not be expected to evolve without such outside influence. Young was fully cognizant that his work in Haiti was preparing the way for the possibility of U.S. occupation; rather than harboring any regrets, however, he welcomed this as the march of progress.[38]

NOTES

1. Larry M. Dilsaver and William C. Tweed, *Challenge of the Big Trees of Sequoia and Kings Canyon National Parks: A Resource History* (Tucson, Ariz., 1990), 91.

2. Alfred Vagts, *The Military Attaché* (Princeton, N.J., 1967), 33; Brian Shellum, "Captain Charles Young in Hispaniola, 1904–1907: Point Man for an Invasion" (paper presented at U.S. Army History Conference, Washington, D.C., summer 1998), 5.

3. Shellum, "Charles Young in Hispaniola," 5–6.

4. Report of the Acting Superintendent of Sequoia and General Grant National Parks, 15 October 1903, 4, 15–16, National Park Service, Sequoia and Kings Canyon Museum, Three Rivers, Calif. [hereinafter SKCM].

5. William C. Tweed, "Captain Charles Young: Military Superintendent, Sequoia National Park, 1903," www.nps.gov/seki/young.htm.

6. John R. White and Samuel J. Pusateri, *Sequoia and Kings Canyon National Parks* (Palo Alto, Calif., 1952), 32–33.

7. Ibid.; Tweed, "Charles Young."

8. Report of the Acting Superintendent, 15 October 1903, 6, SKCM; Charles Noel Young, "Biography of Charles Young," Coleman Collection, Akron, Ohio; Tweed, "Charles Young."

9. Report of the Acting Superintendent, 15 October 1903, 6–10, SKCM.

10. Report of the Acting Superintendent, 15 October 1903, 8–11, 14–15, SKCM; Dilsaver and Tweed, *Challenge of the Big Trees*, 91, 118.

11. Report of the Acting Superintendent, 15 October 1903, 3, SKCM; Inspector General's Office to Secretary of War, 28 January 1904, Letters Received by the Appointment, Commission, and Personal Branch, Adjutant General's Office, 1871–1917, Record Group 94, National Archives, Washington, D.C. [hereinafter ACP File]; Visalia, California, Board of Trade to Adjutant General's Office, 19 November 1903, ACP File; Miscellaneous notes on the life of Charles Young, Coleman Collection.

12. Charles Young File, Caroline Bond Day Papers, Peabody Museum, Harvard University, Cambridge, Mass.; Typescript on Colonel Charles Young, Young File, Ripley Museum; Oral interview with Tarea Hall Pittman conducted by Joyce Henderson, 25 August 1971, Earl Warren Oral History Project, University of California, Berkeley, Calif.; M. A. Broadstone, ed. *History of Greene County, Ohio: Its People, Industries and Institutions, II* (Indianapolis, 1918), 950; Miscellaneous observations on the life of Charles Young by Harry O. Atwood, Coleman Collection; Charles Young to Ada Young, 24 August 1916; Coleman Collection; Charles Noël Young, "Biography of Charles Young," Coleman Collection.

13. "The Desert and the Solitary Place," Notes on the life of Charles Young by Ada Young, 1922, Coleman Collection; Clipping from the *Philadelphia Daily News*, 1 December 1906, Coleman Collection.

14. David Levering Lewis, *W. E. B. Du Bois: Biography of a Race, 1868–1919* (New York, 1993), 174–175, 318–323.

15. *Daily Palo Alto*, 9 December 1903, cited in Robert E. Greene, *Colonel Charles Young: Soldier and Diplomat* (Washington, D.C., 1985), 69.

16. John Hay to Charles Young, 23 April 1904, Diplomatic Instructions of the Department of State, 1801–1906, Haiti and Santo Domingo, RG 59, National Archives II, College Park, Md. [hereinafter DIHSD]; William Powell to John Hay, 8 June 1904, Dispatches from U.S. Ministers to Haiti, 1862–1906, Records of the Department of State, RG 59, National Archives II, College Park, Md. [hereinafter DUSMH]

17. Shellum, "Charles Young in Hispaniola," 8–9; *Army and Navy Journal* 41 (7 May 1904): 939.

18. Vagts, "Military Attaché," 34; *Army and Navy Journal* 41 (7 May 1904), 939; "Colored Officer Chosen," *New York Times*, 1 May 1904, 4.

19. William Powell to John Hay, 8 June 1904, DUSMH; William Powell to John Hay, 4 June 1904, DUSMH; John Hay to William Powell, 28 June 1904, DIHSD.

20. W. H. Furniss to Elihu Root, Dispatches from the Haitian Legation, Records of the Department of State, RG 84, National Archives II, College Park, Md. [hereinafter DHL]; William Powell to John Hay, 8 June 1904, DUSMH; Murville Ferere to William Powell, 3 June 1904 [with attached newspaper clipping], DUSMH; Nancy Gordon Heinl, "Colonel Charles Young: Pointman," *Army Magazine* 27

(March 1971), 31; Robert Debs Heinl and Nancy Gordon Heinl, *Written in Blood: The Story of the Haitian People, 1492–1995* (Lanham, Md., 1996), 313.

21. See correspondence concerning Haiti between Charles Young and the Military Information Division, 1904–1906, Office of the General Staff, Army War College, Records of the War Department, RG 165, National Archives, Washington, D.C. [hereinafter MID]; See Dispatches from U.S. Ministers to Haiti, 1904–1906, DUSMH.

22. Only a fraction of Young's work on Haiti and the Dominican Republic is still extant. His intelligence reports and monograph were destroyed in the early 1920s when the War Department cleaned out its "dead" files. His French-English-Creole Dictionary is housed in the library of the Army War College in Carlisle, Pa., and some of his maps survive in the National Archives II, in College Park, Md. Young's cable communications with the military information division (see MID) and the dispatches of the U.S. minister to Haiti to the State Department (see DUSMH) only hint at the voluminous and detailed nature of his reports and monograph; Heinl, "Pointman," 31.

23. William Powell to John Hay, 5 April 1905, DUSMH; William Powell to Elihu Root, 20 October 1905, DUSMH; W.H. Furniss to Elihu Root, 7 March 1906, DUSMH.

24. Military Intelligence Division to Charles Young, 26 January 1905, MID; Charles Young to Military Information Division, 3 February 1905, MID; Charles Young to Military Information Division, 28 April 1905, MID; William Powell to John Hay, 5 April 1905, DUSMH; W.H. Furniss to Elihu Root, 1 March 1907, DHL.

25. W.H. Furniss to Elihu Root, 1 March 1907, DHL; W.H. Furniss to Elihu Root, 13 March 1907, DHL.

26. Charles Young to W.H. Furniss, 15 March 1906, DHL; Nancy Gordon Heinl, "Charles Young," in *Dictionary of American Negro Biography*, ed. Rayford W. Logan and Michael R. Winston (New York, 1985), 678 [hereinafter DANB]; Charles Young to Benjamin O. Davis, 5 May 1905, Benjamin O. Davis Papers, United States Military History Institute, Carlisle, Pa [hereinafter Davis Papers]; Charles Young to Arminta Young, 4 September 1906, Coleman Collection.

27. Charles Young to Benjamin O. Davis, 5 May 1905, Davis Papers; Shellum, "Charles Young in Hispaniola," 12.

28. There is a draft of Young's Toussaint L'Ouverture drama together with notes and music related to the work in the Coleman Collection; "The Negro Officer," Letter to the Editor from Charles Young, *New York Evening Post*, 5 April 1919, editorial page; Charles Noël Young, "Biography of Charles Young," Coleman Collection; Heinl, "Charles Young," DANB, 678; Heinl and Heinl, *Written in Blood*, 767; Charles Young to the Military Intelligence Division, 2 August 1905, MID.

29. Heinl and Heinl, *Written in Blood*, 767; Heinl, "Charles Young," DANB, 678; E.H. Lawson, "One Out of Twelve Million: Unrevealed Facts in the Life Story of Col. Charles Young, West Pointer," *Washington Post*, 26 May 1929, 14.

30. Notes on Jamaica, 1906, Charles Young Papers, National Afro-American Museum and Cultural Center, Wilberforce, Ohio [hereinafter Young Papers].

31. Charles Noël Young, "Biography of Charles Young," Coleman Collection.

32. Individual Service Reports, 15 August 1903, and 26 September 1906, ACP File; Charles Young, *The Military Morale of Nations and Races* (Kansas City, Mo., 1906).

33. Young, *Military Morale*, 20–21.

34. Young, *Military Morale*, 41–42.

35. Theodore Roosevelt to Harry Pratt Judson, 27 July 1911, Elting E. Morison, ed., *The Letters of Theodore Roosevelt, vol. 7* (Cambridge, Mass., 1954), 313.

36. Young, *Military Morale*, 23.

37. William Loeleb to Charles Young, 2 May 1907, Young Papers; Heinl and Heinl, *Written in Blood*, 313, 395.

38. Lt. Colonel Jones to Charles Young, 30 October 1907, Coleman Collection; Lawson, "One Out of Twelve Million," 14; Charles Noël Young, "Biography of Charles Young," Coleman Collection.

Gabriel Young wearing his Civil War Medal.
(Courtesy of the Coleman Collection)

Charles Young at West Point. (Courtesy of the Coleman Collection)

Young, the only Black cadet in the West Point class of 1889. (Courtesy of the Coleman Collection)

Young, front row, center, and work gang in Sequoia National Park in 1903. (Courtesy of the Coleman Collection)

On frontier duty in Wyoming, circa 1909. (Courtesy of the National Afro-American Museum and Cultural Center, Wilberforce, Ohio)

Young, center, with group in Liberia, circa 1913. (Courtesy of the National Afro-American Museum and Cultural Center, Wilberforce, Ohio)

Charles Nöel, Marie, Ada, and Charles (left to right). (Courtesy of the Coleman Collection)

With the punitive expedition in Mexico in 1916. (Courtesy of the National Archives Record Administration)

Entertaining a guest on the steps of "Youngsholm." (Courtesy of the National Afro-American Museum and Cultural Center, Wilberforce, Ohio)

Young's signature dedication, "For Race and Country." (Courtesy of the Coleman Collection)

Scenes from Charles Young's funeral procession in Washington, D.C., in 1923. (Courtesy of the Coleman Collection)

CHAPTER 6

Back to Africa

Charles Young's service in the Philippines and Haiti reflected the expanding global reach of American foreign policy in the early twentieth century. As the extent of America's international commitments continued to grow, so too did the frequency of Young's overseas postings. He would spend much of the rest of his career in uniform outside the United States, punctuated by intermittent domestic assignments, many of which were directly related to his foreign service. His return from Haiti in 1907 was followed by a year with the Second Division (military intelligence) in the Office of the General Staff in Washington, D.C., before he shipped out with the Ninth Cavalry for a second tour of duty in the Philippines in 1908. He returned to the United States in the summer of 1909, spending two years at Fort D. A. Russell in Wyoming before heading overseas again, this time as the new United States military attaché to the Republic of Liberia in West Africa.

The U.S. decision to appoint a military attaché to Liberia in 1911 is particularly illustrative of the transformation of American foreign policy in this era. Inspired by a variety of motives, ranging from abolition to a desire to rid the United States of an unwanted Black population, the American Colonization Society had founded Liberia as a haven for freed American slaves in 1820. Even though it failed to inspire a mass exodus of free Blacks from the United States, there were a sufficient number of people of Americo-Liberian stock to support the declaration of a republic there in 1847. The fledgling state struggled to survive from the outset and faced increasingly stiff competition for territory and resources from the European imperial powers as the century wore on. Pleas from Monrovia, the Liberian capital, for American assistance in the face of British and

French encroachments fell on deaf ears in Washington until the early twentieth century.

Consistent with its aggressive approach to foreign policy in other parts of the world, the administration of Theodore Roosevelt began to take an active interest in Liberia as a possible foothold for the United States on a continent that had been largely devoured by European imperialists in the late nineteenth century. Whereas the existence of Liberia had served in the nineteenth century only to remind the United States of its own slave past, sectional divisions, and race problems, in the twentieth century it held out the promise of natural resources, investment opportunities, and strategic value. Young's appointment as military attaché was an integral part of the U.S. State Department's strategy to establish a controlling American presence in Liberia.[1]

Far from resenting his role in what some critics would come to see as a veiled imperialist venture, Young embraced the Liberia assignment as an opportunity to extend the benevolent arm of American assistance to mother Africa. Like many African Americans of his generation, Young had an idealized image of Africa, and of Liberia in particular. Liberia was a symbol of Black self-rule, and as such it served as a counterweight to the racial assumptions that underpinned Western imperialism. Together with Haiti and Africa's other independent Black state, Ethiopia, Liberia provided inspiration for African Americans struggling to escape from prejudice, discrimination, and segregation in the United States. Young's eagerness to serve in Liberia reflected more than his genuine faith in the munificence of American foreign policy. He shared with Booker T. Washington, Emmett Scott, W. E. B. Du Bois, and other leading African American figures, the belief that American intervention in Liberia was necessary to save the Black republic from the clutches of the European imperialist powers. The survival of Liberia in the colonial age was critical to African American morale.

Young won acclaim both in Monrovia and Washington for his performance as military attaché and his additional assignment of overseeing the retraining of the Liberian Frontier Force. The value of his contribution to the African American community was recognized when he was awarded the NAACP's Spingarn Medal on his return to the United States in 1915. Despite the frustrations resulting from his dealings with the entrenched, privileged, Americo-Liberian oligarchy, Young developed a strong bond with Liberia and its people. The seeds of interest in African culture that had been sown during his time in Haiti grew and blossomed in West Africa. The tangible experience of three years in Liberia transformed an abstract curiosity into a deep-seated fascination and heartfelt affinity for the continent of his ancestors.

Following his somewhat hasty retreat from Haiti in the spring of 1907, Charles Young returned to Washington, D.C., where he spent a year briefing officials in the Military Information Division on matters pertaining to Haiti and collating and deciphering the material he had gathered during his tour of duty there. These were heady times for the youthful captain. He was working on a daily basis in the nerve center of U.S. Army operations, and his work in Haiti was winning high praise from his military superiors and from President Roosevelt. Such recognition would have been cause for considerable satisfaction to any ambitious army officer, but for Young it was all that more rewarding given his unique status in the military.[2]

This was also a time for Young to catch up on events in the United States that had taken place in his absence. In particular, Young had to come to terms with the death of his close friend Paul Laurence Dunbar, who had passed away in February 1907. Dunbar's losing battle with alcohol and tuberculosis robbed a generation of one of African America's greatest literary talents. While Young was in Haiti, Dunbar had written that he was very sick and joked that perhaps he should come down to join his friend, "the finest Negro soldier that we ever had," and avail of the healing climate. Young endeavored to make up for his absence during Dunbar's final days by pouring his energy into a campaign to fund a monument at the poet's gravesite in Dayton, Ohio. The year he spent in the nation's capital, his second home away from Wilberforce, was also a time to cultivate surviving friendships. Young developed a lasting affection for this "dear town...with the many cherished friends it holds." Foremost among them were William Broad and Charles Cuney, a physician and a lawyer, respectively, both students of Young's at Wilberforce in the 1890s. Like so many of the young men he educated or commanded throughout his life, they would remain his lifelong friends.[3]

Young's year in Washington came to end in the summer of 1908 when he received orders to sail to the Philippines for a second tour of duty on the U.S-occupied archipelago. In August accompanied by Ada and his infant son, Charles Noel, Young sailed from San Francisco on the transport ship *Thomas*. He spent the next year in command of the Third Squadron based at Camp McGrath in Batangas Province. This second tour of duty "differed widely in its routine garrison duty from the arduous days of the insurrection." Football, baseball, boxing, and horse training as well as a fair amount of drinking, dancing, and gambling, broke the monotony of the duty for the enlisted men. Discipline was nonetheless strict, and the "West Point Men" earned a particular reputation among the troops for efficiency and leadership.[4]

Having his wife and son with him largely offset Young's isolation as the lone Black commissioned officer at Camp McGrath. The routine nature of the tour gave Young considerable time to enjoy the presence of his family, and years later he would reminisce about "the days of delight" he and Ada spent together in Asia. The decision to travel as a family to the Philippines was most likely related to Ada's pregnancy; she was already three months pregnant with their second child when they left the United States. On March 26, 1909, Charles and Ada Young welcomed a daughter, Marie Amelie, into the world, and the proud father penned "a sweet, tuneful, little cradle song" to mark the arrival of the newborn girl. It was fitting that both the Young children were either conceived or born outside the United States, as they would spend much of their youth being educated in Europe. Charles and Ada Young were determined that their children's horizons should be both figuratively and literally wider than those available to most African American children in the United States at that time.[5]

Two months after Marie Amelie was born, the Young's were on their way back to the United States. While Ada and the children returned to Wilberforce, Charles took up his new post in command of the Second Squadron at Fort D. A. Russell in Wyoming. Fort Russell was established in 1866 three miles from Cheyenne to provide protection for Union Pacific railroad workers laboring on the first transcontinental railroad, brought into being by the Railroad Act of 1862. By the time Young arrived at Fort Russell in 1908 it had become the largest cavalry post in the United States, and the small cluster of wood frame barracks that had occupied the original barren site had given way to an impressive tree-lined facility with rows of stately red-bricked buildings and stables capable of accommodating thousands of horses and mules. The excellent facilities somewhat compensated for the hostile Wyoming climate, which Young complained was "absolutely rotten because of the wind."[6]

Young's rank ensured that he had comfortable accommodations at Fort Russell, unlike in his days at Fort Robinson, with room enough to house his piano, which his colleague Benjamin Davis noted formed an ever present part of his luggage. In addition to playing for the men, Young sought to cultivate their musical talents by taking charge of the regimental band at Fort Russell and leading performances at the Rough Rider rodeo and other events in Cheyenne. Wyoming proved to be a fairly comfortable assignment, and a welcome interlude from the stress and fatigue of overseas duty. However, Fort Russell provided no escape for Young from the racial animosity that was so often directed at him by White officers. On the occasion of President William Howard Taft's visit to the fort in 1909, Young was in command of the exhibition guard mount when a junior White officer refused to repeat the Black captain's orders to the troops. When this occurred a second time, Young was compelled to have his first sergeant execute the order.[7]

Young also encountered the widespread public hostility that existed toward African Americans in uniform when he traveled to Fort Sam Houston in San Antonio, Texas, with the Second Squadron for maneuvers in the spring of 1911. While Young initially welcomed this opportunity for a break from the Wyoming weather, he soon found that there was little to endear him to his new post; he wrote his mother that "the whites don't like the colored soldiers at all here." The local citizens were sufficiently unreceptive to the presence of the Ninth Cavalry to prompt one Texas congressman to write President Taft asking that they be removed. The locals charged that the Black troops were guilty of creating disturbances on streetcars and flouting local segregation laws. Young and his men had a different perspective, maintaining that the attitude of the White population to the Blacks troops, in stark contrast to Wyoming, was one of unbridled prejudice.[8]

The presence of Black troops in Texas had on many previous occasions incited local hostility and often resulted in violence, most notably in Brownsville in 1906. The Brownsville incident involved a rampage through the streets of the small Texas town by a number of armed men who local people claimed were Black troops from the 25th Infantry. On the basis of earlier altercations with locals, the troopers, on the other hand, concluded that a party of civilian raiders preparing to attack the fort had carried out the shooting. The subsequent handling of the incident by the military and the government, specifically President Roosevelt's decision to discharge without honor 167 troopers from the 25th for denying knowledge of the incident, outraged many Black Americans. Brownsville was just the most celebrated of many such incidents involving Black troops stationed in the South between the end of the Civil War and the integration of the armed services in 1948. More than any other case, it appeared to confirm that racial prejudice pervaded the very fiber of the military, reaching all the way to the civilian commander-in-chief, and that the army was unwilling to protect Black soldiers from the constant harassment they faced in the South.[9]

Young, however, was determined that southern bigotry should not be allowed to jeopardize the right of African Americans to serve in the military, for if "permission [to soldier] is taken away our people must sink to a lower caste, far lower than even slavery entailed." While in San Antonio, Young wrote a heated letter to Booker T. Washington asking him to speak to the president and other people of influence to assure them that what they were hearing about his troops in Texas was not true. Young was at pains to point out that, despite what the newspapers might say concerning the breaking of Jim Crow laws and drunken brawling, "the conduct of the soldiers has been exemplary," with both officers and men making a concerted effort to avoid trouble. As far as Young was concerned, the stories of Black troopers "riding down...white people or flourishing...revolvers" were fabrications born of local hostility, and he was anxious that Washington should make every effort to counter "the lies...in the newspapers [that were] simply echoes of Brownsville, no more."[10]

The two men were engaged in correspondence again the following November, this time on a more heartening subject, when Washington wrote to urge Young to accept an assignment as military attaché to Liberia. Washington enclosed a letter from Reed Paige Clark, the head of the U.S.-led receivership in Liberia, outlining the reasons for Young's selection. According to Clark, officials from the State and War Departments decided that Young was "just the man for a position where considerable tact and great executive ability are required." Clark noted Young's West Point and Haiti experience and his "admirable record" in uniform as significant factors in determining his suitability for the position. What remained unstated was that the State and War Departments required an African American officer for the job, and so the color of Young's skin was as much a consideration as anything else. Young, long used to taking advantage of his uniqueness among the commissioned ranks, embraced this as another opportunity "to aid in...work for the good of the country in general and our race in particular, whether that race be found in Africa or in the United States."[11]

The decision to appoint a military attaché to Liberia was an integral part of U.S. strategy to preserve the existence of Liberia from the twin pressures of territorial encroachments by the European powers and insurrection on the part of the native African population. The Americo-Liberian oligarchy that ruled the West African republic had managed to fend off successive threats in the late nineteenth century, but matters had reached an unprecedented point of crisis in 1908, prompting the dispatch of a commission from Monrovia to the United States to appeal for Washington's intervention. In contrast to earlier administrations' coolness to such appeals, Theodore Roosevelt's administration welcomed the Liberian delegation's visit as an opportunity to access an open door into an otherwise closed continent.[12]

The accession to the White House of William Howard Taft enhanced American interest in Liberia, as it now became part of the new administration's global dollar diplomacy strategy. Taft dispatched an American commission to Liberia with a view to discerning a possible course of action for the United States in the republic. The American commission confirmed the imminent danger posed to Liberian independence from British and French territorial encroachments, British and German economic pressure, and internal unrest among the disgruntled native African population. To whet the Taft administration's appetite for intervention, the commission also noted Liberia's tremendous potential as a source of tropical raw materials such as rubber, coffee, and palm oil, citing "stores of wealth" lying untapped in the country's "extensive forests." To secure American access to these resources, the commission recommended that the United States undertake a loan to Liberia to pay off its debts, secured by an American-administered receivership that would take control of Liberian finances. Furthermore, to stabilize Liberia's borders and interior, the commission report included a call for the United States to sell arms to Liberia and undertake the reorganization of the Liberian Frontier Force.[13]

Acting on the commission's recommendation, the Taft administration, following the dollar diplomacy model it employed in China and Central America, negotiated a $1.7 million loan for Liberia to be funded by private bankers and secured by a U.S.-led receivership that, to assuage European fears of American competition in Africa, involved British, German, and French receivers in subsidiary roles. Among the numerous additional actions on the part of the United States detailed in the agreement was the appointment of a military attaché to the republic. First Lieutenant Benjamin O. Davis, Young's protégé from Fort Duchesne, was given the initial task of surveying the strength and capability of Liberia's existing military forces. Davis spent just over a year in Liberia and during that time he witnessed sufficient turmoil and inefficiency to conclude that the country's army and militia were "worthless and should be reorganized." Frustrated by the limitations of his orders, which prohibited him from playing an active role in the reorganization process, and suffering from frequent bouts of blackwater fever, Davis was recalled to the United States at his own request in the fall of 1911.[14]

On the basis of Davis's depiction of the Liberian military as grossly inadequate and inept, the U.S. State Department requested that his replacement as military attaché be given latitude, in accordance with the terms of the loan agreement, to act as advisor to the country's main military body, the Liberian Frontier Force (LFF). In addition, the State Department suggested and the Liberian government consented to the appointment of three American officers to command and retrain the LFF. Having agreed to take up the attaché's post with its expanded responsibilities, Young was given the additional task of recruiting the American officers for the LFF and assembling his team for immediate departure.[15]

As he had done when recruiting officers for the Ninth Ohio Battalion during the Spanish-American War, Young turned to his former students at Wilberforce for volunteers. He recruited Wilson Ballard at the rank of major to serve as the field commander of the LFF, and he was to be assisted by Arthur Brown and Richard Newton, who would both serve as captains. Ballard and Brown were products of Young's military science and tactics courses at Wilberforce and both had served with him in the Ninth Ohio. Ballard had gone on to serve as a first lieutenant in the 48th Infantry during the Philippine insurrection, before returning to school at Ohio State University, where he received a degree in dentistry in 1904. Brown had also continued his education after the Spanish-American conflict, pursuing graduate studies at Howard and Kansas State before opening a private podiatry practice in Chicago in 1911. Newton was the odd man out, coming to his new position from the non-

commissioned ranks of the army, having served under Young as a sergeant with the Ninth Cavalry. While the $1,200 annual salary served as
an enticement, each of the three men agreed to serve out of loyalty and
respect for Young.[16]

Accompanied by his wife and his three designates, Charles Young
arrived in Liberia on May 1, 1912. It was in all likelihood a thrilling
moment for him to set foot on African soil for the first time. Young and his
three military colleagues joined Reed Paige Clark, the American receiver;
William Crum, the American minister; and Richard Bundy, American
chargé d'affaires, to form a fairly tight-knit American presence in Monrovia. The affable Young, with his traveling library and "the only piano at
that time in all of Liberia," proved an immediate hit with the American
social circle, which in addition to the official presence, included a number
of missionaries and traders. Young was pleasantly surprised to find Monrovia to be a pretty town, "all different from what I had imagined," and
the family rented a delightful two-story brick house with a veranda over-
looking the sea. Ada quickly made friends among the other American
wives, Nellie Bundy in particular, and became active in the community,
running a school for small children and hosting the women of Monrovia
for social events.[17]

The other African American officials, Bundy in particular, had additional reason to celebrate Young's arrival. Although Bundy was nominally
second in command at the American legation, according to Young, he was
"the brains of our ministership here." Bundy was a rising star in the
African American community in Ohio and one of the few Blacks of that
era to earn entry into the lily-White ranks of the U.S. State Department. He
had taught engineering at Wilberforce while Young was there, and both
men had been active members of Beta Kappa Sigma fraternity, or "Black
Cats." Reunited in Monrovia, they formed a close alliance over the next
three years, intent on casting an African American influence over the
direction of U.S. policy in Liberia.[18]

The euphoria of reaching Africa's shores must have been somewhat
dampened for Young and his colleagues as the scale of the task facing
them in Liberia became clear. Even the news in August of his promotion to
major in the U.S. Army, after successfully completing the promotion exam
at Fort Riley the previous spring, can have done little to assuage Young's
growing frustration with the task at hand. Young confirmed Davis's
assessment of the poor state of the LFF, observing that the leadership of
the force had "lost complete control" and that the men, bereft of morale
and supplies, were reduced to preying on private property, and themselves posed a greater threat to order than any internal or external enemy.
Far from being superficial, the malaise extended all the way to the Liberian secretary of war, who, Young maintained, was utterly ill suited for his
position.[19]

Young identified numerous roadblocks standing in the way of the American contingent's ability to rectify this state of affairs. Delays in implementing the loan agreement, ineptitude and corruption on the part of Liberian officials, and the continued interference of the European powers in Liberian affairs, all hampered efforts to reorganize the LFF. Most debilitating of all, however, was the bureaucratic foot dragging and orchestrated opposition on the part of certain Liberian officials. Secretary of War W. E. Dennis was particularly hostile toward Young, charging him with exceeding his authority and threatening the integrity of the Liberian constitution. Young, for his part, claimed that Dennis was guilty of gross irregularities in accounting, and his charges were backed by Bundy who attributed Dennis's hostility to the threat posed to his power and patronage by Young's "rigid system of money accountability" pertaining to the LFF.[20]

Despite these difficulties, the American officers did experience some success, particularly in the area of recruitment, with an increase in the force during the first six months of American leadership, from 356 men and 4 commissioned officers to 540 men and 17 officers. The full complement of this expanded force would be needed during the coming months, as the implementation of the American reform plan appeared to coincide with increasing disorder in Liberia's interior and along its borders. Young charged that, far from being happenstance, these disturbances were the result of collusion on the part of the European powers, who wished to place pressure on Liberia to settle long-standing border disputes in their favor, at the same time undermining American goals in the republic. Young urged Bundy to convince his superiors in the State Department of the need to expedite the American loan plan, which had not yet gone into operation because of protracted negotiations with the European partners over the terms of operation of the receivership; otherwise the United States "shall be made ashamed, while the English, French and Germans rejoice at our weakness."[21]

Germany, whose commercial interests in Liberia had grown considerably in the early twentieth century, was particularly uncooperative in the matter of the American receivership and appeared determined to promote instability in the republic. In the fall of 1912 there was widespread unrest among the coastal Kru people, one of many ethnic minorities in Liberia, the majority of whom resented the imposition of Americo-Liberian authority. The unrest led to German charges of property damage and prompted Berlin to dispatch gunboats to Liberian waters on the pretext of protecting German citizens residing in the troubled region. Only American diplomatic intervention prevented German military action following a clash between LFF troops and German marines on shore leave. The French and British, meanwhile, were applying continuous pressure along their common borders with Liberia.[22]

It thus became imperative to the success of American goals in Liberia to quell internal unrest in the country and pacify the border regions. The American officers were required to divide their small force on numerous occasions to suppress simultaneous uprisings. In addition to the coastal Kru revolt of 1912–13, which occupied the largest LFF contingent under Major Ballard, revolts erupted among the Mano, Kpele, Bandi, and Kissi peoples at different times between 1911 and 1912. With his forces stretched to the limit, the Liberian president, Daniel Howard, was compelled to ask Young to lead a party in relief of Captain Brown, who was "surrounded by hostile natives" in Bassa County on the border with French Guinea. Young was instructed to proceed to Zorzor in eastern Liberia, where he would take command of a contingent of one hundred Liberian troops and advance on the rear of the Mandingo warriors who were besieging Brown and his men.[23]

The expedition in relief of Captain Brown was Young's first foray outside Monrovia, beyond the Americo-Liberian enclaves that hugged the coast and into the native African interior. He left Monrovia on November 25, 1912, with a party of six soldiers and two carriers. Ironically for a cavalry officer, almost the entire journey had to be made on foot, as dense forest and bush covered the Liberian interior and the presence of the trypanasomiasis-carrying tsetse fly precluded the use of horses. Nine days and one hundred miles after leaving Monrovia, Young arrived in Zorzor on the Guinea border, where he took command of a large contingent of LFF troops. Imbued with the same civilizing mission that stimulated most Western perceptions of Africa, Young speculated continuously, as he cut through bush and waded streams, about the potential agricultural and industrial wealth of the interior were it opened up by roads, bridges, and railroads. The interior opened his eyes to the maladministration of the Liberian government and the hostility it engendered in the African population. Young was highly critical of what he saw as the laziness and pride of the Americo-Liberian population. In Monrovia people subsisted on imported food because they were too proud to farm or to switch to a diet of native fare. Meanwhile, in the interior Young discovered what he called "a natural paradise" that would make "thousands rich" if Americo-Liberians would just discard their lethargy and their pretensions. As it was, revenues from the vibrant trade of border towns such as Zorzor escaped across the border to the French railway line leading to Conakry. Despite the Kiplingesque images with which he often portrayed the interior, there was more to Africa in Young's mind than warlike tribes and hostile jungle. He became convinced on this trip that the future prosperity of Liberia depended on Monrovia's ability to tap into the potential of the native population and the latent wealth upriver from the capital.[24]

After a week gathering government forces and supplies at Zorzor, Young and a party of well over a hundred, including a contingent of pro-government African chiefs and their followers, proceeded south along the Guinea border to the besieged town of Tappi. Progress was now considerably slower as the column moved through difficult terrain, stopping regularly to recruit carriers to transport the supplies and provisions from one village to the next. Their arrival occasionally generated hostility among the local population, while at other times their reception was more cordial. They subsisted largely on rice that they carried with them or on whatever they could procure from the local population by trading tobacco. In the village of Sarraya, Chief Cotta Gaou provided them with 100 carriers and 30-day rations. Young was impressed with the organization and industry of Sarraya, and found Cotta Gaou to be a "fine fellow," but was a little shocked when he got "roundly drunk" on gin and tried to steal Young's shoe and hat. It was the theft, not the drunkenness, that he found offensive. Young was not averse to imbibing, indeed he was remembered by members of the expatriate community in Monrovia as a man who "swore like a trooper and drank like a gentleman."[25]

Realizing that many of his men were raw recruits, the ever-meticulous Young devoted a portion of each day to "drill and fire discipline," an endeavor that proved valuable soon after they entered the area where the hostilities were taking place. On December 22, a local guide led them into an ambush, and over the course of the next few days Young and his men fought their way from town to town. Young himself received a gunshot wound in the right arm. The "bullet," which was in fact a two inch rusty leg from a cast iron pot, entered his arm below the elbow and ranged up toward his shoulder. Proper medical attention was lacking (the bullet would not be removed for three weeks), and the wound soon became infected. It was the only wound Young ever received in action during his military career.[26]

On Christmas Day 1912, a month after leaving Monrovia, a wounded Major Young found himself and his charges "lost in the jungles of Liberia, surrounded by man-eating Manos, with about four clips of ammunition to the soldier." Despite this desperate state of affairs, Young did manage to locate Captain Brown and his men in Tappi four days later. Bolstered by this relief, Brown was able to drive off the assailants and pacify the area before Young and his party departed for Monrovia. Taking a shorter route via Grand Bassa and the coast, they reached Monrovia on January 15. Young returned to the capital convinced of the need for wholesale reforms in Liberia. It was clear to him that much of the trouble in the interior was chiefly attributable to the corruption and brutality of the interior administration. Instead of focusing their energies on developing the country's resources, interior administrators spent more time alienating the rural population by endorsing practices such as nailing the skulls of natives killed in battle to the doors of official buildings as a lesson to those who might challenge official authority. As in Haiti, Young was convinced that, for Liberia, American intervention and directed reform were vital to the future stability of Black rule.[27]

Soon after his return to Monrovia, Young began to experience some tension between his role as military adviser to the Liberian government and his duty as U.S. military attaché. In his view, he was "over here to help...both the Republic and the Receivership." During his mission in relief of Brown, Young had repeatedly acted to win "hearts for the government" while extending the reach of Liberian authority in the interior. In the same vein, soon after his return from that expedition, Young traveled down the coast to negotiate a peace settlement with the Kru chiefs. In return for his service, and that of the other Americans, he expected the Liberians to accept the "controlling hand of the U.S." and preserve Liberia as a heritage for "Black men the world over." However, Young also had a duty to gather intelligence for the United States military and prepare a monograph on conditions in Liberia. He reported to his military superiors in the United States that the Brown expedition was indicative of how his services had been "taken advantage of," and offered this episode, together with the transitory state of affairs in Liberia as a whole, by way of explanation for his failure to begin work on the monograph.[28]

Young's efforts to catch up on his attaché duties were stymied in the spring of 1913 when he contracted blackwater fever, a form of malignant malaria. It was the same ailment that had forced Davis to relinquish his post as military attaché, and it now compelled Young, who was so weak he was "practically unable to walk," to apply for leave to return to the United States for medical treatment. With his arm in a sling from the bullet wound he had received in the interior, he was forced to dictate his correspondence to his friend Emory Ross, a Methodist missionary who had arrived in Liberia the previous year, and in this manner he sent word to his mother that he had been extremely sick for several weeks and that he was now waiting for Ada to come to take him home. Ada herself had been forced to return to the United States because of the detrimental impact the tropical environment was having on her health. Young now looked forward to the prospect of recuperation in "Old Ohio" and vowed that when he got there he would "*stay* home."[29]

Young's condition deteriorated rapidly, and before Ada could secure passage to Monrovia, his friends determined that he must be shipped home right away. Bundy wrote to Ada that Young was "too disregardful of his own personal welfare" and would attempt to minimize his illness and that she must do her best to keep him there until he was fully recovered. By the time he was carried aboard a German steamer to begin the homeward journey, Young was delirious with fever and close to death. Emory Ross, who accompanied him on the journey home, remembered that Young spent much of the journey lying in his cabin recounting "the many phases of his life, some bitter, some pleasant." At one point, close to tears, he turned to Ross and asked suddenly, "Lad, how would you like to be a nigger?"[30]

When Young arrived at his home in Ohio in June he was extremely ill, still not "able to handle a pen," and in August he applied for and was granted an additional three months leave of absence. Before leaving Liberia, he had been told that he had albuminuria and other "symptoms of acute nephritis." The examining doctor noted the high quantity of albumen in Young's urine and the serious inflammation of his liver. Gradually Young's strength returned sufficiently for him to get out of bed, and Youngsholm provided the perfect tonic to boost his recovery. Although he had survived, the impact of this bout of blackwater fever would have serious repercussions for his health in later years.[31]

With his gunshot wound fully healed and his fever abated, Young was too restless to abide by his earlier promise to stay home for good. "Liberia called again to duty" and at the end of October 1913 he returned to "the boiling pot of hard work." Although the widespread internal unrest of the previous 12 months had subsided, there were numerous other issues requiring Young's immediate attention on his return. Most pressing of all was the matter of personnel. The three American officers of the LFF were feeling overburdened. Newton's frustration with his Liberian bosses had brought him to the brink of resignation before he too fell ill, and Brown's relationship with the Liberian government had become so strained that he was forced to resign. While Eldridge Hawkins, the clerk of the legation, was pressed into service to replace Brown, with the urgent demands of "men to be trained, battles...to be fought, tribes of the interior to be restrained, [and] roads to make," Young pleaded for the appointment of additional American officers. For this request, which was duly granted, and subsequent appointments needed because of turnover, Young again turned to Wilberforce University and to his old volunteer unit for recruits.[32]

The nature of Young's role in Liberia was itself still a matter of concern. Before taking leave, Young had accepted an appointment from the Liberian government as a military adviser with wide-ranging powers. Although this was technically a violation of U.S. Army rules, which prohibited him from accepting a commission from a foreign government, the Office of the Chief of Staff chose to overlook the matter in "view of all the circumstances in connection with Major Young's assignment to Liberia." Young was frank and diligent in his reports to Washington, and both the U.S. State Department and the War Department were satisfied that his performance in Liberia, however unorthodox, was fulfilling the purpose of strengthening America's hand in the republic.[33]

By the spring of 1914 the LFF had grown to one thousand men, armed with five hundred new carbines and commanded by an increasingly disciplined and well-trained officer corps. The Kru coast and the interior had for the most part been pacified, and the border disputes with France and Britain were well on their way to settlement. Young was determined that the graft and opposition of certain Liberian officials should not now be allowed to stand in the way of an "American solution" to the Liberian question. These officials, Young maintained, needed to understand "that this country is a heritage for the blacks of the U.S. and their children's children for all time," and that "for the sake of the Negro...[and] every American who believes in a square deal for the Negro" the United States government should do everything in its power to preserve the Liberians from their own ineptitude and from the imperial designs of Europe.[34]

The outbreak of war in Europe in August 1914, however, paralyzed the republic's foreign trade and appeared to jeopardize the progress Young and his colleagues had made with the LFF. Without the revenue generated by customs receipts, the American-led receivership was rendered largely inoperable and there was no money to fund the military. By the end of 1914 the LFF had lost half of its troops and the rest had not been paid in months. The situation was compounded by a general state of unrest among the American officers, a number of whom were threatening to return to the United States, and by the death of Captain Newton from tuberculosis at Young's home in July. Young feared that the enormous strides made toward achieving American hegemony in Liberia during the previous two years might now be in jeopardy. Without the effective functioning of the LFF, which Young viewed as "an arm both of the Loan Agreement and the General Government," the very future of Liberia was in question.[35]

The outbreak of hostilities in Europe also precipitated a major crisis for the Young family. In search of opportunities and horizons denied them at home, the Youngs enrolled their children in the School of Notre Dame de la Compassion in Pieton, Belgium. The whole family had made the Atlantic crossing following Young's return from sick leave in October 1913, and Charles Noel and Marie were entrusted into the care of the nuns at Pieton early in 1914 before their parents traveled on to Liberia. The cornerstones of the children's Belgian education were French, music, and religion, clearly reflecting the values of their parents. It was a place where they would be safe from the stifling prejudice of the United States. However, when Pieton, along with much of the rest of Belgium, succumbed to the overwhelming pressure of the German military offensive the following fall, Charles and Ada were faced with the agonizing uncertainty of not knowing the whereabouts of their five-year-old daughter and eight-year-old son or whether they were well. Acting swiftly, Ada made her way to Europe to search for the children, while Young pressed the American minister in Monrovia into service to gather information from his superiors in Washington.[36]

Eventually the children surfaced in Rotterdam, where they had found refuge in the home of one of their schoolmates, and in May 1915, after much bureaucratic maneuvering, Ada received a permit from the British government to travel to Holland. With "the kiddies" in tow, Ada returned to London to stay with her friend Nina Du Bois, wife of Will Du Bois. Nina had taken up residence in London to offer moral and logistical support during her own daughter's European education. Young was relieved that his family was "outside the zone of that beastly war," although the occasional bomb dropped on London tempted him to order their return to the United States. Ada, despite the fact that the West African climate had taken its toll on her health, was nonetheless determined to continue her children's continental education and so in June 1915 she booked passage on a steamer across the Channel to enroll them in a Paris lycée. While Young was somewhat anxious about his family moving so close to the front, he was ultimately willing to defer to Ada's judgment in this matter.[37]

During the summer of 1915 Young found some diversion from his anxiety about his family's safety by directing the backbreaking labor of cutting a road from Monrovia into the Liberian interior. His undertaking of this task exemplified the broad latitude Young took with his position in Liberia. Road building was clearly outside the purview of a military attaché and it was not directly related to his role in reorganizing the LFF. To Young, however, this road through the "big bush" to the hinterland was symbolic of what he and other African Americans could do to save Liberia. The Americo-Liberian population had done all it could for the country; now it was the turn of industrious, honest Americans of African ancestry to develop this "blood treasure" to its full potential.[38]

Before the Manchu Law, which prohibited regular army officers from serving away from troops for longer than three years, brought his service in Liberia to an end, Young was determined to put every last ounce of effort into what had become for him a personal crusade. The reality that his departure would leave this work unfinished was brought home to him in the fall when a large uprising plunged the Kru coast once again into turmoil, precipitating what Young characterized as "the most serious juncture in the affairs of the Republic since I have been here." Young realized that, as with earlier unrest, behind the Kru grievances was the manipulating hand of the Europeans bent on undermining the American rehabilitation plan. Given the lack of available funds and the decline in the number of officers and men in the LFF, Young believed that concerted action on the part of Washington, in this instance the dispatch of a U.S. Navy cruiser to the Liberian coast, was needed to avert the undoing of the previous three year's work.[39]

By the time the U.S.S. *Chester* arrived in Liberian waters, however, Young had already received orders to return to the United States. His departure from Monrovia on November 25, 1915, engendered both official regret and personal lament. So impressed were U.S. State Department officials with his work in promoting American influence in Liberia that they endeavored unsuccessfully to suspend the Manchu Law so that he could continue to serve as military attaché. Both Liberia's president and secretary of state bemoaned his departure and offered glowing praise and appreciation for his service to their country. Meanwhile, Young's closest friend in Liberia, Dick Bundy, praised him for leaving an indelible mark on Liberia and expressed personal gratitude for his "sympathy, counsel and help, always so unselfishly given."[40]

The effects of Young's energy and commitment were to be found everywhere in Liberia, from Mrs. Sharp's American school, where he volunteered his advice and labor, to the road from Monrovia into the interior, which marked the republic's first major infrastructure venture beyond the coast in its 70-year history. He had taken over the LFF in disarray, with its corrupt Americo-Liberian officers and reluctant troops drawn from disparate tribes in the interior, and transformed it into a cohesive and efficient unit. Although the LFF had been hit hard as a result of wartime belt tightening, it was generally accepted in both Washington and Monrovia that under the direction of Young and his colleagues the LFF had been critical in stabilizing Liberia's disputed borders and volatile interior. The continued maintenance of such order in Liberia was essential to Washington's designs on preserving an American foothold in Africa.[41]

What was less clear was the extent to which Young fulfilled his duties as military attaché. He did file regular lengthy reports on conditions in Liberia and, with his usual eye for detail, he completed a monograph including a comprehensive study on native customary laws and practices. Young was one of the first westerners to recognize the important function of secret societies and ritual magic among the African peoples of Liberia. In addition to the monograph, Young compiled a detailed map of Liberia, much of the interior of which was previously uncharted. When the State Department's map division fielded requests for a map of Liberia at the outset of World War II, "the best one available was the one drawn by Young." At the end of the day, however, the War Department recognized that, although designated a military attaché, Young's primary function was in fact to advise the Liberian government and effect the reorganization of the LFF. His role in Liberia was to support the efforts of the State Department to establish a guiding American influence there. The greatest tribute to his effectiveness in this role was paid by Secretary of State Robert Lansing's plea to the War Department to override the Manchu Law and keep Young in service in Liberia.[42]

Young had come to Africa imbued with the ethos of Western civilization and its attendant civilizing mission. Borrowing heavily from European sociologists, he characterized native Africans as "rude and backward peoples" in *Military Morale,* in which he posited that "it must be evident to any students of the origin and growth of civilization that the regeneration of [Africa] must come in the same manner as it has come to all countries in the past—i.e. from the outside." Unlike most White Europeans and Americans, however, Young was in no doubt that people of African descent the world over had "the natural capacity and aptitude" to match any other race or ethnicity given adequate resources and education. Young transposed to Africa Du Bois's vision of the Talented Tenth, in which a handful educated and sophisticated African Americans would marshal the uplift of the masses. Young expected that he and Bundy and Ballard, along with the civilized Americo-Liberians, would fulfill a similar function in Liberia.[43]

During his three years in Liberia, Young's belief in the transforming power of outside influence grew stronger. However, at the same time, his preconceptions were seriously challenged by the complex reality of Africa. The Americo-Liberian elite proved to be a sore disappointment to Young. While there were certain officials such as President Howard whom he liked and admired, there were far too many who were, at best, lazy and inefficient and, at worst, venal and corrupt. Nonetheless, he believed that "the Americo-Liberian with all his faults and failings is head and shoulder above" the colonial subjects of the British, German, and French. Therefore, Young concluded, an obligation fell on the United States, and particularly its officials in Liberia, to intervene to preserve "this land of promise for...[the] black man" and prevent its falling into the hands of the "land-grabbing" Europeans.[44]

Young was cognizant of the fact that his government's interest in Liberia was more practical than idealistic, but the establishment of an American economic protectorate in Liberia was worth the price of preserving the "Liberian idea," an independent Black republic in otherwise colonial Africa. Unlike the State Department officials in Washington who saw in Liberia only the untapped wealth of rubber, coffee, and other tropical products, Young viewed the native African as "the best asset of the Republic." He was appalled by the exploitation and abuse of these people by Americo-Liberian officials and he recognized that until the repressive nature of this relationship changed, the internal unrest that periodically ravaged the republic would continue indefinitely. Young saw no contradiction in his role in retraining the LFF and leading the campaign to crush native revolt. He was not opposed to Monrovia exercising authority over the African peoples of the interior; he simply wanted to promote more enlightened administration. Thus, with the support of the U.S. government and under the guidance of educated African Americans, "the rehabilitation of the African race as of old" could begin in earnest in Liberia.[45]

However paternalistic Young's views of Africa may appear to today's readers, his passion for the continent of his ancestors was deep-seated and genuine. In the native villages of Liberia's interior he encountered a richness and vitality of life that he found inspirational, and when he returned to Ohio he brought a little bit of Africa with him. Various pieces of West African art were added to the materials he had collected earlier in Haiti and the Caribbean; an African suite became the latest addition to his growing body of musical composition; the outline for an African play, "The Lake of Life," lay on his desk awaiting the day when he would find time to finish it; guinea fowl joined the eclectic animal population on his Ohio farm; and, as he had done in the Philippines, he became a sponsor to a number of young Liberian natives seeking an education in the United States.[46]

More so than any of the other places he visited, Africa had an enormous impact on the way Young viewed the world. In contrast to his frustrations with the chronic instability of the Liberian republic, Young was inspired by the diversity and spirit of the indigenous African people. He began to gather notes in Liberia for a book on the history of the Black race that might serve as an "energizer in the renaissance of the Negro of today both in the old and the New World." He was anxious to demonstrate that the Black man was not simply put on this earth as a "servant to hew wood and draw water," nor was he a "caricature of mankind...a quasi-modo makeshift between man and monkey." Young was determined to demonstrate that Black people were "an important division of the human family...consisting of differing peoples each having its own natural spirit of ideals as much as the boastful Europeans." Young noted the irony in the prevailing image of Africa as savage and superstitious at a time when the Christian nations of Europe were "cutting each other's throats...in the name of progress and civilization." Observing the war from Africa, Young echoed the emerging concept of collective security by calling for a "brotherhood of nations and races" as a fundamental matter of "natural law." He believed that to create an environment in which such an eventuality might occur, strenuous efforts had to be made to promote a fuller understanding of the world's disparate histories, literatures, and languages. Similarly, Young was convinced that education and understanding held the key to overcoming racism and prejudice in the United States. Exposure to African history would contribute to Black self-esteem, for if Black people were made aware of the achievements of their ancestors they would "thank God for every drop of black blood" in them. All of America should know the "glorious history of that proud race that gave civilization to the white race."[47]

NOTES

1. David P. Kilroy, "Extending the American Sphere to West Africa: United States Relations with Liberia 1908–1926" (unpublished dissertation, University of Iowa, 1995).

2. Lt. Colonel Jones to Charles Young, 30 October 1907, Coleman Collection, Akron, Ohio; William Loeleb to Charles Young, 2 May 1907, Charles

Young Papers. National Afro-American Museum and Cultural Center, Wilberforce, Ohio [hereinafter Young Papers].

3. Paul Laurence Dunbar to Charles Young, 16 December 1904, Coleman Collection; Charles Young to W. E. B. Du Bois, 29 June 1907, W. E. B. Du Bois Papers, University of Massachusetts, Amherst, Mass. [hereinafter Du Bois Papers]; Charles Young to William Broad, 12 October 1921, Charles Young File, Moorland-Spingarn Research Center, Howard University, Washington, D.C. [hereinafter Young File MSRC].

4. Nancy Gordon Heinl, "Colonel Charles Young: Pointman," *Army Magazine* 27 (March 1971), 174; Lieutenant Colonel George Rodney, "History of the Ninth Cavalry," n.d., Regimental Records, Records of the U.S. Regular Army Mobile Units, RG 391, National Archives, Washington, D.C. [hereinafter Regimental Records]; Army Service Experience Questionnaire [ASEQ] John B. Johnson, ASEQ Vance Hunter Marchbanks, Jr., ASEQ Edward York, Spanish American War, Philippine Insurrection, Boxer Rebellion Veteran Research Project, U.S. Military History Institute, Carlisle, Pa. [hereinafter Spanish American War Project]

5. Charles Young to Ada Young, 6 December 1920, Coleman Collection; Nancy Gordon Heinl, "Charles Young," in *Dictionary of American Negro Biography*, ed. Rayford W. Logan and Michael R. Winston (New York, 1985), 678; Bernice Young Mitchell Wells, "A Versatile Relative of Mine: Colonel Charles Young," in Herman Dreer, ed., *American Literature by Negro Authors* (New York, 1950), 181.

6. Charles Young to Arminta Young, 8 March 1911, Coleman Collection.

7. Survey response for Charles Young [Completed by Charles Noel Young], Research for Black Soldier, Marvin Fletcher Collection, U.S. Military History Institute, Carlisle, Pa. [hereinafter Fletcher Collection]; E. H. Lawson, "One Out of Twelve Million: Unrevealed Facts in the Life Story of Col. Charles Young, West Pointer," *Washington Post*, 26 May 1929, 14; Greene, Robert E. *Colonel Charles Young: Soldier and Diplomat* (Washington, D.C, 1985), 76.

8. Charles Young to Arminta Young, 8 March 1911, Coleman Collection; Charles Young to Arminta Young, 28 April 1911, Coleman Collection; ASEQ John B. Johnson, Spanish American War Project; Survey response for Charles Young, Research for Black Soldier, Marvin Fletcher Collection, U.S. Military History Institute, Carlisle, Pa. [hereinafter Fletcher Collection].

9. Marvin E. Fletcher, *The Black Soldier and Officer in the United States Army, 1890–1917* (Columbia, MO, 1974), 119–152.

10. Charles Young to Booker T. Washington, 3 April 1911, in Louis R. Harlan, ed., *The Papers of Booker T. Washington* (Champaign, Ill. 1975), 11, 77–78.

11. Reed Paige Clark to Booker T. Washington, 10 November 1911, Young Papers; Booker T. Washington to Charles Young, 18 November 1911, Young Papers; Charles Young to Booker T. Washington, 24 November 1911, in Harlan, *Papers of Booker T. Washington*, 11, 377.

12. Kilroy, "Extending the American Sphere," 1–32.

13. "Report of the American Commission to the Republic of Liberia," 6 October 1909, Senate Document no. 457, 61st Congress, 2nd Session (1910).

14. Kilroy, "Extending the American Sphere," 82; Marvin E. Fletcher, *America's First Black General: Benjamin O. Davis Sr., 1880–1970* (Lawrence, Kans., 1989), 40–44; U.S. Department of War Memorandum for the Chief of Staff, War College Division, General Staff, General Correspondence, Records of the Department of War, Record Group 164, National Archives, Washington, D.C. [hereinafter WCD]

15. Philander Knox to the Secretary of War, 14 November 1911, Records of the Department of State Relating to the Internal Affairs of Liberia, 1910–1929, Record Group 59, National Archives, Washington, D.C. [hereinafter RDSL]; William Crum to Philander Knox, 10 January 1912, RDSL; Office of the General Staff to Charles Young, 15 January 1912, RDSL.

16. Claude Clegg, "'A Splendid Type of Colored American': Charles Young and the Reorganization of the Liberian Frontier Force." *International Journal of African Historical Studies* 29 (winter 1996): 55–56; Frank N. Schubert, *On the Trail of the Buffalo Soldier: Biographies of African-Americans in the U.S. Army, 1866–1917* (Wilmington, Del., 1995), 25, 173; U.S. Department of War Memorandum, n.d., RDSL.

17. Entry for 23 April 1950, Diary of Rayford Logan, Rayford Logan Papers, Library of Congress, Washington, D.C. [hereinafter Logan Diary]; Charles Young to Arminta Young, 13 May 1912, Coleman Collection; Charles Young to Arminta Young, 3 August 1912, Coleman Collection; "Speech in honor of Ada Young on the occasion of her departure from Liberia," no author, n.d. [1912], Coleman Collection.

18. Charles Young to U.S. Department of War, 7 October 1915, RDSL.

19. Charles Young to William D. Crum, 9 October 1912, in U.S. Department of State, Papers Relating to the Foreign Relations of the United States, 1912 (Washington, D.C.), 666 [hereinafter FRUS].

20. Charles Young to Richard C. Bundy, 9 October 1912, RDSL; Richard C. Bundy to the Secretary of State, 14 April 1913, RDSL.

21. Clegg, "Splendid Type of Colored American," 60; Charles Young to Richard C. Bundy, 9 October 1912, RDSL.

22. Richard Bundy to Philander Knox, 12 October 1912, RDSL; Richard Bundy to Philander Knox, 11 November 1912, RDSL; Philander Knox to the American Legation, Monrovia, 19 December 1912, RDSL.

23. Daniel Howard to Charles Young, 23 November 1912, RDSL.

24. Richard Bundy to Secretary of State, 28 January 1913, with enclosure, Major Charles Young, U.S.A., "Report on Browne [*sic*] Relief Expedition," 16 January 1923, RDSL; Charles Young to Arminta Young, 3 August 1912, Coleman Collection; Charles Young Diary, Part I, 15 November 1912, Coleman Collection.

25. Richard Bundy to Secretary of State, 28 January 1913, with enclosure, Major Charles Young, U.S.A., "Report on Browne [*sic*] Relief Expedition," 16 January 1923, RDSL; Charles Young Diary, Part I, 15 November 1912 Coleman Collection; Entry for 23 April 1950, Logan Diary.

26. Richard Bundy to Secretary of State, 28 January 1913, with enclosure, Major Charles Young, U.S.A., "Report on Browne [*sic*] Relief Expedition," 16 January 1923, RDSL; Newspaper clipping from unidentified Louisville, Kentucky, publication, 16 August 1912, Young Papers; Extracts from Colonel Charles Young's Military Record, Fletcher Collection; "The Desert and the Solitary Place," Notes on the life of Charles Young by Ada Young, 1922, Coleman Collection.

27. Richard Bundy to Secretary of State, 28 January 1913, with enclosure, Major Charles Young, U.S.A., "Report on Browne [*sic*] Relief Expedition," 16 January 1923, RDSL, Charles Young Diary, Part I, 15 November 1912, Coleman Collection.

28. Charles Young to Secretary, War College Division, General Staff, 20 April 1914, RDSL; Richard Bundy to Secretary of State, 28 January 1913, with enclosure, Major Charles Young, U.S.A., "Report on Browne [*sic*] Relief Expedition," 16 January 1923, RDSL; Clipping, *Liberia Times,* n.d., Young Papers; Charles

Young to Secretary, War College Division, General Staff, 19 January 1913, WCD.

29. Charles Young to the Adjutant General's Office, 6 August 1913, with enclosed doctor's certificate dated 16 May 1913, Letters Received by the Appointment, Commission, and Personal Branch, Adjutant General's Office, 1871–1917, Record Group 94, National Archives, Washington, D.C. [hereinafter ACP File]; Charles Young to Arminta Young, 11 May 1913, Coleman Collection.

30. Richard Bundy to Ada Young, 31 May 1913, ACP File; Entry for 23 April 1950, Logan Diary.

31. Charles Young to the Adjutant General's Office, 6 August 1913, with enclosed doctor's certificate dated 16 May 1913, ACP File; Charles Young to Alexander Pipers, 26 July 1915, reprinted in Patricia W. Romero, *I Too Am an American: Documents from 1619 to the Present* (New York, 1968), 190; J. B. Moore to Philander C. Knox, 26 May 31 1913, WCD; Richard Bundy to Philander Knox, 31 May 1913, WCD.

32. Charles Young to Alexander Pipers, 26 July 1915, Romero, *I Too Am an American*, 190; Richard Bundy to the Secretary of State, 14 February 1913, RDSL; Richard Bundy to Secretary of State, 7 October 1913, RDSL; Charles Young to Secretary, War College Division, General Staff, 6 September 1913, WCD; Charles Young to Richard Bundy, 27 October 1913, RDSL.

33. Dennis Howard to Charles Young, 8 February 1913, RDSL; U.S. Department of State Memorandum, Office of Third Assistant Secretary of State, 15 April 1913, RDSL.

34. Charles Young to the Secretary, War College Division, General Staff, 20 April 1914, RDSL.

35. Charles Young to the Secretary, War College Division, General Staff, 31 December 1914, RDSL; Richard Bundy to the Secretary of State, 8 June 1915, RDSL; Charles Young to the Secretary, War College Division, General Staff, 17 April 1914, RDSL.

36. Charles Young to George Buckner, 7 October 1914, Uncataloged Boxes, Charles Young Papers; Charles Noel Young to Grandparents, n.d., Charles Young Papers, National Afro-American Museum and Cultural Center, Wilberforce, Ohio [hereinafter Young Papers Uncataloged]; Marie Young to Grandpapa, 28 April 1914, Young Papers Uncatalogued.

37. Note dated June 1915, author unknown, Charles Young File, Ripley Museum, Ripley, Ohio; Travel Permit to Holland, issued by His Majesty's Government of Great Britain, 31 May 1915, Young Papers; Charles Young to Nina Du Bois, 6 July 1915, Du Bois Papers; David Levering Lewis, *W. E. B. Du Bois: Biography of a Race, 1868–1919* (New York, 1993), 457; Ada Young to Arminta Young, 7 October 1915, Young Papers Uncatalogued; Charles Young to Arminta Young, 10 January 1915, Coleman Collection; Charles Young to Arminta Young, 30 June 1915, Coleman Collection.

38. Charles Young to Delamare Skerrett, 26 July 1915, Charles Young File, United States Military Academy Archives, West Point, New York. Charles Young to Secretary, War College Division, General Staff, 20 April 1914, RDSL.

39. Charles Young to Richard Bundy, 26 September 1915, Young Papers; Charles Young to U.S. Secretary of War, 7 October 1915, RDSL; U.S. Secretary of War to U.S. Secretary of State, 24 November 1915, with enclosed report from Major Charles Young, U.S.A., Military Attaché to Liberia, n.d., RDSL.

40. Robert Lansing to U.S. Secretary of War, 4 December 1915, ACP File; C. D. B. King to Richard Bundy, 17 November 1915, ACP File; Daniel Howard to Charles Young, 24 November 1915, ACP File; Richard Bundy to Charles Young, 20 November 1915, ACP File.

41. C. K. Bolton to Charles Young, 18 February 1915, WCD; Charles Noel Young, "Biography of Charles Young," Coleman Collection; U.S. Department of War Memorandum for the Chief of Staff, February [n.d.] 1916, WCD; C. D. B. King to Richard Bundy, 17 November 1915, ACP File; Daniel Howard to Charles Young, 24 November 1915, ACP File.

42. Synopsis of Native Customary Laws of Liberia, n.d., Young Papers; Entry for 23 April 1950, Logan Diary; U.S. Department of War Memorandum for the Chief of Staff, February [n.d.] 1916, WCD; Robert Lansing to Secretary of War, 4 December 1915, ACP File.

43. Charles Young, *The Military Morale of Nations and Races* (St. Louis, 1912), 208, 212, 269–70.

44. Charles Young to Daniel Howard, 12 October 1915, Young Papers; Charles Young to Richard C. Bundy, 9 October 1912, WCD; Charles Young to Secretary, War College Division, General Staff, 20 April 1914, RDSL.

45. Charles Young to U.S. Department of War, 7 October 1915, RDSL; Charles Young to Richard Bundy, 9 October 1912, WCD; Young, *Military Morale,* 270.

46. Wells, "A Versatile Relative of Mine" (New York, 1950), 179–181.

47. Charles Young Diary, Part I, "Big or Little Ns?" n.d. [1915], Coleman Collection; "Colored Young Men of American," Speech by Charles Young, n.d., Coleman Collection.

CHAPTER 7

On the Trail of Pancho Villa

Charles Young's stock as a leader in the African American community rose significantly following his three years of service as the military attaché in Liberia. His exploits in Africa were widely reported in the Black press and even formed the basis for a character in a romantic novel. The symbolic significance of Liberia to African Americans of this era can be gauged by the decision of the National Association for the Advancement of Colored People to award Young the Spingarn Medal in 1916, an award given annually to an African American man or woman who demonstrated significant achievement in any field during the previous year. Young's work in Liberia, contributing as it did to the continued independence of the Black republic and winning the acclaim of U.S. and Liberian government officials, was welcomed by Black America as a significant contribution to the cause of "racial uplift." The Spingarn award recognized Young's performance in a role in which he was growing increasingly comfortable, a warrior in the cause of racial equality.[1]

Young was approaching the pinnacle of his career. Promotion from major to lieutenant colonel was imminent and, as American entry into the European war became an ever-increasing possibility, a general's star was not an improbable expectation. President Woodrow Wilson's decision to send a "punitive expedition" to Mexico in 1916 in pursuit of the rebel leader Pancho Villa following his deadly assault on the border town of Columbus, New Mexico, afforded Young another opportunity to prove his ability as an officer in the field. Young commanded the Second Squadron, 10th Cavalry, in a number of actions in Mexico, including the timely relief of Major Frank Tompkins at Parral. His performance earned him the admiration of the expedition's commander, General "Black Jack"

Pershing, who noted that he was an "active, energetic and able" officer who had "shown very high efficiency throughout the campaign."[2]

Young's rise into the senior ranks of the military brought his status as the army's highest-ranking Black officer into sharper focus. His promotion to the rank of lieutenant colonel during the course of the Mexican campaign increased the number of White officers who fell under his command and raised the potential for incidents of insubordination. Pershing observed that through his exemplary performance of duty, Young "won the respect of his fellow...officers," while Young's regimental commander, Colonel William Brown, noted that he always used tact and good judgment in dealing with White officers. The problem was not Young's ability to effectively command, however, it was the prejudice of a small number of junior White officers who openly resented taking orders from a Black officer. Even before he returned from Liberia to join the 10th Cavalry, news of his assignment prompted a young southern lieutenant named John Kennard to request a transfer to the all-White Seventh Cavalry, which he was granted. The increasing politicization in 1917 of the issue of a Black officer giving orders to White subordinates eventually set in motion a series of events that would contribute to the unraveling of Young's career.[3]

Young was unaware as he led his men on a 300-mile chase across northern Mexico that this would be his last campaign in the uniform of the United States Army. It is somewhat fitting that it should also have been the last campaign of the "Old Army." The punitive expedition marked the passing of an era, as it was the final time that mounted cavalry would play a significant role in U.S. military history. There were signs of change in Mexico, with motorized and airborne units deployed for the first time, albeit with limited success. Men on horseback, however, bore the brunt of the grueling hunt for Villa. Young relished the rugged challenge of Old Army life, and it was apposite, therefore, that he should play such a central role in its swan song.

On returning to the United States at the end of 1915, Young requested and secured leave to attend to private business. He returned to Youngsholm, which would prove increasingly important as a refuge and source of comfort during the next few turbulent years of his life. Even with the children away at school in Paris, Youngsholm was a bustling hive of activity. Arminta Young served as the matriarch of an eclectic extended family, which in addition to Charles, Ada, and their children, included a large number of farmhands and houseguests, many of whom were "adopted" by Young during his service both at home and overseas. Over the years the Youngs added 80 acres of land and an additional small house to the original property. A new wing was added to the main house to accommodate the ever-increasing number of permanent residents, increasing the total number of rooms from 12 to 16. However, the constant flow of visitors and guests ensured that Youngsholm was often full to overflowing.[4]

The vitality of Youngsholm was due partly to Charles Young's attitude that "there is always room for one more," invited or not, and partly to the fact that it stood at the center of a fully functioning farm. When confronted with the assertion that he was a gentleman farmer, Young liked to display the dirt on his "britches" as evidence that his commitment to the vocation was of the hands-on variety. In truth, however, while Young was not averse to toiling in the fields, his presence on the farm was intermittent and the day-to-day care of the livestock and crops was left to the resident manager and hands. In addition to the revenue generated by the farm, Young also supplemented his army income through returns generated on property he and Ada owned in Denver, Oakland, and Dayton. These additional revenues enabled Young to sustain his country gentleman lifestyle, supporting a large household in Wilberforce while educating his children in Europe.[5]

In addition to taking care of his business interests, Young took advantage of his leave to catch up on correspondence with old friends. His most consistent correspondent remained his "Good Friend" Will Du Bois. Young was one of the few people willing to talk openly and frankly to Du Bois, and the two regularly sought each other out for advice or simply to pour out their troubles. As they had done on so many occasions around the piano at Youngsholm when the two of them were teaching together at Wilberforce, they continued to collaborate on artistic projects. In October 1913, Du Bois raised the curtain on one of his most ambitious projects, a three-hour musical extravaganza called *The Star of Ethiopia* highlighting epochal moments in Black history. Young was among the chief contributors to the musical score for the pageant, which ran to rave reviews at the 12th Regiment armory in New York. The success of the initial production, staged to mark the fiftieth anniversary of the Emancipation Proclamation, led to three additional runs for the three-thousand-dollar extravaganza, at Washington, D.C.'s America League Ballpark in 1915, Philadelphia's Convention Hall in 1916, and the Hollywood Bowl in Los Angeles in 1925. Du Bois intended the pageant as an exercise in raising race consciousness rather than a money-making entertainment venture. Young's contribution consisted of a prelude and five additional pieces, which he composed and sent to Du Bois while he was still in Liberia and which, not surprisingly, drew heavily on his experiences in the republic's interior. Pieces such as "Chant of the Savages," "Song of the Faithful," and "The African Chant" caught the attention of critics. The 1915 performance prompted the *Washington Bee* to report, "the primitive and African savage music of Major Young is most weird and peculiar...the rhythm is irregular and the score is full of unexpected intervals." The critic for the *Bee* was convinced nonetheless that the challenge it presented the musicians was eminently

worthwhile. An exuberant Du Bois wrote his friend after the initial performance that the pageant had been a remarkable success, drawing a total
of thirty thousand people (other figures put the number at half that total),
and that Young's music had gone over particularly well.[6]

The bulk of Young's correspondence with Du Bois in early 1916 concerned preparations for the Spingarn Medal ceremonies. Du Bois, the editor of the NAACP journal *The Crisis*, had been instrumental in putting
Young's name forward for the award, and now he was determined that his
friend should overcome his antipathy to publicity and sacrifice himself
"for the good of the race." In particular, Du Bois was anxious that Young
should appear for the award in full-dress uniform, as anything less would
disappoint those who came to honor his achievements. Young duly
obliged, and the event at the Boston Tremont Temple on February 22, 1916,
proved to be a glittering affair. Although Young professed that such occasions were "absolutely foreign to an Army Officer's trade," he agreed to
participate and accept the award "only for the Cause of Advancement of
my Race." Ironically, Du Bois and Joel Spingarn, the former Columbia
humanities professor and benefactor of the award, were unable to attend
as a wreck had caused the cancellation of their train from New York to
Boston. These notable exceptions aside, the assembled audience of three
thousand people contained many of the leading figures in the African
American community and the civil rights movement. The gold medal, valued at one hundred dollars, was presented by the governor of Massachusetts, Samuel W. McCall, and there was a long parade of speakers, who
one by one came to the podium to heap lavish praise on the achievements
of America's highest-ranking Black officer.[7]

Young was genuinely surprised by the decision to award him the Spingarn Medal, believing himself to have "done so little to deserve [it]," and
he accepted it with humility, suggesting that perhaps the absent Du Bois
might have been a more deserving recipient. He expressed his hope to the
audience at the Tremont Temple that this recognition might serve to
encourage other Black Americans to answer the call of military service. In
closing, Young observed that there were two ways to subjugate a Black
man. One was to convince him that he was worthless and that he was
incapable of rising in the world; the second was to persuade him that "he
is it" and he has nothing left to achieve. Young informed his listeners that
this was the first time the second approach had been tried on him, imply-
ing that he was no stranger to the former tactic. He vowed, to ringing
applause and laughter, not to be subdued by flattery.[8]

The event, widely reported in the Black press, marked the intersection
of Young's military career and his growing significance as a figure of
prominence in the struggle for civil rights. One or other theme provided
the subject of all the speeches made in his honor at the Tremont Temple.
Black newspapers across the country uniformly reported the remarks of

Major General Leonard Wood, the army's former chief of staff who, in a written statement read out by the War Department's representative at the meeting, lauded Young's ability as an officer and noted that "his service...had been highly creditable to his race from every standpoint." The success of Charles Young and other African Americans in public service was vital to the advancement of the NAACP's nascent civil rights strategy, and such testimonials from the White establishment were important building blocks. In a letter thanking him for soliciting the letter from Wood, Young sought to impress upon Spingarn "how helpful—far more than any financial aid—are such words...to men of our race." The achievements of men like Charles Young in public institutions such as the army had important implications for all African Americans. As Moorfield Storey, the former chairman of the American Bar Association who served as the NAACP's first president in 1910, remarked at the Spingarn ceremony, every citizen demonstrating allegiance to "the Stars and Stripes" ought to enjoy the full protection afforded by the flag.[9]

With his leave at an end, Young returned to regimental duty in March for the first time in four years. His orders took him to Fort Huachaca, Arizona, where he took command of the Second Squadron, 10th Cavalry. Located in the Huachaca Mountains of southern Arizona, Fort Huachaca was among the remotest of all U.S. Army posts in the United States. Young nonetheless found it to be "delightfully situated" and, in contrast to Liberia, with its tropical heat, the days were pleasantly warm while the nights were blissfully cool. Originally established in 1877 as a base of operations against the Apache, Huachaca's proximity to the Mexican border ensured its survival during the systematic closure of forts throughout the Southwest following the capture of Geronimo in 1886. In early 1916 the troops at Fort Huachaca, like all those stationed along the border with Mexico, were on a state of heightened alert. The murder in January of 17 American mining engineers at Santa Ysabel, Mexico, by a band of men loyal to the rebel leader Pancho Villa had inspired widespread calls for military action on the part of the United States. Despite the fact that President Wilson expressed satisfaction in the Mexican government's pledge to restore order in the northern province of Chihuahua, tensions remained high along the border as Young settled into his new post.[10]

Young was excited to be returning to regimental duty, although a little apprehensive having been on detached service for so many years. He felt somewhat out of touch with cavalry life, as there had been numerous changes in order, regulation, and drill in his absence. "Everything is to relearn," he lamented in a letter to Ada. However, these difficulties were more than offset by the fact that he knew most of the men and NCOs from previous commands and they welcomed his return with enthusiasm. His old friend from Philippine days Chaplain George Prioleau, whose presence ensured that Young would not have to endure complete social isolation at the post, also greeted him on arrival at Fort Huachaca. Moreover, his new commanding officer, Colonel William Brown, had been a tactical officer at West Point during Young's cadet years. Brown welcomed Young and informed him that he was glad to have an officer who could get in "touch [with the regiment] where he could not."[11]

Shortly after Young's arrival in Arizona, the stunning news of Villa's raid on Columbus, New Mexico, reached Fort Huachaca. In the predawn hours of March 9, Villa and approximately five hundred of his followers crossed into the United States and converged on the dusty border town of Columbus. The 13th U.S. Cavalry, which garrisoned the town, was caught completely unawares, and for six hours the Mexican invaders rampaged through Columbus shouting "Viva Villa" and "Viva Mexico" before being driven off by regrouped American forces. As the dust settled, 19 Americans, including 13 U.S. soldiers, lay dead and fires raged in numerous buildings across town. In addition to loot from private homes and businesses, one hundred U.S. cavalry horses were taken in the raid. An outraged and angry American public found little comfort in the fact that Villa had lost as many as 62 men during the fighting.[12]

Villa's attack on Columbus was less predicated on military success than on creating enough indignation in the United States to inspire U.S. military intervention in Mexico's ongoing civil war. The roots of Villa's "quixotic adventure" lay in his feeling of betrayal at the hands of Woodrow Wilson and his own deteriorating military fortunes vis-à-vis the forces of the Mexican government in Chihuahua. Since Wilson came to office in 1912, his Mexican policy had been based firmly on the principle of promoting constitutional government south of the Rio Grande. At one point Wilson had hoped that Villa might become Washington's man in the Mexican imbroglio, a possible alternative to the Constitutionalist leader Venustiano Carranza, whom the American president distrusted. However, as Carranza's army gained the upper hand over Villa's forces in northern Mexico in 1915, and with events in Europe demanding increasing U.S. attention, Wilson sought to extricate himself from the diplomatic quagmire by dumping Villa.[13]

Interpreting Wilson's recognition of the Carranza government in the fall of 1915 as evidence of a deal to establish an American protectorate in Mexico, Villa cast himself in the role of Mexico's savior from "Yanqui imperialism" when he launched his raid against Columbus. The killings at Santa Ysabel had been designed to elicit an American military response that would serve to undermine the Carranza regime while rallying support to Villa as Mexico's nationalist champion. When that action failed to elicit the requisite response, Villa launched his attack on Columbus. This time public and political pressure were so great that Wilson was left with little option but to launch a retaliatory military assault against the Villistas.[14]

Just six days after the Columbus raid, on March 15, 1916, the first troops from the punitive expedition, approximately five thousand strong (the number would gradually increase to over ten thousand), crossed into Mexico. The Americans advanced in two columns, one from Culberson Ranch, Arizona, and the other from Columbus. The 10th Cavalry arrived at Culberson Ranch on March 14, having left Fort Huachaca five days earlier. In the early morning hours of March 16, Charles Young and the Second Squadron formed part of the long, winding column of men and horses that followed Pershing across the border into Mexico. Young was exhilarated about the prospect of returning to action and, having endured weeks of anticipation, the men were elated that "at last our dream is to come true." In less than 48 hours this flying column traveled 125 miles to Colonia Dublan, where they were to rendezvous with the main force coming from Columbus with the supply wagons.[15]

Having covered 252 miles in less than 10 days, the men and horses of the 10th Cavalry were sorely in need of rest when they arrived in Dublan. No respite was forthcoming, however, as reports of Villa's presence a short distance to the south prompted Pershing to dispatch three separate cavalry columns in pursuit. The 10th Cavalry's Machine Gun Troop and Second Squadron, 14 officers and 258 enlisted men under the command of Colonel Brown, were designated as one of the pursuing columns. They were to have one full day's rest before departing by train for El Rucio. This assignment was to provide early insight into the numerous obstacles that American forces would face in their pursuit of Villa; some were peculiar to Mexico whereas others reflected the poorly planned nature of the U.S. operation.[16]

The decision to send Colonel Brown's detachment south by train was made partly to provide extra rest for the horses and partly to gain time in the pursuit of Villa. However, when the train arrived on the morning of March 19, it was in no condition to serve as a transport for cavalry troops. The officers and men of the 10th Cavalry spent the whole day refitting the train, cutting holes in some of the boxcars for ventilation and repairing others that were smashed or broken. The engine was so short of fuel that wood was requisitioned from a local corral, the owner left with little choice but to accept a promissory note from the U.S. government. The train finally departed later that evening with the horses riding in the cars while the men rode on the roofs.[17]

"Five times in ten hours the engine ran out of fuel and the troops had to disembark and scrape up mesquite roots, old ties, telegraph poles...anything that would burn." A full 24 hours after leaving Dublan, the 10th Cavalry troops detrained at El Rucio, a distance of approximately twenty-nine miles. After the stock had been watered and fed, the column advanced across a rocky, hilly trail toward San Miguel, where Villa had been reportedly sighted. Having entered Mexico without their pack wagons, the troops of the 10th Cavalry carried only the supplies in their saddlebags and two days of rations. For much of the ensuing campaign they would be required to follow General Pershing's orders to "live off the country." Shoes for the horses were in short supply, and the constant movement of the column over difficult terrain took its toll on the animals, many of which were destroyed and replaced only when abandoned horses were recovered from fleeing Villistas. Officers were often required to use their own money to purchase supplies, or reluctant Mexicans were given little choice but to accept U.S. government receipts for slaughtered cattle or feed for the horses. The men survived on a diet of beef jerky and corn ground in coffee grinders, which were useless for little else, as coffee, sugar, and fruit were rarities. They had no tents, just a bed and saddle blanket for cover on those cold Mexican nights.[18]

It was a hard campaign, made all the more difficult by the seemingly elusive nature of the quarry. From the moment the Brown column chased down its first lead at San Miguel, it appeared that Villa was always once step ahead. Each new reported sighting drew the pursuing columns further south only to find that Villa and his men had moved on. The snow and frost of the mountains and the heat and dust of the plains, combined with the general distrust and hostility of the local population, added to the discomfort of the Americans. Charles Young's body and soul appeared to rise to the challenge of these privations and adverse conditions. He wrote to Joel Spingarn from Mexico that the punitive expedition was "for me and my squadron strenuous indeed at times; but full of adventure and movement—never banal." "We have it hard," he wrote Ada, but "I am healthy and have never felt better in my life save the dirt." This despite the fact that his shoes were falling apart, he had been forced to borrow $20 from Colonel Brown to buy underwear after his own wore out, and that he had lost his horse and was for a time reduced to riding a Shetland. His men were in an even more "disheveled state." His bunkmate in Mexico, Chaplain Oscar Scott, another of his former Wilberforce students who had also served with him in the Philippines, noted that Young showed greater concern for the morale of his men than he did for his own welfare. Young's concern extended to taking "the blanket off his own bed to keep others warm," dividing "the last piece of bread," and giving "the last drop from his canteen to another."[19]

Young not only earned the respect of his men but also their deep affection. He was pleased with the performance of the officers and men of his squadron, particularly when called on to fight, and he noted that as the campaign went on the White officers were "becoming accustomed" to having a Black officer in charge. Occasionally he would walk the picket line with one of his junior White officers recounting stories of Africa and the West Indies, and a couple of his White subordinates had gone out of their way on his behalf, sharing food and washing his clothes. However, although "highly esteemed by his fellow officers," Young remained socially isolated from the upper ranks, and his social interaction in Mexico was limited largely to the Black chaplains, NCOs, and troops. As a result, it was a common site in camp to see Charles Young holding court with a large number of "non-commissioned officers sitting around his tent."[20]

Young developed a close working relationship with his commanding officer, Colonel Brown. Brown recognized that Young's "position—a colored officer with white officers under him—was peculiarly trying" and was impressed by the fact that "not a single complaint" reached his ears during the course of the campaign. Brown admired Young for his "energy, good judgment, and loyalty," the last of which qualities Brown would demonstrate in turn when Young turned to him for help in 1917. Their mutual respect was reinforced by acts of personal sacrifice, as on the occasion when Young used his watch and diamond ring as security to ensure that a messenger carried an urgent dispatch to Brown or when Brown used 100 pesos of his own money to purchase a new horse for Young to ride. At the end of the day, however, even Brown could not see past the color of Young's skin. In his efficiency report, he noted that Young was "an excellent officer, handicapped only by the fact that he is a colored man."[21]

Brown and Young were riding at the head of the column on March 31 when they encountered a large contingent of Villa's troops at a ranch named Aguas Calientes. As the Villistas attempted to abandon some of the adobe buildings on the ranch, Young led two troops in an effort to cut them off. A number of Villistas took cover behind a low stone wall and proved particularly difficult to dislodge, so Brown passed the order for Young to mount up and lead a charge against their right flank while the regiment's machine gun unit provided covering fire. Without hesitation, Young and his men dropped back from the firing line, mounted their horses and, with pistols drawn, galloped down a steep hill toward the enemy. At a signal from Young the troops let out a blood-curdling yell and increased the pace of their advance, prompting the Villistas to abandon their positions before the troopers were even within range to discharge their pistols. Aguas Calientes was one of the first times in the army's history that machine gun fire had been used to cover advancing troops, and its success added to the 10th Cavalry's reputation as one of the best fighting units in the Old Army.[22]

Incidents like the one at Aguas Calientes typified the punitive expedition. On those occasions when Villa's partisans were encountered, they would retreat rather than engage in large-scale combat with the Americans. While U.S. troops inflicted some casualties in these skirmishes, they were sucked ever deeper into Mexico in pursuit of Villa and the main body of his army. Each advance stretched already taut lines of communication and contributed to mounting tension with Mexican government forces in northern Mexico, one of Villa's goals in inciting American intervention in the first place. The Carranza government had initially recognized the need to accept the entry of the punitive expedition into Mexico to avoid a crisis with the United States, but it had such a difficult time selling it the Mexican people that no formal approval was ever granted. The presence of a growing contingent of American troops some three hundred and fifty miles south of the Rio Grande proved increasingly unpalatable for the Mexican government. Nationalist sentiment fueled mounting opposition to their presence on Mexican soil, and tensions between the United States and Mexico became progressively more strained.[23]

These mounting tensions eventually erupted into clashes between American forces and Mexican government troops. On April 12 in the town of Parral, the furthest point to which American troops would advance during the expedition, troops from the 13th Cavalry under the command of Major Frank Tompkins came under fire from a mixed contingent of Mexican government troops and civilians. A number of Americans were killed or wounded in the initial skirmish, and Tompkins led his men in a hasty retreat from Parral. The Mexican regulars pursued them to the village of Santa Cruz de Villegas, where Tompkins and his men took up a defensive position, and outriders were sent north to seek relief. Help duly arrived in the form of the 10th Cavalry, who identified themselves in the gathering dusk by sounding the distinctive American cavalry bugle calls. A disheveled and slightly wounded Tompkins reportedly greeted this relief exclaiming, "By God! They were glad to see the Tenth Cavalry at Santiago in '98, but I'm a damn sight gladder to see you now. I could kiss every one of you." Young, riding at the head of the advance guard, quickly tempered his colleague's exuberance by retorting "Hello, Tompkins! You can start in on me right now."[24]

The clash at Parral was followed by the gradual withdrawal of the flying columns north to Colonia Dublán. With many of their horses so exhausted that they could no longer be ridden, the haggard and weary troops retraced their steps at the end of April to the site from which they had departed the previous month. With the return of the pursuers from the south and the arrival of reinforcements from the north, a great sprawling U.S. encampment grew up around the little Mormon settlement of Colonia Dublan in the summer of 1916. Although the troops of the 10th Cavalry were reunited here with their wagons and thus received regular supplies and rations for the first time in over a month, camp life proved monotonous after the excitement of the active pursuit of Villa. The Carranza government now insisted that the only direction American troops could move without coming to blows with government forces was north, and so the future of the punitive expedition became uncertain.[25]

With tensions at a fever pitch, a second clash between U.S. and Mexican forces in June 1916 brought the two countries to the brink of war. On June

20 a scouting party consisting of two troops from the 10th Cavalry encountered opposition from Mexican forces as it attempted to enter the town of Carrizal, approximately sixty miles west of Dublan. The resulting firefight left 13 Americans dead, with scores wounded or taken prisoner, and an even higher number of fatalities on the Mexican side. Although Young had not been part of the scouting party, he knew all the men who had been killed, including a young man from Xenia whose mother he now prepared to write. As the survivors of the Carrizal fight slowly drifted back into camp, many of the troops in Dublan "longed for an opportunity to come to real hand-grips with the Mexicans." Young was more circumspect; in his view a war with Mexico would be "unfortunate." If it did come to that, however, his professional ambitions were such that he hoped to be given the opportunity of commanding "a regiment of my own people" in the conflict.[26]

With Wilson insisting that Pershing be allowed to complete the task of capturing Villa, and Carranza demanding immediate American withdrawal, the prospect of such an opportunity arising seemed likely indeed. Feverish diplomacy took place against a backdrop of large troop movements on both sides, including mobilization of the U.S. National Guard along the border. Eventually cooler heads prevailed and the crisis was defused, but negotiations over the terms of American withdrawal and prisoner exchange dragged on through the summer and fall. Throughout this period of diplomatic disengagement, the forces of the punitive expedition were essentially confined to the camp at Colonia Dublin.[27]

Although the quality of camp life gradually improved as truck convoys from the United States became more frequent, life for the soldiers at Colonia Dublan from the time of the Carrizal fight to the day of the withdrawal in January 1917 was tedious and uncomfortable. Without an adequate supply of tents, the men had to improvise with makeshift shelters to protect them from the dust storms, swarms of "pestiferous flies," and tropical heat of the summer and the snow, rain, and freezing cold of winter. The men and officers grew increasingly "restive and quarrelsome" as each new rumor about imminent departure proved unfounded. Regular athletic events, including a regimental football league in which the 10th Cavalry was runner up, provided some respite from the boredom of camp life. Training and exercises dominated the daily routine and took on greater urgency as the realization of the likelihood of American entry into World War I permeated the camp. As always, Young continued to work his men hard, gaining satisfaction from the fact that at the end of squadron exercises "some butts are sore."[28]

Oscar Scott, the chaplain, made the mistake of accompanying Young's squadron on one of their exercises but was forced to turn back and return to his bed by the pace of the ride. Young was fond of Scott and encouraged the men to attend his services, where he would play the piano and lead the men in hymns. In addition to nurturing their souls, Young also cultivated his men's commitment to the struggle against racial violence in the United States by leading a collection for the NAACP's antilynching fund. The 10th Cavalry's contribution eventually amounted to six hundred dollars, prompting a letter of appreciation from W. E. B. Du Bois. Young hoped the money would "help a little to swell the fund of $10,000 they are raising toward the end of breaking up that shame to the country."[29]

The confinement of the expedition at Dublan provided Young with the opportunity to take his promotion exam for lieutenant colonel at the end of June 1916. Facing a board headed by Brigadier General Pershing himself, Young's elevation was duly approved. The doctors who conducted his physical exam noted his contraction of blackwater fever in 1913 but deemed him otherwise fit for service. It was another historic promotion, and Young welcomed it as such. He professed that he cared for "these advanced grades only so far as they help my people and the 'cause'," but nonetheless he took great personal satisfaction in the achievement and the seamless promotion augured well for further advances in the near future. Buoyed by promotion, Young devoted some of his boundless energy to relieving the monotony at Dublan. With the assistance of the regiment's NCOs, he organized "a very clever program" to celebrate the 50th anniversary of the founding of the 10th Cavalry. The pageant was performed on July 28 in front of a large crowd that included numerous dignitaries from the top brass and it even earned a detailed report in the *New York Times*.[30]

The 10th also took the lead in organizing elaborate Christmas celebrations. Unfortunately, on December 25 a cold storm blew in the from the north, whipping up clouds of dust that destroyed the planned festivities and rendered "whole steers that were being barbecued...uneatable." It was the fifth Christmas in a row that Young had spent away from his family, all of them forgetful. In 1912 he lay wounded and lost in the "African wilderness"; the following year he was negotiating with warring tribes on the Bassa coast. In 1914 he was deep in jungle making a road, and a year later he was on the high seas during a wicked storm. As bad as these were, Christmas 1916 was worse. "Of all the days that were ever born from the bowels of the earth from the years of my life," Young wrote Ada, "this has been the...worst." The years of separation were taking their toll, and Young was ready to go home.[31]

Letter writing relieved some of the loneliness, and during the long hiatus at Dublan Charles and Ada exchanged regular missives. Charles Young's letters to his beloved "Johnnie" reveal the depth to which he loved his wife. In one letter, he wrote "life would mean absolutely nothing to me since I have begun to love you so." Their marriage, however, had its strains. Ada's health had not been good since her time in Africa, and her letters to Charles betrayed an increasingly nervous and agitated disposition. She worried about her husband's health and his past fidelity, her children's education, their financial situation, and the management of the house and farm. Young's letters are full of reassurances; he told Ada not to worry about money, that the farm would pay and the work should be left to the hands, that there was "no vacancy in his heart," and that contrary to rumors of his death then circulating in Wilberforce he felt "like a fine old fiddle." Part of Ada's unhappiness was rooted in the strained relationship she had with her mother-in-law, Arminta. "You are the absolute boss there," he assured her, adding that she should remain strong and patient. Ada's melancholy posed a threat to Young's idyllic vision of retirement at Youngsholm surrounded by his extended family and good friends. He was ready to return home to restore equilibrium to his personal life. He hoped that being "the *only officer* available" he might be returned to Wilberforce University and thus he could spend time getting both the farm and the family in order.[32]

Another major theme of Charles and Ada's correspondence was the education of their children now that they were back in Wilberforce. Both parents wanted Marie's education built around music and language, the basis of her convent studies in Europe, while Charles was anxious that Tonton should "learn agriculture," with a view to eventually forging a career in tropical agriculture. Young was worried about the prospect of sending his children to school in southern Ohio, where he believed prejudice would hinder their growth. If need be he was prepared to send them to school on the East Coast regardless of the expense and in any case they were to go back to Europe as soon as the war was over. The rugged cavalry officer was a little concerned that his son was not robust and strong enough, and so emphasized a regimen of physical exercise for the boy. To this end he bought a horse for Tonton and arranged to have the stream and woods behind the house stocked for hunting and fishing. There was no shortage of gifts and souvenirs from overseas for either child, from a pot-bellied pig to a set of elephant tusks, and Young clearly loved his children. Ultimately, though, much of his parenting was done from afar.[33]

The new year brought news that American forces were finally to quit Mexico. With a diplomatic settlement finally reached, Pershing received orders in January 1917 to return to the United States. Villa had cleverly eluded his American pursuers and almost succeeded in causing an irreparable breach between Wilson and Carranza. Although Villa was never in a position to challenge for control of the whole country again, after the punitive expedition departed Carranza was unable to break his power in Chihuahua. Somewhat weakened by the crisis, Carranza was ousted from power in 1920, and Villa survived to make peace with his successor. To the United States Villa would always be a killer and a bandit, but to many Mexicans he became a heroic figure who stood toe-to-toe with the "Colossus of the North" and survived.[34]

By early 1917, however, the Great War and the deepening crisis in the Atlantic reduced the Villa debacle to the status of a sideshow in the United States. Wilson's hesitancy with regard to Mexico reflected his growing anxiety over affairs in Europe, which is where the attention of the American public was increasingly focused in this period. Preparations for American involvement in the European conflict dominated the thoughts of the officers and men of the punitive expedition as they returned home in February. Before leaving Mexico, General Pershing took the initiative of forwarding to the War Department a list of officers whose performance in the punitive expedition warranted their being granted command of a brigade in the event of general mobilization. Among those the general tagged for this honor was Lieutenant Colonel Charles Young.[35]

Young looked toward the prospect of war with the resolve of a professional soldier, prepared to answer the call to duty when it came. He was also particularly anxious that African Americans be permitted to play an active and integral part in the U.S. war effort, one befitting their rights as full citizens. With this in mind, he overcame stiff opposition from White officers at Fort Huachaca and established an officer training school for the enlisted men on the post following his return from Mexico. The school proved popular with the men of the 10th Cavalry, as well as a number of White NCOs at the fort, all of whom relished the instruction they received from this "strict disciplinarian" and "past master of the military game." Young's ability to pass on "all the answers to military problems" served his charges well, as 65 Black NCOs from Fort Huachaca went on to officer training school in Fort Des Moines and 62 of them subsequently received commissions during the World War.[36]

American involvement in World War I became official on April 6, 1917, when Congress adopted a resolution declaring war on Germany, four days after President Wilson's blistering condemnation of Berlin's "warfare against mankind." Young shared his commander in chief's disdain for the Kaiser and his goals, warning of dire consequences were the United States to fail to do its part in destroying the "German military machine." Expanding on Wilson's call to fight to make the world "safe for democracy," Young pressed Black Americans to focus on the U.S. war effort in terms of "our aspirations for racial betterment." This was not just a chance for African Americans to demonstrate "loyalty and leadership," it was an opportunity to prevent a German victory, a victory that would mean a return to slavery for Black people around the world "more galling and hopeless than [that] of ante-bellum days in the United States." The future of Western civilization depended on the defeat of Germany, and Young urged that unless they were willing to relinquish "the heights of a half century of...awakening," African Americans must respond to the president's call to action without qualification.[37]

Young implored Black Americans to stand by the flag in this hour of need and he shared with Du Bois and others the belief that loyal participation in this war could serve as a springboard for significant gains in the civil rights cause. Proponents of this vision expected Young to be the standard bearer for the cause. It was generally anticipated in the African American community that Young would lead a Black volunteer division on the battlefields of Europe or, at the very least, be placed in command of Joel Spingarn's proposed officer training school for Black officers. In the words of Du Bois, "he was strong, fit and only 49 years of age [he was in fact 53 in 1917], and in the accelerated promotion of war he would have been a general in the army by 1918." As America's first Black general, Young would help to secure victory for the United States in this "war to end all wars" and in the process help to usher in a new era of equality and freedom.[38]

Charles Young welcomed American entry into World War I, not with the enthusiasm of a militarist eager to indulge in the exhilaration of combat, but as a reformer convinced that this conflict could inaugurate a new, more tranquil and equitable age. Young was a product of the progressive era and, although there is much to question the benevolent motives America attached to its intervention in the Philippines, Haiti, Liberia, and Mexico, a great deal of his army career to this date had been taken up with tasks such as battling disorder and building roads. Like many American progressives, Young believed that World War I offered an opportunity to move beyond the piecemeal contributions these interventions afforded and to promote American principles of democracy and freedom on a grand scale.

Young had every reason to believe that he would play a central role in the American war effort. Twice during the course of the punitive expedition to Mexico he had taken command of the 10th Cavalry in the absence of Colonel Brown and after returning to Fort Huachaca he served for a brief period as post commander. In Mexico he had literally rubbed shoulders with Generals Pershing and Bliss and other ranking members of the military hierarchy, and he demonstrated himself to be an officer of considerable ability. His promotion to lieutenant colonel had gone smoothly, and his superior officers in Mexico were unanimous in their praise for his capacity to command. Of particular note, in light of later events, was the fact that the medical examiners in Mexico had raised no doubts about his fitness to serve. In fact, a physical exam conducted immediately before the return of the punitive expedition from Mexico found that the grueling ride back to Fort Huachaca posed no danger to "the life of the officer." Given the inevitable expansion of the regular army and the introduction of a general mobilization, Young's seniority guaranteed that he would secure promotion.[39]

There were, however, storm clouds on the horizon. Although the doctors in Mexico gave him a clean bill of health they detected the presence of albumen in his urine, a problem that Young confessed had appeared intermittently for several years past. Meanwhile, his efficiency report for 1917 contained an alarming note of censure from his commanding officer at Fort Huachaca, Colonel Ellwood Evans. Evans noted that Young was an excellent officer, morally and mentally fitted for all duties, but added the considerable qualification that Young was "hampered by the characteristic racial trait of losing his head in sudden emergencies." Evans's report ran completely contrary to the assessment of Young's service in Mexico by both Colonel Brown and General Pershing, and was utterly inconsistent with the critical role played by Young at Aguas Calientes and Parral. Evans's hostility toward Young was based solely on the issue of race; although he recognized Young's ability as an officer, he did not think he could be trusted "in cases involving the color line." Evans offered the opinion that Young was inclined to great prejudice in favor of his race—this hampers his usefulness." For Colonel Evans, Young's steady rise through the ranks was an intolerable challenge to White supremacy in the officer corps, one that he and others of a like mind were determined to check.[40]

NOTES

1. Henry F. Downing, an American expatriate working for a British cotton company in West Africa, based the central character in his 1917 novel, *The American Cavalryman*, on Young. Henry F. Downing, *The American Cavalryman: A Liberian Romance* (College Park, Md., 1969).

2. Adjutant General's Office to Charles Young, 16 September 1916, W. E. B. Du Bois Papers, University of Massachusetts, Amherst, Mass. [hereinafter Du Bois Papers].

3. John J. Pershing to Nathum Daniel Brascher, 21 February 1922, John J. Pershing Papers, Library of Congress, Washington, D.C. [hereinafter Pershing Papers]; Letter of Recommendation for Charles Young by Colonel William C. Brown [n.d.], 1916, Charles Young Papers, National Afro-American Museum and Cultural Center, Wilberforce, Ohio [hereinafter Young Papers]; Robert E. Greene, *Black Defenders of America, 1775–1973* (Chicago, 1974), 162; Woodrow Wilson to Newton D. Baker, 25 June 1917, Newton Diehl Baker Papers, Library of Congress, Washington, D.C. [hereinafter Baker Papers].

4. Bernice Young Mitchell Wells, "A Versatile Relative of Mine: Colonel Charles Young," in Herman Dreer, ed., *American Literature by Negro Authors* (New York, 1950), 179–83; Charles Young to Arminta Young, 3 January 1906, Coleman Collection, Akron, Ohio; Charles Young to Ada Young, 8 September 1915, Coleman Collection; Charles Young, Last Will and Testament, n.d., Coleman Collection.

5. Wells, "A Versatile Relative of Mine," 179–183; Notarized statement, 26 December 1919, Young Papers; Ellis Wood to Ada Young, 21 August 1920, Young Papers; William Hass to Ada Young, 22 October 1920, Young Papers.

6. W. E. B. Du Bois to Charles Young, 14 January 1916, Young Papers; *Washington Bee*, 23 October 1915, clipping in Du Bois Papers; David Levering Lewis, *W. E. B. Du Bois: Biography of a Race, 1868–1919* (New York, 1993), 460–61; W.E.B.

Du Bois to Charles Young, n.d., November 1913, Coleman Collection; Lewis, Biography of a Race, 459–60.

7. W. E. B. Du Bois to Charles Young, 21 January 1916, Du Bois Papers; W. E. B. Du Bois to Charles Young, 31 January 1916, Young Papers; Charles Young to Joel E. Spingarn, 26 January 1916, Joel E. Spingarn Papers, Moorland Spingarn Research Collection, Howard University, Washington, D.C. [hereinafter Joel Spingarn Papers]; Newspaper clippings pertaining to Spingarn Medal Ceremony, 22 February 1916, Box 209C, Records of the National Association for the Advancement of Colored People, Library of Congress, Washington, D.C. [hereinafter NAACP Papers].

8. Charles Young to R. G. Randolph, Clipping, Joel Spingarn Papers; Clipping, "Medal Given to Maj. Young," *Boston Daily Globe*, 23 February 1916, NAACP Papers.

9. Clipping, *New York Evening Post*, 24 February 1916, NAACP Papers; Charles Young to Joel E. Spingarn, 26 January 1916, Joel Spingarn Papers; Clipping, *Boston Daily Globe*, 23 February 1916, NAACP Papers.

10. Lieutenant Colonel George Rodney, "The Punitive Expedition," n.d., Regimental Records, Records of the U.S. Regular Army Mobile Units, RG 391, National Archives, Washington, D.C. [hereinafter Regimental Records]; Charles Young to Ada Young, 1 March 1916, Coleman Collection.

11. Charles Young to Ada Young, 1 March 1916, Coleman Collection.

12. Frank Tompkins, *Chasing Villa: The Last Campaign of the United States Cavalry* (Harrisburg, Pa., 1939), 48; Friedrich Katz, "Pancho Villa and the Attack on Columbus, New Mexico," *American Historical Review* 83 (February 1978): 101.

13. Katz, "Pancho Villa and the Attack on Columbus," 106.

14. Katz, "Pancho Villa and the Attack on Columbus," 128.

15. Tompkins, *Chasing Villa*, 72–77; Rodney, "Punitive Expedition," 1–3, Regimental Records; Charles Young to Ada Young, 11 March 1916, Coleman Collection.

16. Tompkins, *Chasing Villa*, 78; Rodney, "Punitive Expedition," 3–4, Regimental Records.

17. Tompkins, *Chasing Villa*, 79; Rodney, "Punitive Expedition," 4, Regimental Records.

18. Rodney, "Punitive Expedition," 4–11, Regimental Records; Tompkins, *Chasing Villa*, 89–94; Charles Young to Ada Young, 16 April 1916, Coleman Collection.

19. Rodney, "Punitive Expedition," 4–17, Regimental Records; Charles Young to Joel E. Spingarn, 3 July 1916, Joel Spingarn Papers; Charles Young to Ada Young, 16 April 1916, Coleman Collection; O. J. W. Scott, "Colonel Young—The Friend," Oration delivered on the occasion of funeral services for Charles Young, 1 June 1923, reprinted in Abraham Chew, *A Biography of Colonel Charles Young* (Washington, D.C., 1923), 16–17.

20. Survey response for Jerome W. Howe, Research for Black Soldier, Marvin Fletcher Collection, U.S. Military History Institute, Carlisle, Pa. [hereinafter Fletcher Collection]; Survey response for J. C. Pegram, Research for Black Soldier, Fletcher Collection; Charles Young to Ada Young, 24 August 1916, Coleman Collection; Charles Young to Ada Young, 16 April 1916, Coleman Collection.

21. Efficiency Report filed by William C. Brown, 13 January 1916, Letters Received by the Appointment, Commission, and Personal Branch, Adjutant General's Office, 1871–1917, Record Group 94, National Archives, Washington, D.C.

[hereinafter ACP File]; Letter of Recommendation for Charles Young by Colonel William C. Brown [n.d.], 1916, Young Papers; Tompkins, *Chasing Villa,* 147, 52.

22. Bernard Nalty, *Strength for the Fight: A History of Black Americans in the Military* (New York, 1986), 98–99; Tompkins, *Chasing Villa,* 145–46; Clarence C. Clendenen, *Blood on the Border: The United States Army and the Mexican Irregulars* (New York, 1969), 257.

23. Katz, "Pancho Villa and the Attack on Columbus," 128; Arthur S. Link, *Wilson: Confusions and Crises, 1915–1916* (Princeton, N.J., 1964), 280–318; Edward P. Haley, *Revolution and Intervention: The Diplomacy of Taft and Wilson in Mexico, 1910–1917* (Cambridge, Mass., 1970), 187–223.

24. Tompkins, *Chasing Villa,* 137–44, 261–63.

25. Rodney, "Punitive Expedition," 12–13, Regimental Records; Tompkins, *Chasing Villa,* 207–208.

26. Rodney, "Punitive Expedition," 14–16, Regimental Records; Tompkins, *Chasing Villa,* 209–212; Charles Young to Ada Young, 16 July 1916, Coleman Collection; Charles Young to Joel E. Spingarn, 3 July 1916, Joel Spingarn Papers.

27. Link, *Crises and Confusion,* 280–318; Haley, *Revolution and Intervention,* 187–223; Tompkins, *Chasing Villa,* 213–15

28. Rodney, "Punitive Expedition," 16, Regimental Records; Survey response for Benjamin J. Hoge, Research for Black Soldier, Marvin Fletcher Collection, U.S. Military History Institute, Carlisle, Pa. [hereinafter Fletcher Collection]; Tompkins, *Chasing Villa,* 214; Charles Young to Ada Young, 20 July 1916, Coleman Collection; Charles Young to Ada Young, 6 August 1916, Coleman Collection; Charles Young to Ada Young, 8 September 1916, Coleman Collection.

29. Charles Young to Ada Young, 8 September 1916 Coleman Collection; Charles Young to Ada Young, 10 September 1916, Coleman Collection; O. J. W. Scott, "Colonel Young—The Friend," oration delivered on the occasion of funeral services for Charles Young, 1 June 1923, reprinted in Chew, *A Biography of Colonel Charles Young,* 16–17; Charles Young to Ada Young, 27 September 1916, Coleman Collection; W. E. B. Du Bois to Charles Young, 22 September 1916, Coleman Collection.

30. Promotion and Physical Exam, 28 June 1916, ACP File; Charles Young to Joel E. Spingarn, 3 July 1916, Joel Spingarn Papers; Charles Young to Ada Young, 6 August 1916, Coleman Collection; Rodney, "Punitive Expedition," 12, 17, Regimental Records; *New York Times,* 3 August 1916, 6.

31. Rodney, "Punitive Expedition," 12, 17, Regimental Records; Charles Young to Ada Young, Christmas 1916, Coleman Collection.

32. Charles Young to Ada Young, 8 September 1915, Coleman Collection; Charles Young to Ada Young, 20 July 1916, Coleman Collection; Charles Young to Ada Young, 30 July 1916, Coleman Collection; Charles Young to Ada Young, n.d., August 1916, Coleman Collection; Charles Young to Ada Young, 8 September 1916, Coleman Collection; Charles Young to Ada Young, 31 December 1916, Coleman Collection; Charles Young to Ada Young, 17 February 1917, Coleman Collection.

33. Charles Young to Ada Young, 8 September, 1915, Coleman Collection; Charles Young to Ada Young, 8 September 1916, Coleman Collection; Charles Young to Ada Young, 27 September 1916, Coleman Collection; Charles Young to Marie Young, 1 January 1917, Coleman Collection; Charles Young to Charles Noel

Young, 4 July 1915, Coleman Collection; Charles Young to Charles Noel Young, 1 January 1917, Coleman Collection.

34. Katz, "Pancho Villa and the Attack on Columbus," 128–130.

35. John J. Pershing to Adjutant General, 21 August 1916, reproduced in extracts from Colonel Charles Young's Record, Fletcher Collection; Adjutant General to Charles Young, 16 September 1916, Du Bois Papers.

36. John H. Purnell, "Colonel Charles Young, U.S.A.: Soldier, Diplomat, Philanthropist, Man of Culture," *The Oracle* (winter 1979): 7; Vance Hunter Marchbanks, Sr., "Forty Years in the Army," Young File, Fort Huachaca Museum, Fort Huachaca, Ariz.; Charles Young to T. Montgomery Gregory, 14 May 1917, T. Montgomery Gregory Papers, Moorland Spingarn Research Library, Howard University, Washington, D.C.

37. Charles Young, "A Comrade to Comrades," *The Crisis* 16, no. 2 (June 1918): 59–60.

38. Charles Young to Harry Smith, 23 March, 1917, Young Papers; Wesley A. Brown, "Eleven Men of West Point," *Negro History Bulletin* 151 (April 1956), 147–157; E. H. Lawson, "One Out of Twelve Million: Unrevealed Facts in the Life Story of Col. Charles Young, West Pointer," *Washington Post*, 26 May 1929, 14; Clipping from the *Chicago Defender*, 26 May 1917, Coleman Collection; W.E.B. Du Bois, *Dusk of Dawn: An Essay Towards an Autobiography of a Race Concept* (New York, 1940), 250.

39. Physical Exam, Mexico, 7 December 1916, ACP File.

40. Efficiency Report by Colonel Ellwood Evans [n.d.], 1917, ACP File.

CHAPTER 8

The Glass Ceiling

The decision of the Wilson administration to declare war on Germany in 1917 ended a century and a half of self-imposed isolation from the great power politics of Europe. U.S. participation in the conflict severely tested the loyalty of immigrant groups with strong ties to the home country in Europe, most notably German-Americans, prompting the president to issue a stern warning that "the most un-American thing in the world is a hyphen."[1] To Black Americans the issue of loyalty was clear; the "hyphen-ates" were immigrants, they were Americans. There were those, most notably the socialist newspaperman A. Philip Randolph, who questioned why young Black men should die in Europe for democratic ideals denied to them at home, but the majority of African Americans were patriotic in their support for the war. Black enthusiasm for the conflict rested squarely on the expectation that the ideals invested in this new departure in American foreign policy would be applied with equal measure on the domestic scene, spelling a new dawn for people of color in the United States.

Ultimately, however, World War I proved to be a bitter disappointment for African Americans. Despite its impressive progressive credentials in other areas, the Wilson administration compiled a poor record in the area of civil rights for Black Americans. Himself a transplanted Virginian, Wilson stocked his administration with southern appointees, and the general bias of the White House in these years was reflected in policies such as the decision to segregate the civil service. Wilson supported the continuation of the army's policy of racially segregating units, and limited the number of Black combat regiments during the war to eight. In all, 380,000 African Americans served in World War I, but 89 percent of them were confined to duty as stevedores and laborers, often under deplorable conditions. Two

Black combat divisions were sent to Europe, but one, the 93rd, was essentially expunged from the American force, serving instead under the flag of France. The service of African Americans went largely unrecognized by the U.S. government, and the uniform of the United States afforded no protection for Black veterans who returned in 1919 to one of the worst summers of racial violence in American history. Rather than fulfilling the promise of progress, the Black experience in World War I was largely one of regression.[2]

One of the earliest and most stinging blows to Black morale in World War I was the forced retirement of Charles Young in the summer of 1917. Young had emerged during the previous two decades as a prominent and respected, and increasingly heroic, figure in the African American community, and each successive advance he made through the ranks of the army was welcomed as an advance for the race as a whole. His promotion to general and command of a Black combat division was eagerly anticipated. News of his retirement on medical grounds was greeted with astonishment and a great degree of skepticism throughout Black America. To many observers it appeared that Young had been done a great disservice and that the government had concocted a "scheme to keep [him] out of the present game." The swirling controversy that ensued over Young's "non-assignment" during the war was a matter of deep concern to "nearly twelve million loyal colored Americans."[3]

Charles Young was stunned by the decision of the army to press his retirement at the most critical moment in American military history since the Civil War. As soon as he learned that he was to be placed on the retired list, Young initiated a dogged, but ultimately fruitless, campaign to secure reinstatement. He wrote dozens of letters to friends and colleagues and people of influence imploring them to do all they could to convince the army and the War Department that he was fit and anxious to serve his country in its hour of greatest need. With his pleas falling on deaf ears in Washington, Young undertook a 500-mile horseback ride from his home in Wilberforce to Washington, D.C., to convince the Secretary of War of his fitness. Outwardly, despite the failure of these efforts, Young maintained a steadfast commitment to the United States and its government. Behind the steely resolve, however, Young was disillusioned and the experience of his retirement left him bitter.

On May 7, 1917, Charles Young took the exam for promotion to the rank of colonel. The examination board found him "entirely fitted" for promotion, but the medical examiners reported that he was suffering from symptoms of albuminuria and high blood pressure. The board was inclined to overlook these findings in view of the pronounced need for capable officers to lead the campaign in Europe, but recommended nonetheless that Young be sent to the Army General Hospital for further observation to determine the seriousness of his ailment. In early June, as steps were being taken to mobilize American forces for action in Europe, Young traveled to Letterman General Hospital in San Francisco for a battery of tests that would determine his future in the army.[4]

Alarmed by implications of the medical findings, Young began a personal campaign before leaving Huachaca to remain in active service no matter what diagnosis the doctors in San Francisco offered. American entry into the Great War had inspired Theodore Roosevelt, the former president and self-styled colonel, to propose raising a "colored" regiment for service in Europe. On the day after his promotion exam, Young wrote to the old Rough Rider requesting inclusion in his plans. Young lamented that the medical findings had come like "a bolt out of a clear blue sky" and that now, "instead of scrapping in this war, I am . . . to be scrapped." He felt no ill effects from the high blood pressure he was informed that he had, and in any case he was willing to shed his blood "for the flag." "I must and will have a chance in this war," Young pleaded with the former president, adding that he was willing to serve under the French flag if necessary. He asked Roosevelt to recommend him to the French Military Commission then visiting the United States. With a proficiency in French and knowledge of Africa, Young felt suitably qualified to command French African troops. The thought of his own obsolescence and mortality compelled Young to seek one final opportunity to serve. "If I'm to die any ways soon," he reflected, "I must now both push and pull for my race and country."[5]

On June 2 Young was ordered before a second examining board, this time at the headquarters of the Western Division. The members of this board recommended that, in view of his past record and the army's need for experienced officers, "the physical condition of this officer be waived and he be promoted to next higher grade." The chief medical officer dissented, however, reporting that Young's disability was permanent and that he should therefore be disqualified from promotion. Young adamantly maintained that he was fully fit, with a "constitution of iron and sense enough to know when to quit." He pleaded with the adjutant general to waive the medical reports and allow him to return to active duty. Confined to Letterman Hospital throughout much of June and into July, Young became increasingly frustrated and despondent. "It seems to me," he wrote Ada, "that they have discovered very little wrong with me" yet with all the work to be done "they let me loaf this way." His frustration mounted after news reached him of the government's decision, following an intensive lobbying campaign led by the NAACP, to establish Fort Des Moines as a training school for Black officers. Bemoaning the fact that he was stuck in a hospital bed "twirling my thumbs . . . when I should be . . . in Des Moines helping to beat those colored officers into shape," Young worried about the impact this "seemingly enforced retirement would have upon our people" and their morale. He pleaded with Du Bois to advertise the fact that he was "not slacking to run for cover. To work with my own in this war is all I want for the good we can do our country."[6]

What Young did not know was that there were forces other than his medical condition at play in the question of his retirement. While Young languished in Letterman Hospital, Woodrow Wilson penned a letter to his secretary of war, Newton D. Baker, concerning an issue raised by Senator John Sharp Williams of Mississippi. During a visit to the White House on June 20, Williams related to the president a concern he had about one of his constituents. Albert Dockery, a captain with the 10th Cavalry stationed at Fort Huachaca, had complained to his father, who then contacted Williams, about having to serve under a Black commander. Dockery's complaint came shortly after Young had taken charge of the post at the end of May. Wilson informed Baker that Dockery finds it not only "distasteful but practically impossible to serve under a colored commander." The president was worried that Dockery's feelings might lead to a serious incident of insubordination were he "left under Colonel [sic] Young," and he asked if Baker could engineer the Mississippian's transfer and replacement with a man "who would not have equally intense prejudices."[7]

Baker, a former Cleveland mayor and one of the racially moderate members of the Wilson administration, was initially inclined to instruct Dockery to "either do his duty or resign." However, the receipt of similar complaints from several other senators, together with the personal interest shown by the president in this "very embarrassing" affair, compelled him to action on Dockery's behalf. The wheels quickly began to turn, and Army Chief of Staff Tasker Bliss notified the secretary of war somewhat cryptically that "the matter is under way towards settlement." Baker then informed his boss that he was endeavoring to have Young removed from the 10th Cavalry and assigned to officer training at Fort Des Moines, a move that might enable the administration to "tide over this difficulty...for at least a while." In any case, somewhat surreptitiously, Baker added that Young was not in the best of health and that he was at the time of writing undergoing tests at Letterman Hospital to determine whether he was fit to return to active service. He concluded by assuring Wilson that "there does not seem to be any present likelihood of his early return to the 10th Cavalry so the situation may not develop to which you refer." The Adjutant General's Office, meanwhile, instructed the commander of the Western Department to call Young before yet another board to "make a definitive finding and recommendation" in the matter.[8]

Even though Young's fate had yet to be conclusively decided, Wilson sought to placate Williams at the end of June with the assurance that Young was in "ill health and likely when he gets better he will be transferred to some other service." The senator from Mississippi was apparently not fully assuaged, for Wilson pressed Baker again in early July to bring closure to the affair, reiterating his fear that "there is some danger of trouble of a serious nature if this officer is not separated from his present command." Within three days Baker was able to offer such finality when he reported to the president that the surgeon's report indicated that Young was suffering from Bright's disease (chronic nephritis) and was therefore to be retired on medical grounds. As soon as his retirement became official, Young was to be ordered to join the Ohio National Guard, which had requested his services. "This, I think," the secretary of war concluded, "will remove the cause of trouble."[9]

The final diagnosis of the doctors at Letterman Hospital, delivered in mid-July, was brutally conclusive. Young was suffering from "chronic interstitial nephritis of an advanced grade." His symptoms included high blood pressure and hypertrophy of the heart, and the Medical Corps report concluded that he was unfit for service as strong physical exertion would cause a danger to his life. On July 10 he was ordered to report to the adjutant general of Ohio to train Black volunteers in the state militia. At the end of July the surgeon general of the army endorsed the findings of the medical examiners, and the president approved Young's retirement at the rank of colonel. The door was firmly closed on Charles Young's military career.[10]

Young's retirement initiated a maelstrom of controversy in the Black press and precipitated an avalanche of protest from his friends and supporters. Even in the absence of public knowledge of the Dockery affair, there was a widespread feeling among African Americans that the highest-ranking Black officer in the army had been forced out "by unfair means." Ada Young was far from alone in her view that the Wilson administration had engineered the "forced retirement" of her husband to avoid his promotion. The Dockery affair confirms that Woodrow Wilson, anxious not to alienate the southern power base of the Democratic Party, was eager to embrace any opportunity to remove Young from the active list. The medical diagnosis of chronic nephritis was accurate, and indeed Young would succumb to this ailment just five years later. However, in the absence of political pressure from the White House it is conceivable that the army might have accepted the recommendation of the two examining boards that Young's medical condition be "waived." His retirement, while ultimately legal, was certainly politically expedient. Once Young's status as a lieutenant colonel in command of white officers came to the attention of the Wilson administration, his future became a political hot potato. Even Baker's suggestion of placing him in command of Fort Des Moines was too controversial a solution, and so he was shunted away to the Ohio National Guard.[11]

The decision to promote Young to colonel at retirement, although lauded as a historic milestone by the *Army and Navy Journal*, did little to quell anger in the African American community. As the news spread

throughout the country, the Black press poured scorn on the army's decision to prematurely terminate Young's career. A *Cleveland Advocate* editorial offered the view that "this retiring of Colonel Young when...every
experienced officer is needed, arouses suspicion in the minds of Colored
men." The decision to remove him from the active list when a general's
star beckoned was an injustice to "the race" as a whole. The *Advocate*
charged that the retirement of Young, together with the posting of Benjamin O. Davis and John E. Green, the only other Black commissioned
officers in the army, to the Philippines and Liberia, respectively, indicated
the intention of the Wilson administration to place all Black conscript
units in the World War under the exclusive command of White officers.
"If President Wilson expects Colored soldiers to be filled with enthusiasm
over taking up arms against a foreign foe," the editorial concluded, "we
cannot understand why he continues to ignore, insult, and degrade the
race."[12]

These sentiments were echoed in dozens of newspaper clippings gathered by Emmett Scott, Booker T. Washington's former secretary, and R. R.
Moton, who succeeded Washington as head of the Tuskegee Institute and
who now endeavored to carry on the spirit of the Atlanta Compromise following the Washington's death in 1915. Moton forwarded to President
Wilson the clippings that he and Scott collected together with an appeal to
retain Young in the army, intimating that the issue was politically loaded,
as "colored people are very much concerned about this matter." Wilson,
who had long since abandoned his brief flirtation with the Black vote in
1912, dismissed the concerns echoed in the Black press and advised Moton
that he was "laboring under a misapprehension." The president categori-
cally denied the assumption that Young was "in any way being discrimi-
nated against," and he offered Moton the disingenuous assurance that the
highest-ranking Black officer in the army "will be treated as any other officer would be in similar circumstances."[13]

Young meanwhile remained hopeful of returning to active service.
There was widespread talk of his being placed in command of Roosevelt's
proposed colored regiment. In reply to Young's earlier appeal for inclusion, Roosevelt wrote that he would have no hesitation in placing Young
in command, as "you would handle it in the best possible fashion." Roosevelt was convinced that "Young was physically, and in every other way,
fit to command a regiment or even a brigade." Rumors of a "Roosevelt
Division," with Young at the helm of a Black regiment, brought letters to
Wilberforce from eager volunteers, men who had been exposed to the
Black colonel's "spirit of real genuine hard soldiering" in earlier commands. Roosevelt's hopes of resurrecting the spirit of the Rough Riders
came to naught, however, and another lifeline slipped from Young's
hands. Roosevelt, who resented what he saw as President Wilson's delib-
erate opposition to his plan, commiserated with Young that they were

both now in the same boat, "not being needed by their government in a time of war."[14]

Young's friends and former colleagues continued to work hard on his behalf. His former commander from Mexico, Retired Colonel William C. Brown, willingly took up the call to have his former subordinate returned to active service. Brown wrote numerous letters endeavoring to have Young assigned to service at Fort Des Moines, and even secured permission from the camp commander, Colonel Charles Ballou, for Young to visit the camp. The official army line remained, however, that Young's retirement was final and nothing could be done to override the decisions already made. Brown nonetheless advised Young to persevere and he would "win out" in the end as "[your] case seems to be a reasonable one." One possible course of action, Brown suggested, was to see a civilian specialist to examine his "supposed malady."[15]

Following his discharge from Letterman Hospital in early July, Young boarded a train bound from San Francisco to Columbus where he was to begin duty with the Ohio National Guard (O.N.G.). En route, he disembarked at Des Moines to take up General Ballou's offer to visit the Black officer training camp. Young had been a vocal supporter of the campaign to establish the camp, reminding Black critics who saw it as a token gesture that loyal participation in the war was a likely springboard to full equality and that capable Black officers would be needed to lead the way. "It seems that with certain people," Young noted, "there is doubt as to the ability of the colored American to qualify as an officer and in other minds if he seems capable of becoming one that to allow it would be of doubtful social policy, as it would lead to social equality." Young argued, however, that the Black officer was not seeking social equality but social equity. The man who many African Americans had hoped would be given command of the camp received a magnificent reception from the Des Moines recruits on his arrival.[16]

Young was a Herculean figure in the eyes of these prospective officers, and his name was always spoken at the camp with "reverence." His supporters noted that his career was a limitless source of inspiration in "the lives of hundreds of Black boys...in uniform." Many of the young men there had cried when they heard of his dispatch to Letterman Hospital, and it was widely felt throughout the camp that the army had retired him because "they didn't want him to have that much power." His review of the recruits had the feel of a "royal reception," and his address to the men was greeted with a thunderous ovation. Stirred by the sight of twelve hundred Black officers and by his own deepening crisis, Young delivered an emotional challenge. With the eyes of the whole country on them, he reminded the men that they would be "given the chance not only of independent initiative to lead your own, to prove your valor and do your duty nobly, but a chance to strive to do that duty as finely, as splendidly, as any white man performed his duty." With his own career suddenly in abeyance, Young emphasized the importance of success for the men of Fort Des Moines, for from this group would come the postwar leaders of the race. For nearly 30 years he had stood alone; now it was the turn of others to take up the challenge.[17]

From Des Moines, Young traveled on to Columbus, where his return was feted by Ohio's Black press. The editor of the *Cleveland Advocate* informed the mothers and fathers of the young men called to serve in the state's planned Black militia regiment that they could now rest assured that their sons were in the capable hands of an "officer of the highest efficiency." There was intense interest in the mobilization of Black volunteers among the "150,000 Colored people of Ohio...whose hearts are wrapt [*sic*] up in and whose hopes are pinned to the regiment." Unfortunately for Young, this added a poisonous political element to the assignment. The negative experience of his service with the Ninth Ohio Battalion in the Spanish-American War convinced Young that the ability to appoint his own staff and line officers was absolutely vital to make volunteer service sufferable. The decision of the adjutant general of Ohio to grant this authority to Young set off a firestorm of protest from veteran guardsmen and their supporters who were disgruntled at being passed over. Critics, charging that Young's uniform selection of outsiders had precipitated an open rebellion in the ranks of the Ninth Ohio, lobbied the state's adjutant general and governor to override the colonel's authority. Young defended his appointments as "the best men available for officers of the Ninth regiment."[18]

From the moment Young unpacked his trunk at the Litchferd Hotel in Columbus on July 14, the O.N.G. assignment had served only to add to his torment. After a month of political bickering, he received notice that his mission in Ohio had expired as the War Department determined that it did not need the regiment that Young was scheduled to command. Rumors abounded that the regiment had been shelved for political and racial reasons. In actuality, rather than reflecting sinister design on the part of the War Department, the decision not to raise the Ninth Ohio to regimental status bore testimony to the haphazard nature of America's mobilization efforts in World War I. The state of Ohio had acted without the full authority and approval of the federal administration. When the last element of the O.N.G. was mustered into service, Young was left with nothing to do, and until his retirement order placing him on active duty with the Ohio militia was countermanded he felt compelled to remain in the state. Perplexed by this "peculiar status," Young returned home to Wilberforce to continue his campaign for reinstatement.[19]

Now more than ever, Youngsholm provided a refuge for Young from the trials of his professional life. Enveloped in the warmth of his bustling household, Young was able to find here at least momentary relief from the anguish of his enforced redundancy. During the day, he would put on his old "britches" and take to the fields or tend to the livestock, which in addition to his beloved horses included cows, hogs, poultry, bees, dogs, and "whole families" of cats. Some evenings after supper "the family, the farm hands, the servants...and [any] guests who happened to be there" would gather "around the piano in the huge old-fashioned music room" to sing for an hour or two. Young was a "voracious reader," and could regularly be found in the library surrounded by his priceless collection of literature from around the world, or hidden away in his attic den lost in the pages of a book. "A staunch friend of the University," Young volunteered his services as chair of the Military Science and Tactics Department at Wilberforce, making the one-mile trip to campus to teach every day. At the weekend, he would throw open his house for "the further instruction of the young men." For a time he contemplated beginning work again on the Toussaint L'Ouverture drama he had begun in Haiti. He was intrigued by its potential but ultimately gave up because of his inability to "boil it down into dimensions that are playable." He was too restless to concentrate. The circumstances of his retirement incessantly gnawed at his soul, and over and over again he was drawn back to his desk to engage in an endless stream of correspondence seeking a way out of his dilemma.[20]

Young received numerous letters from friends offering sympathy and support and proffering theories on the motivations behind his retirement; and there were frequent requests for speaking engagements, offers of honorary degrees, and appeals to conduct military drill for college students. But foremost on Young's mind remained the possibility of returning to active service. He wrote Joel Spingarn that his sole ambition was "to give all that is within me during the period of the war." All he could do was to be "patient, keep my temper, my health, and continue to study along professional military lines pending a need which may possibly come." He was anxious not to appear egotistical or disloyal, and so he publicly played the role of loyal patriot and accepted his own fate in stoic silence. He appealed to those who were outraged by his retirement not to "embarrass the administration" in this time of crisis, for "we love our country too well not to desire its early success in this war," and he would not consent to "tying for one moment the hands of the government by agitation" even were this to result in "the complete rehabilitation of my race." In private, however, Young vented his bitterness with the army brass, whose message appeared to be "keep your mouth shut," and with the government for using a "doctor's dodge" to shelve him "until such a time as they can find out whether they need Negro troops and Negro officers." He was in little doubt that race was the clinching factor in his retirement.[21]

Young's plea to all Americans to put aside their "racial differences until after the war" followed a summer of unchecked lynching and frequent racial disturbances. African Americans were growing increasingly hostile to the Wilson administration and its Jim Crow mentality. Frustration with the widespread antagonism shown by White America to Blacks in uniform exploded in the Houston riots of August 1917. Nineteen people lost their lives when troops from the Black 24th Infantry rampaged for two hours through the streets of Houston in response to a racially motivated assault on one of their number by a White police officer. In stark contrast to its response to the racial pogrom in East St. Louis earlier in the year, the government took swift and decisive action in the aftermath of the Houston riots. To Black America, the hanging of 18 alleged ringleaders had all the appearances of a military lynching.[22]

The October appointment of Emmett Scott as the War Department's special assistant for "Negro affairs" was designed as a palliative to Black ire. Scott's elevation to this post initially raised expectations that the Wilson administration was preparing to moderate its position on Blacks in the military. It also offered a potentially fruitful new avenue of exploration for Young, who immediately penned a letter congratulating Scott on his new position and offering his support. Scott was quickly inundated with mail from African Americans complaining about a host of issues pertaining to the mistreatment and misuse of Black soldiers and recruits. One matter of particular concern was the confinement of the majority of Blacks in uniform to "stevedore regiments," regardless of their level of education or professional expertise. There were also angry letters calling for the assignment of Colonel Young where "his services would count for much towards downing the 'Hun.'"[23]

Hampered by his own timidity and the token nature of his position, Scott's record as special assistant on "Negro affairs" was checkered at best. He did succeed in generating a small degree of sympathy for Young's plight among some of his superiors in the War Department, but not enough to challenge the army's official position that the colonel had been legally retired and that any attempt to restore him to active service would create an undesirable precedent. The best that Scott could offer Young was a position in his office as a consultant or supervisor of a student army training camp in Washington, D.C. Young was not to be placated by such sops. Having accepted the burden of public expectation throughout his career, he felt compelled to seek nothing less than active service with troops. In his mind, his retirement was not just a personal concern; it was a matter of importance to the race as a whole. He had disproved countless detractors since graduating from West Point and advancing through the ranks of the army, and now all he wanted was to prove his ability to command in the "regular establishment."[24]

Others lobbying on Young's behalf encountered the same official obduracy that stymied Scott. Oswald Garrison Villard, the influential White journalist, publisher, and former chairman of the NAACP, added his considerable influence to that organization's efforts to secure reinstatement for Young. Villard was initially certain that "a miscarriage of justice" had taken place, as "Young is the huskiest retired officer I have ever seen." He drafted a series of letters on the matter to the third assistant secretary of war, Francis "Dean" Keppel, noting that settling the issue would "have a profound effect upon the colored people in the country." Despite his influence, however, he too made little headway. In fact, the War Department's uniform insistence that nothing untoward had taken place, gradually wore him down and ultimately he became convinced that, while mistakes might have been made, there was no "prejudice in the case." Villard's advice to Young was to secure statements from a number of private physicians endorsing his fitness for duty, and on that basis apply for reinstatement through "regular channels."[25]

This is the same course of action that Colonel William Brown had earlier recommended that Young take. He balked at his suggestion, claiming that while he felt sure that he could secure such a clean bill of health, he did not want to antagonize the army by challenging the findings of the surgeons. The army had in fact, however, made this very offer to Young and he had refused, suggesting instead that he undertake a 90-mile horseback ride to prove his fitness. Young knew that he could not challenge the veracity of the medical diagnosis. His contraction of blackwater fever in Liberia in 1913 had almost proved fatal, and the doctor who examined him in Monrovia at that time noted numerous "symptoms of nephritis" in his report. Young had informed the doctors who examined him in Mexico that he had been intermittently found to have albumen in his urine going all the way back to 1910. During his confinement at Letterman he had written Ada that he "feared...the albumen might be the cause" of the medical findings. Young nonetheless was sincere in professing that he felt fit and able to serve. While he may have recognized that his health was ailing, he genuinely believed himself physically capable of commanding troops in the field. His passionate desire to participate in the war was so all-consuming that he was willing to risk bringing on the complications the army doctors warned would result from his continued service. In the meantime, he continued to hope that "when they need men and officers badly enough they will drop some of the fatuous policies that are paralyzing the army as a fighting force."[26]

Instead of taking issue with the medical findings, Young grasped at the possibility his retirement was the result of a technical error. He believed that Secretary of War Baker intended to accept the examining board's recommendation and retain him in active service for the duration of the war, but the mistaken substitution of the words "active duty" for "active service" had brought about his retirement. The army, however, steadfastly denied that any such error had taken place and noted that, in any case, the law would not allow his return to active service. Young was convinced, largely on the basis of correspondence forwarded to him by Scott, Villard, and others, that Secretary Baker was willing to reinstate him but that all efforts to do so were being stonewalled by Adjutant General McCain. His direct appeals to Baker were wasted, however, for as the Dockery affair illustrated, regardless of the merits of the case, returning Young to active service posed the reactivation of a political issue that the administration would rather avoid.[27]

It was Du Bois who had spotted the semantic loophole, and it was to him that Young turned repeatedly as his situation became more desperate. Knowing that his friend was prevented by his own humility and sense of duty from trumpeting his own cause, Du Bois had led the charge in "belling the cat." Together with Joel Spingarn, Du Bois was the driving force behind the NAACP's efforts to bring attention to the case, urging Villard and others to use their influence on Young's behalf. He was undoubtedly also the most forceful advocate of the position that ulterior motives lay behind his friend's retirement. Du Bois pushed Young's case in *The Crisis,* charging that the army's primary motivation in the whole affair had been to avoid promoting his friend to the rank of brigadier general and that he had been deliberately confined to a paper assignment in Ohio, where it was hoped he would simply fade away. Du Bois's letters of support were a critical boost to Young's morale, occasionally prompting a jocular response, such as the note thanking "thee, oh mighty Dubois, if I come out, foh delivering dis Jonah from de belly ob de Army Whale."[28]

Following the public outcry that had greeted Young's retirement, the army was anxious to contain further controversy by preventing Young from participating in public speaking engagements. The adjutant general blocked an invitation from the Chicago YMCA on the grounds that "it is contrary to the policy and wishes of the Secretary of War to permit officers of the Regular Army to make public addresses." After repeated appeals, the YMCA reluctantly withdrew its offer in the face of the "insuperable obstacle" of the opposition of the adjutant general, who maintained throughout that "the services of all officers [were] urgently necessary in the performance of their strictly military duty." Even Dean Keppel in the War Department was astounded by this rationale, noting incredulously that the army was "not giving Young anything to do!" Although confined to the retired list, Young continued to be viewed as a dangerous liability by the army brass.[29]

In June 1918, with his appeals exhausted and the walls closing in around him, Young decided on one last desperate effort to secure a return to service. "As soon as the school year was over," the 54-year-old retired colonel prepared to undertake a grueling 497-mile horseback ride to Washington, D.C., to "rid myself of this 'case'" and "to show the Secretary of War that I am still physically fit." Sending one of his favorite horses, Dolly, ahead on the Baltimore and Ohio railroad, Young saddled his huge black Kentucky-bred mare, Blacksmith, and set off for the nation's capital from his home in Wilberforce. His nonstop, unassisted ride took him "through town and hamlet, by stream and river, over the Appalachians," through Athens, Parkersburg, Clarksburg, Winchester, and on to Washington. "Walking on foot fifteen minutes in each hour" to rest his horse, Young crossed the M Street bridge into Georgetown 16 days after leaving his home. He had averaged 31 miles per day with only one rest day during the whole ride. An "agreeably surprised" Black public greeted his arrival in Washington on June 22 with enthusiasm, and the Black press reported that after days in the saddle "the Colonel looks fit...for service at the front."[30]

Young's horseback ride to Washington captured the imagination of the American public and succeeded in drawing renewed attention to his case. In the most public fashion possible, Young offered his services "gladly at the risk of life, which has no value to me if I can give it for the great ends for which the United States is striving." Newton Baker had little choice but to grant him an informal hearing, and Young noted that the secretary of war "received me kindly and offered me consideration." However, two months later Young was back pacing the floors of Youngsholm, "a combination of caged lion and antagonized schoolboy," and he was reluctantly drawn to the conclusion that Baker was "too busy to remember." His final appeal was to General Pershing, commander of the American Expeditionary Force in France and the man who had recommended him for a brigade at the end of the Mexico campaign. In September Young beseeched Pershing to intercede with Baker, who was then in France, promising the four-star general that "despite the doctor's findings...I will not be sick on your hands nor lumber up the line." Young appealed to Pershing as one old soldier to another, "Have I not served the country well enough and you loyally enough to ask to finish my army career in active service under you?" Pershing, like Baker, was apparently too busy to respond.[31]

In an ironically cruel final twist to the saga of his retirement, the Wilson administration, in what was in essence a token gesture to a seething Black public, restored Charles Young to active duty five days before the German armistice. On November 6, 1918, Young was ordered to proceed to Camp Grant in Rockford, Illinois, for "assignment in connection with the colored development battalions." The so-called "stevedore regiments," to which the majority of Black men conscripted under the Selective Service Act were assigned, had been a source of bitter controversy throughout the war. Deplorable working conditions and mistreatment by White officers served to further deplete the already low morale of men confined to institutional servitude. Ever since Houston, the administration had feared the prospect of further trouble at Black encampments around the country, and complaints from Black conscripts, no matter how legitimate, were automatically treated by the army as "Negro subversion." Young's assignment to Camp Grant coincided with a rising volume of protest from the Black conscripts there in the fall of 1918.[32]

The Development Unit at Camp Grant was bubbling with discontent when Young arrived to take command. The conscripts, many of them recently arrived from the South, complained bitterly that the tents and the clothes they were issued offered inadequate protection from the harsh Midwestern winter. Letters from men in the camp arrived on the desk of Emmett Scott, adding inadequate food, poor sanitation, and general filth to the list of complaints. One of the complainants noted that "we would not expect anything better...were we on the fighting line, [but] we are doing nothing here to assist our Government." To add insult to injury, Black troops at Camp Grant charged that many of the southern White officers serving with the unit were "unfit to be slave drivers." Scott diligently forwarded these grievances to his superiors and received assurances from the army that efforts were being made to improve conditions at the camp. By posting Young to Camp Grant in November the army evidently hoped to rid itself of two troublesome issues with one move, the controversy surrounding his retirement and the danger of "Negro subversion" at the camp. As Rayford Logan noted, however, the assignment of Young to "obscure duty in Illinois" did little to assuage the "distress, anger, and wry laughter" his retirement had caused.[33]

The timing and nature of Young's return to active duty ensured that the two things he had hoped to achieve in the war, promotion and service in Europe, remained outside his reach. The army and the Wilson administration, having successfully sidelined the most visible and public symbol of challenge to military segregation for the duration of the conflict, returned him to service at the very end in a seemingly innocuous post. Young was determined, however, not to be used as a token figure. He was delighted to have the opportunity to work again and he resolved to bring order to the lives of the eight thousand men under his command. Within a month of his arrival he reported that he was "as busy as a blue hen with new chicks." When the Chicago branch of the NAACP forwarded anonymous letters of complaint from Black soldiers to him at Camp Grant, Young immediately took the matter up with "the authorities." At issue was the continuous harassment and abuse of Black conscripts by southern White officers. Young declared in response to the NAACP request for assistance that "no embarrassment can come to me by helping to plead the cause of humanity be it black or white." The number of complaints emanating from Camp Grant gradually tapered off, and at the time he was relieved of this duty in February 1919, Young felt satisfied that he had "cleaned up a bad situation." Young's commitment to service remained as strong as ever, but his personal experience during World

War I had clearly prompted him to reconsider his penchant for acting quietly behind the scenes.[34]

His unexpected retirement in 1917 had come as a stunning blow to Charles Young, and his subsequent efforts to secure reinstatement ushered in what he called "the hardest fight of my life." Soon after his return from his Washington, D.C., ride, he wrote his friend Billy Broad that it all seemed like "a blasted night-mare, I wonder if I may wake up and find that I have been dreaming in a shack in Mexico." The experience gradually wore the old soldier down and took a serious toll on his spirit. Ada noted that the whole episode shattered his "high hopes," and his efforts to maintain the "high ground came near to proving too great a tax." After so many years of "hard service" and patriotic duty, it was impossible for him to accept that he was not needed at this critical moment. According to Ada, he was extremely upset at the notion that his retirement had been mishandled and that his reinstatement had been "pigeonholed." Rather than self-pity, his chief emotion was embarrassment at his own obsolescence, compelled to offer "endless excuses and explanations...to people of both races." His greatest fear was that his inactivity might be interpreted as cowardice or, worse still, disloyalty. Thus, when Senator Atlee Pomerene of Ohio took it on himself to investigate reports that Young was a German sympathizer, the retired colonel, "wounded to the core," offered a heartfelt and detailed defense of his military record and his "strenuous protest" against retirement. "If I have ever prided myself on anything," he reproved the senator, "that one thing has been my services to the country that educated me, put shoulder straps on me, and gave me equal show to pass through all the grades from Cadet at West Point to Colonel in the Regular Army." This retort prompted a swift retraction from the senator.[35]

Try as he might, Young could not suppress occasional bouts of bitterness over his retirement. To General Hugh S. Johnson of New Deal fame, he confessed that if he "wanted complete revenge on a super-enemy, I wouldn't send him to hell...I would make him a Negro officer in a white man's army." While still at Camp Grant, he received a letter from a young high school student from Cincinnati named Clarence Smith. Smith expressed his tremendous admiration for the retired colonel and wished to emulate him by entering West Point. In response to Smith's request for advice on how to proceed, Young bluntly advised against pursuing a military career. Not only did the military academy offer "a dog's life," but he could expect "for years after you graduate, a pittance of a salary as a subaltern and in the end retirement on a mere competence, which does not pay if you have a little girl in view that wishes to wear diamonds." Young advised Smith, "as a brother who has been over the whole road," to channel his energies into more profitable fields. He lamented that had he devoted himself to cultivating his knowledge of Spanish and learning the skills of tropical agriculture he "would have been a rich man now instead of a Colonel on the scrap heap of the U.S. Army."[36]

Young certainly had grounds to be bitter. Although the medical findings would ultimately prove to be fatally accurate, Young's examiners had recommended that he remain in active service for the duration of the war. He was baffled and angered by the steadfast refusal of the adjutant general and the secretary of war to revisit the issue, despite the concerted campaign on his behalf led by political heavyweights such as Du Bois, Scott, Moton, Villard, and Joel Spingarn. He was mistaken, however, in concluding that the secretary of war was sympathetic to his plight, for it was political pressure placed on the War Department by the White House that prevented any possibility of his return to active service during the war. Not even his dramatic horseback ride from Wilberforce to Washington, D.C., could sway what had become immovable obstacles to his reinstatement.

Anger dueled with patriotism for primacy in his heart. Patriotism, albeit tempered now by a dash of skepticism, ultimately won out. Young at one point offered the somewhat untenable claim that "in spite of me and without my assent" others have "made a 'case' out of my retirement." In fact, from the very beginning he had asked Du Bois and others to take up his cause. There is considerable truth to Young's assertion, however, that he was always anxious that his case be promoted on the merits of his career and his own willingness to serve, and not as a political issue to be used to embarrass the government. Loyalty in time of war was paramount; "duties not rights" was his motto throughout America's participation in the conflict. Although his faith had been badly shaken, his belief in America remained intact. To the actor Charles Borroughs, who was among the scores of former pupils and protégés who saw action in Europe during the war, Young dedicated the song "There's a Service Flag in the Window." Young promised to fly the service flag, a custom widely adopted in the United States during World War I, for the duration of the war in honor of his friend and all the "brave Yankee men" who served to "make the wide world free."[37]

NOTES

1. Speech by Woodrow Wilson, St. Paul, Minnesota, 9 September 1919, reprinted in Woodrow Wilson, *War and Peace: Presidential Messages, Addresses, and Public Papers* (1917–1924), vol. 2, ed. Ray S. Baker and William E. Dodd (New York, 1970): 78.

2. Bernard Nalty, *Strength for the Fight: A History of Black Americans in the Military* (New York, 1986), 107–112; Gail Buckley, *American Patriots: The Story of Blacks in the Military from the Revolution to Desert Storm* (New York, 2001), 163–166.

3. *Southwestern Christian Advocate*, 6 September 1917, clipping in Charles Young Papers, National Afro-American Museum and Cultural Center, Wilber-

force, Ohio [hereinafter Young Papers]; Dock Seward to Charles Young, 19 June 1917, Young Papers; Charles Cuney to Emmett J. Scott, 11 September 1918, Office of the Chief of Staff, Executive Division, Military Intelligence Branch, Correspondence regarding Negro troops, 1917–1924, Records of the Department of War, Record Group 165, National Archives, Washington, D.C. [hereinafter Scott Files].

4. Examination for Promotion, 7 May 1917, Letters Received by the Appointment, Commission, and Personal Branch, Adjutant General's Office, 1871–1917, Record Group 94, National Archives, Washington, D.C. [hereinafter ACP File]; Charles Young to W. E. B. Du Bois, 20 June 1917, W. E. B. Du Bois Papers, University of Massachusetts, Amherst, Mass. [hereinafter Du Bois Papers].

5. Charles Young to Theodore Roosevelt, 8 May 1917, Private Collection of John H. Motley, Hartford, Conn. [hereinafter Motley Collection]; Charles Young to William Jay Schieffelin, 30 May 1917, Motley Collection.

6. Department of War Memorandum on the case of Colonel Charles Young, U.S.A. Retired, n.d. [filed 30 July 1917], Military Information Division, General Correspondence, 1917–1941, Records of the Department of War, Record Group 165, National Archives, College Park, Md. [hereinafter MID]; Charles Young to Examining Board, 7 May 1917, ACP File; Charles Young to Ada Young, 10 June 1917, Coleman Collection, Akron, Ohio; Charles Young to W. E. B. Du Bois, 20 June 1917, Du Bois Papers.

7. Wilson erroneously cited Dockery's rank as first lieutenant. Woodrow Wilson to Newton D. Baker, 25 June 1917, Newton Diehl Baker Papers, Library of Congress, Washington, D.C. [hereinafter Baker Papers]; Many years later, when surveyed on the subject of serving with a Black regiment, Dockery made no mention of his discomfort with having to serve under Charles Young. See Survey response of Albert Dockery, Research for Black Soldier, Marvin E. Fletcher Collection, United States Military History Institute, Carlisle, Pa.

8. Note from Newton D. Baker to Tasker Bliss, n.d. [June 1917], Baker Papers; Memorandum by Tasker Bliss, n.d. [June 1917], Baker Papers; Newton D. Baker to Woodrow Wilson, 26 June 1917, Baker Papers; Adjutant General's Office to Commander, Western Department, 27 June 1917, ACP File.

9. Woodrow Wilson to John Sharp Williams, 29 June 1917, Baker Papers; Woodrow Wilson to Newton D. Baker, 3 July 1917, Baker Papers; Newton D. Baker to Woodrow Wilson, 7 July 1917, Baker Papers.

10. Medical Corps Report for the Surgeon General of the Army, 18 July 1917, ACP File; Department of War Memorandum on the case of Colonel Charles Young, U.S.A. Retired, n.d. [filed 30 July 1917], MID.

11. William Reeves to Charles Young, 18 August 1917, Coleman Collection; W. E. B. Du Bois to Walter Lippman, 29 June 1917, Du Bois Papers; Ada Young to John J. Pershing, 12 October 1921, John J. Pershing Papers, Library of Congress, Washington, D.C. [hereinafter Pershing Papers].

12. *Army and Navy Journal*, 21 July 1917, clipping in Charles Young File, United States Military Academy, West Point, N.Y. [hereinafter Young File USMA]; "Colonel Young's Retirement," *Cleveland Advocate*, 18 August 1917, 8.

13. Robert R. Moton to Woodrow Wilson, 7 July 1917, in Arthur S. Link, ed., *The Papers of Woodrow Wilson*, 69 volumes (Princeton, N.J., 1987), vol. 43, 119; Woodrow Wilson to Robert R. Moton, 9 July 1917, in Link, *Papers of Woodrow Wilson*, vol. 43, 132.

14. Theodore Roosevelt to Charles Young, 15 May 1917, Motley Collection; Theodore Roosevelt to Wilson Ballard, 23 July 1918, Motley Collection; Sam B. Wallor to Charles Young, 18 October 1917, Young Papers; Ada Young to John J. Pershing, 12 October 1921, Pershing Papers.

15. William C. Brown to Charles Young, 26 June 1917, Young Papers; William C. Brown to Charles Young, 27 June 1917, Young Papers; Charles Ballou to William C. Brown, 29 June 1917, Young Papers; William C. Brown to Charles Young, 30 June 1917, Young Papers.

16. Charles Young to Harry Smith, 23 March 1917, Young Papers; Notes for "The Colored Officer," n.d. [1918], Coleman Collection; William Sanders Scarborough, "A Tribute to Colonel Charles Young," (Philadelphia, 1922), 11, William Sanders Scarborough Papers, Wilberforce University, Wilberforce, Ohio [hereinafter Scarborough Papers].

17. Arthur B. Chambliss to Charles Young, 10 June 1917, Coleman Collection; A. O. Mitchell to Charles Young, 27 October 1918, Coleman Collection; Interview with James B. Morris, Des Moines, 1 May 1977, cited in Gerald W. Patton, *War and Race: The Black Officer in the American Military, 1915–1941* (Westport, Conn., 1981), 62; Scarborough, "Tribute to Colonel Charles Young," 11, Scarborough Papers; Charles Young speech quoted in Lucy France Pierce, "Shoulder Straps for Colored Men," *Leslie's Illustrated Weekly,* 13 October 1917, 520.

18. "Col. Young at Columbus," *Cleveland Advocate,* 21 July 1917, 1; "Trusting Col. Young," *Cleveland Advocate,* 28 July 1917, 8; "Col. Young's Appointments Cause 'Military Rumpus'," *Cleveland Advocate,* 4 August 1917, 1; "Personal References," *Cleveland Gazette,* 11 August 1917; William W. Giffen, "Mobilization of Black Militiamen in World War I: Ohio's Ninth Battalion," *Historian* 40 (fall 1978): 694.

19. "Col. Young at Columbus," *Cleveland Advocate,* 21 July 1917, 1; Wilson Ballard to Charles Young, 4 August 1917, Young Papers; Charles Young to Adjutant General's Office, 14 August 1917, Young Papers; Charles Young to Emmett Scott, 29 October 1917, Young Papers.

20. Bernice Young Mitchell Wells, "A Versatile Relative of Mine: Colonel Charles Young," in Herman Dreer, ed., *American Literature by Negro Authors* (New York, 1950), 180; Scarborough, "Tribute to Colonel Charles Young," 9, Scarborough Papers; Charles Young to Atlee Pomerene, 20 August 1918, Coleman Collection; Charles Young to William Broad, 30 August 1917, Charles Young File, Moorland Spingarn Research Center, Howard University, Washington, D.C. [hereinafter Young File MSRC].

21. See, for example, Whitefield McKinley to Charles Young, 16 August 1917, and Edwin C. Silsby to Charles Young, 19 November 1917, Young Papers; *Southwestern Christian Advocate,* 6 September 1917, clipping in Young Papers; Charles Young to Joel E. Spingarn, 15 August 1917, Joel E. Spingarn Papers, Moorland Spingarn Research Collection, Howard University, Washington, D.C. [hereinafter Joel Spingarn Papers]; Charles Young to Arthur B. Spingarn, 5 November 1917, Young Papers; Charles Young to W. E. B. Du Bois, 17 December 1917, Coleman Collection; Charles Young to William Broad, 30 August, 1917, Young File MSRC.

22. Charles Young to Arthur B. Spingarn, 5 November 1917, Young Papers; Nalty, *Strength for the Fight,* 101–6.

23. Emmett Scott to Charles Young, 23 October 1917, Young Papers; Charles Young to Emmett Scott, 29 October 1917, Young Papers; Charles Cuney to Emmett Scott, 11 September 1918, Scott Files.

24. Emmett Scott to Charles Young, 21 May 1918, Young Papers; J. E. Cutler to Emmett Scott, 28 September 1918, General Correspondence, Record Group 164, U.S. Department of War, War College Division, National Archives, Washington, D.C. [hereinafter WCD]; Florette Henri, *Black Migration: Movement North, 1900–1920* (Garden City, N.Y., 1975), 283; Emmett Scott to Charles Young, 23 July 1918, Young Papers; Charles Young to Emmett Scott, 23 May 1918, Young Papers.

25. Oswald Garrison Villard to Francis Keppel, 30 January 1918, Oswald Garrison Villard Papers, Houghton Library, Harvard University, Cambridge, Mass. [hereinafter Villard Papers]; Francis Keppel to Oswald Garrison Villard, 2 February 1918, Villard Papers; Oswald Garrison Villard to Francis Keppel, 9 February 1918, Du Bois Papers; Oswald Garrison Villard to John R. Shillady, 9 February, 1918, Du Bois Papers.

26. Charles Young to John R. Shillady, 21 March 1918, Du Bois Papers; Transcript of U.S. Army hearings on the case of Charles Young's retirement, n.d. [July 1917], ACP File; Charles Young to the Secretary of the Army, 6 August 1913, ACP File; Charles Young to Ada Young, 10 June 1917, Coleman Collection; Physical Exam, Mexico, 7 December 1916, ACP File; Charles Young to Joel E. Spingarn, 5 February 1918, Joel Spingarn Papers.

27. Charles Young to John R. Shillady, 21 March 1918, Du Bois Papers; U.S. Department of War Memorandum, prepared by William S. Graves, 30 April 1918, WCD; Oswald Garrison Villard to John R. Shillady, 9 February 1918, Du Bois Papers; Emmett Scott to Charles Young, 21 May 1918, Young Papers; Charles Young to Emmett Scott, 23 May 1918, Young Papers; Charles Young to Newton D. Baker, 26 April 1918, Du Bois Papers.

28. Charles Young to W. E. B. Du Bois, 18 March 1918, Du Bois Papers; W. E. B. Du Bois, "The Retirement of Colonel Young," *The Crisis* 14 (October 1917): 286; Charles Young to W. E. B. Du Bois, 21 March 1918, Du Bois Papers.

29. Memorandum for Third Assistant Secretary of War, prepared by Adjutant General McCain, 9 May 1918, Young Papers; A. L. Jackson to Charles Young, 16 May 1918, Young Papers; J. S. Tichenor to A. L. Jackson, 15 May 1918, Young Papers.

30. Charles Young to Atlee Pomerene, 20 August 1918, Coleman Collection; Charles Young to Peyton C. March, 20 August 1918, Motley Collection; Charles Young to John J. Pershing, 9 September 1918, Motley Collection; Wells, "A Versatile Relative of Mine," 182; E. H. Lawson, "One Out of Twelve Million: Unrevealed Facts in the Life Story of Col. Charles Young, West Pointer," *Washington Post*, 26 May 1929, 14; Itinerary for Charles Young's Washington Ride, 6–22 June 1918, Coleman Collection; "Col. Young Rides to Capitol on Horseback," *Cleveland Advocate*, 29 June 1918, 4.

31. Charles Young to Senator Pomerene, 20 August 1918, Coleman Collection; Wells, "A Versatile Relative of Mine," 182; Charles Young to John J. Pershing, 9 September 1918, Motley Collection.

32. Adjutant General to Charles Young, 6 November 1918, Young Papers; Emmett Scott to J. E. Cutler, with attachments, 15 October 1918, Scott Files; J. E. Moorland to Charles Young, 6 September 1917, Young Papers.

33. Emmett J. Scott to J. E. Cutler, with attachments, 15 October 1918, Scott Files; K. C. Masteller to Emmett J. Scott, 26 November 1918, Scott Files; Rayford Logan, *The Negro in the United States,* I (New York, 1970), 73.

34. Charles Young to Colonel Robinson, 20 December 1918, Young File USMA; Anonymous Soldier to NAACP, 17 November 1918, NAACP Papers, Library of Congress, Washington D.C.; Anonymous Soldier to NAACP, 9 December 1918, NAACP Papers; Charles Young to Arminta Young, 12 December 1918, Coleman Collection; Charles E. Bentley to Walter F. White, 17 December 1918, NAACP Papers; Charles Young to Charles E. Bentley, 15 December 1918, NAACP Papers; Charles Young to Emmett Scott, 14 February 1919, Coleman Collection.

35. Charles Young to Peyton C. March, 20 August 1918, Motley Collection; Charles Young to William Broad, 4 July 1918, Young File MSRC; Ada Young to John J. Pershing, 12 October 1921, Pershing Papers; Charles Young to Atlee Pomerene, 20 August 1918, Coleman Collection; Atlee Pomerene to Charles Young, 27 August 1918, Coleman Collection.

36. General Hugh S. Johnson, testimony collected on the life of Charles Young by Harry Atwood, Coleman Collection; "A Chronicle of Race Relations," *Phylon* 2 (winter 1941): 89–90; Clarence Smith to Charles Young, 26 December 1918, Young Papers; Charles Young to Clarence Smith, 15 January 1919, Young Papers.

37. Charles Young to Peyton C. March, 20 August 1918, Motley Collection; "There's a Service Flag in the Window," words and music by Charles Young, Xenia, Ohio, 1918, Uncataloged Boxes, Charles Young Papers National Afro-American Museum and Cultural Center, Wilberforce, Ohio.

CHAPTER 9

The Making of a Legend

World War I left a gaping hole in Charles Young's life and career. After 28 years of devoted service, broken only by one short spell of sick leave in 1913, he was compelled to retire when a general's command was in reach. Unlike the proverbial old soldier, however, he refused to fade away. His retirement had created outrage among the Black community and by the close of the war, a full four years before his death, he had already become "a martyr to injustice." The belief prevailed among Black Americans that Young's retirement was the result of "rank discrimination;" that he had been sacrificed on the altar of White prejudice. His courage and equanimity in the face of such injustice was widely praised in the Black press, while his famous horseback ride to the nation's capital was the stuff of pure legend. He was, in the words of Du Bois, "a heroic figure."[1]

When in the summer of 1919 his assignment at Camp Grant came to an end, Young made a commitment to take full advantage of his retirement and focus his energies on the cause of "Negro uplift." At the urging of Du Bois, the retired colonel had earlier accepted an invitation to join the board of the NAACP and he also agreed to serve as a consultant on Du Bois's proposed "History of the American Negro in the Great War." He spent the latter part of 1919 stumping for the NAACP, from Cleveland and Philadelphia in the East to Topeka and Kansas City in the Midwest. Unfettered by military obligation for the first time in his adult life, Young eagerly embraced the public platform that his celebrity afforded. In addition to his commitments to the NAACP, Young wrote letters to newspapers, gave speeches on the treatment of Black soldiers during the war, and participated in forums on the "aspirations of the race" in America. For the first time in his life he publicly decried the racism and prejudice that riddled the institutions of American life; yet, ultimately, his remained a voice of moderation calling on African Americans to reject radicalism and embrace the American way.[2]

Young's career as an advocate, however, was short lived. As 1919 came to a close, he received word that the U.S. State Department requested his services in Liberia. The request was made as part of U.S. efforts to replace the multinational receivership established in 1912 with an exclusively American arrangement, a deal sweetened by the offer of a $5 million loan. The State Department specifically requested Young for the post of military attaché, noting that he "would be more useful to them in their work of rehabilitation" than the incumbent attaché, John E. Green. The War Department, which had been considering discontinuing the attaché post in Monrovia, assented to the request, and Young was returned to active duty.[3]

Young, as always, answered the call to duty without question. His family and friends, however, did not share his forbearance. Ada, Du Bois, and others, were incredulous that the War Department, after contending for more than a year that he was too ill to serve in Europe, could now consent to send him to "the unhealthy climate of West Africa" where blackwater fever had almost cost him his life six years before. Even Young recognized that his return to Liberia could be his last act of service. He nonetheless returned, compelled not only by the call of duty but also by the demands of his own boundless energy and by the irresistible appeal Africa held for him. In addition to resuming the rehabilitation mission he had left unfinished in Liberia in 1915, Young looked forward to continuing the detailed study of African civilization that he hoped might "stir in the colored American a pride of ancestry." It was partly for this reason that he was in Lagos, Nigeria where, shortly after returning from an arduous fact-finding mission to the ancient city of Kano, he became extremely ill and died. His death in Africa in January 1922 added a symbolic exclamation to a tragedy that gripped the imagination of Black America and culminated in the celebrated funeral at Arlington Cemetery in 1923.[4]

Harry O. Atwood, a Charles Young protégé from the Spanish-American War who would accompany him on his return to Liberia in 1920, remembered his mentor as someone who had "faith in the elements of greatness within the black man and...came nearer than he knew to stirring a like faith in others." Throughout his military career, Young had endeavored to prepare young Black men for the acute challenges of climbing the ladder of success in a society in which the odds were stacked against them. As a civilian he now sought to continue these efforts and promote his "faith in the black man" through the work of the NAACP. In August 1919 Young's duties at Camp Grant finally came to an end and he returned to Wilberforce "a free man to the retired status." A member of the board of directors since 1918, Young now threw himself into the task of promoting the NAACP. Young's appointment to the board was more than a symbolic gesture; he had been among the 200 notables invited to the landmark Amenia conference in 1916 and he had close relationships with NAACP notables such as Mary Ovington, Joel and Arthur Spingarn and, of course, Du Bois. The zealousness with which he now took up his new role was motivated to some degree by the depth of his friendship with Du Bois. In Young's eyes Du Bois was an intellectual giant who deserved "better treatment at the hands of your people" for his tireless efforts in the cause of racial equality. After all that Du Bois had done to champion his cause during the retirement struggle, Young was eager to return the favor.[5]

The cause to which Young now committed all his energy was more urgent than ever in the summer of 1919, for as he settled into Youngsholm the country was once again in the grip of an orgy of racially motivated violence. By the time the Red Summer of 1919 came to an end, hundreds of people had been killed in riots that flared in cities across the country and the incidence of lynching had sharply increased throughout the South. The aspiration of racial equality now appeared more encumbered than ever; the optimism with which so many African Americans greeted U.S. entry into World War I was now a distant memory. There were signs of change, however. For the nearly four hundred thousand Black veterans, the war may not have altered their circumstances, but it did transform their attitudes and strengthened their commitment to secure positive reform. Begun during the war, the great migration of Blacks from the Deep South to the urban North, from the stifling pressure of Jim Crow to the relative economic and political freedom of Chicago and New York, was the other significant factor in molding what Du Bois dubbed the "New Negro." In the May edition of *The Crisis*, Du Bois issued a call to action. Having fought to save democracy in France, and been rewarded only with continued discrimination and violence at home, Blacks he insisted, "are cowards and jackasses if, now...we do not marshal every ounce of our brain and brawn to fight a sterner, longer, more unbending battle against the forces of hell in our own land."[6]

It was this message that Young carried on the numerous "talk excursions" he undertook in the summer and fall of 1919. In every speech he made, Young urged "our people to join and cooperate with the Association." He was distressed to find opposition during his travels to the NAACP from the Black churches in which, Young wrote Du Bois, the organization was viewed as "a Negro snob affair." In Philadelphia, Kansas City, Topeka, and other stops en route, Young did his utmost to "disabuse their minds of such a preposterous idea," reporting significant converts to the cause along the way. "The NAACP," he told audiences, "are the biggest patriots of America today because they realize that prejudice must be destroyed." To an overflow crowd at the Royal Inn in Cleveland, Young relayed to the audience the constant reminders of racial prejudice he encountered on his speaking tour, such as being forced to ride in a Jim Crow car in Kentucky, and he urged his listeners to work to convince White America to afford its Black citizen the freedom to succeed in "every line of endeavor." As long as "the Negro...still [lived] under the heel of oppression in America," Young concluded painfully, "those who fought for democracy in the world war, died in vain."[7]

Despite the fact that more than a thousand African Americans served as commissioned officers during the war, the fiction persisted that Blacks did not have the ability to fulfill the functions of the field grades. No longer in a position to challenge these assumptions by deed as he had done for so many years, Young took issue in print with those who claimed that Black officers had failed during the war. In a letter to the *New York Evening Post*, Young criticized an article titled "The Negro Officer," which had appeared in the *International Military Digest*. The author of the article contended that attempts to train and deploy Black officers during the war had largely been a failure. Young pointed out that there were enough African American recipients of the Croix de Guerre and the Distinguished Service Medal to refute the broadest generalizations. He decried the "unpatriotic and unwarranted" conclusions drawn in the article and noted that such propaganda was a cause for "just rankling in the hearts of the Negro people." It was unacceptable that America could make "a lower caste of an officer or man of the Negro race that has offered himself for the honor of the country in this war."[8]

Young was determined that Black veterans, although slighted in war, should earn recognition for their service in peace. He rejected as a hollow gesture a suggestion touted on Capital Hill that a war memorial be erected for Black soldiers. Young told a meeting of the National Urban League in New York that if it "wants to do anything for the black soldiers who died in the service of their country, let the Congress of the United States come clean and give them the thing for which they fought—liberty." He urged all Black veterans to join their local posts of the American Legion as a first step in securing the rights they had earned in service. Founded in 1919 by American veterans in Paris, the legion accepted all veterans of military service and welcomed more than half a million members in its first year, developing in the process a powerful lobby for the cause of veteran's benefits. While theoretically apolitical, the legion nonetheless became a focal point of anti-Bolshevik activity during the Red Scare of 1919 and its conservative tendencies bred suspicion among its membership of almost any organization with a reformist agenda. Although membership was open to people of all religious and ethnic backgrounds, the issue of race was considered largely a local matter. This in effect meant that many posts were segregated and in some states, such as Alabama, African Americans were excluded from membership altogether.[9]

Although the American Legion's conservatism and the inconsistencies resulting from regional autonomy may have given him cause for concern, Young was too much the old soldier not to be drawn to the organization and its underlying principles. The struggle to maintain a balance between his patriotism and his commitment to racial justice, ever present throughout his military career, continued in his civilian life. The American Legion held the same attraction to Charles Young as the GAR had to his father. He chose to ignore its limitations and champion instead its "Americanism, fair play to all citizens who have served, irrespective of color," and encouragement of "comradeship of both black and white" veterans. The organization also appealed to his conservative tendencies, particularly after the bloody turmoil of 1919 when he came to see it as a potential bulwark against anarchy.[10]

Speaking in support of the legion to an audience in the Tremont Temple in Boston, where four years before he had accepted the Spingarn Medal, Young urged all Americans to cultivate their patriotism and strive to keep "America intact." While Young accepted that African Americans had a right to struggle for "every privilege any race has" and protect their families and citizenship by any means necessary, the level of violence that flared up across America that summer deeply disturbed him. He believed that Black public opinion had to be brought to bear to effect positive change, but even the violation of the law by Whites and the act of lynching did not justify extremism or riot. The riots and bloodshed had to end, and Black Americans had to accept their interdependence with their White fellow citizens. The alternative was chaos, a future that held "nothing...for the Negro." The fact that Whites instigated much of the violence of the summer of 1919 did not appear to temper Young's position. His greatest fear was that desperation might drive Black Americans to extremism. He recognized the need for African Americans to be assertive in demanding their rights, but not at the expense of "love of country, its very best institutions, and its highest ideals." The key to the future of Black America, in his mind, lay in the patient insistence on "the brotherhood of all men and the ultimate triumph of right." While the American Legion afforded the opportunity of brotherhood, it was the NAACP that would lead the campaign for the "triumph of right." The NAACP as a champion of an integrated America was the "one constant theme" in all his private conversations and his public talks.[11]

Young believed only positive moves toward integration could prevent continued unrest in America; the races must come together to "rout Rowdyism." He agreed with President Wilson's contention that "the nation can not advance faster than the average moral judgment of the masses," but in his view the continued prevalence of petty and unjust discrimination in America had much to do with attitudes in the halls of power. The masses were ready, yet the government continued to ignore such gross injustices as lynching. He took issue with the "southern gentleman" in the Senate who ignored such basic gentlemanly duties as helping the weak and the downtrodden, and the northern politicians who violated the spirit of the Constitution by allowing a portion of the population to be taxed without representation. By availing themselves of the opportunity to vote, northern Blacks could wake their representatives from slumber while demonstrating the ridiculous nature of the rationales employed to deny Blacks access to the ballot below the Mason-Dixon Line. "Suffrage is a practical tool," Young opined, "let us use it."[12]

Young's public prominence, together with his heralded reputation for generosity, brought a flood of mail from a myriad of disparate bodies and individuals seeking his advice and help. Each time he returned to Youngsholm to be with his family and to take care of personal business, he was inundated with solicitations and petitions. He was always willing to contribute to worthy causes, such as Carter Woodson's fund-raising campaign for the Association for the Study of Negro Life and History, and according to his friends he "scattered his money in charity." Every letter received his personal attention, but occasionally he found the demands overwhelming. He could not satisfy every request for "money for operations for small children, care for blind persons, for youngsters who wished to attend college, but who, for lack of funds, were unable to do so." Reduced to tears, he once confessed to his niece, Bernice Wells, "there are too many of them. I can't do what they ask and I can't tell them no."[13]

Young's brief sojourn as a private citizen came to an end. On November 4, 1919, he received orders to resume active duty and to report to the Division of Military Intelligence, where he was to prepare for his return to Liberia as military attaché. After returning briefly to Wilberforce to spend Christmas with Ada and the "kiddies," Young packed his trunks, including a large number of books and office supplies the War Department gave him special dispensation to carry, and left his home for the last time. According to Du Bois, Young's return to Liberia was "suicide" and "he knew it." But duty, "his lode-star," called and "Africa needed him," and so rather than accept a life of "leisure on his retirement pay," he "went quietly, ignoring appeal and protest." It must have been with a heavy heart that he left his mother and the assorted habitants of Youngsholm. Accompanied by Ada and his children, he traveled back East where he accepted one final round of public engagements before departing for Africa.[14]

Young had a melancholy air according to those who encountered him on this farewell tour. In Boston he delivered the keynote address to the Grand Conclave of Omega Psi Phi, one of the nation's oldest and largest Black fraternities. Since 1912, when he was inducted as the fraternity's second honorary member, Young had been a dedicated Omega man and regular participant in the organization's functions. After addressing the conclave, Young accepted an invitation to repair to a local chapter house for dinner, expressing a desire to talk "heart to heart" to the young brothers for fear that this would be his "last opportunity." During a meal that had the feel of a "last supper" to those in attendance, Young adjured the assembled brothers to "always live up to their promises and obligations."[15]

From Boston, Young traveled down to Harlem to address a meeting sponsored by the National Urban League. Harlem was fast becoming a vital center of the African American intelligentsia and artistic community, whose energy and creativity would give rise to a Black cultural renaissance in the 1920s. Harlem derived much of its vigor from the confidence many of its inhabitants had in their future in the United States, a faith that Young increasingly questioned. When introduced to Paul Robeson, then an aspiring young singer and actor recently graduated from Columbia Law School, Young repeated the advice he had given to the West Point cadet Clarence Smith. In his view, the brightest future for young African American men lay in their willingness to "learn to speak the Spanish language fluently and...go to South America." When his New York host, Walter Stevens, asked him what was "the matter with white folks in America," Young reportedly responded "nothing, except that they have left God out of the equation."[16]

While never an advocate of organized religion, Young believed strongly enough in God to regard this as a monumental omission. To his orthodox Christian friends he had "some very original and queer ideas," which he drew from eclectic influences such as his parents' Baptist faith, his wife's Catholicism, and his exposure to the indigenous religions of the Haitian and Liberian interiors. He conceived of God as "the Ocean of Spirit," a "great sea of soul, from which we mortals have bubbled away to form little rivulets, ponds, streams, and the like, but the Mother Sea has her grip on us and in time will attract us back to Her. Then, she will hold us close on her bosom, give us back those atoms that have evaporated away, and will keep us there on and on through eternity." To him religion was the application of the facts of science and the conclusions of philosophy to individual life and conduct. Young believed in destiny and the powerful shaping hand of God. He also believed that faith, whether in God, man, or country, although it may be shaken, could not be destroyed and would ultimately return stronger than ever.[17]

Charles and Ada Young and their children spent their last full day together in the United States visiting friends in New York before boarding the Cunard line steamship *Orduna* bound for Liverpool on January 3, 1920. Their party also included three new designates, Harry Atwood, Allan Bean, and William Nabors, handpicked by Young to take up the task of training and commanding the Liberian Frontier Force. Arriving in Liverpool 10 days later, Young and Ada parted ways, knowing perhaps they might never see each other again. Ada continued on to Paris with Tonton and Marie where they were to live with a family friend, Loulouze Chapoteau, while the children attended school. After four days in Liverpool, Young and his colleagues boarded the Elder Dempster steamer *Onitsha* for Monrovia.[18]

Young arrived in Liberia to find that conditions had deteriorated considerably since his departure in 1915. After inspecting the Liberian armed forces, he concluded that their discipline was "horrible and a disgrace to the Republic." He determined that this state of affairs was due in large measure to the fact that Major Anderson, a retired American NCO then in command of the LFF, was totally unsuitable for the job. Young was confident, however, that his own appointees, Atwood, Bean, and Nabors, could turn the situation around. Meanwhile, the Great War had devastated the Liberian economy and Monrovia, never the most prosperous of capitals, was more dilapidated than ever. The American legation building had fallen into total disrepair, with rotten floorboards and decaying joints making the upper floor largely unusable. Unable to find living or working space in the building, Young rented the "Old Sherman House" on Broad Street and spent $138 of his own money and "many horrid cuss words" making it livable. The ramshackle state of the legation building would prove to be an ominous omen for Young's second tour as military attaché in Liberia. From the moment he returned to Monrovia, his mission, loosely defined to begin with, was beset by problems.[19]

The combined effects of a British naval blockade of West Africa and the loss of its most valuable European trading partner, Germany, had brought the Liberian economy to the brink of collapse during World War I. In 1918, with the survival of the republic again in jeopardy, Monrovia turned once more to the United States for a lifeline, this time requesting a loan of $5 million. The U.S. State Department embraced the loan request as an opportunity to remove the Europeans completely from Liberian affairs by establishing an exclusively American receivership in place of the multinational arrangement established in 1912, while instituting a program of internal reforms whereby American officials would gain considerable control over the republic's internal administration. The loan was to be floated by the U.S. Treasury under the terms of the Second Liberty Loan Act, on the pretext that it would make Liberia an effective ally against the Central Powers. Liberia had little to offer the American war effort and bore no strategic relevance to the campaign in Europe; the liberty loan was simply an expedient tool with which the State Department hoped to shape its long-term policy in the republic. The ultimate goal of the loan was to establish an American protectorate in Liberia and provide a secure economic and strategic foothold for the United States in West Africa.[20]

However, when Young arrived in Monrovia early in 1920, the loan still had not gone into effect. The Liberian government, while in desperate need of capital, was reluctant to accept the reforms and controls that

Washington insisted accompany the loan. Liberian misgivings about its sovereignty, and fears among the Americo-Liberian elite about the future of their monopoly on power, gave rise to a concerted campaign against U.S. reform plans in the republic. Washington insisted, however, that any American assistance, financial or otherwise, would have to be accompanied by wholesale alterations in the country's administration. By 1920 an impasse had been reached; the Liberians desperately needed the loan but were unwilling to accept the conditions that the United States regarded as critical to the loan's security. While Washington professed only to be interested in promoting prosperity and stability in the West African republic, the streets of Monrovia were abuzz with rumors of American plans to "establish [a] white dictatorship over Liberia."[21]

The State Department's specific request for Young's services appears to have been motivated by its desire to counteract this emergent anti-American atmosphere in Liberia. Although his strict emphasis on regulation and procedure had rankled a few officials, Young had earned the genuine respect and trust of many Liberians during his first tour of duty there. Continued American oversight of the Frontier Force was an integral part of U.S. policy in Liberia, hence the State Department's insistence on the maintenance of a military attaché in Monrovia. Young was preferred to Captain John E. Green in this role, however, because of his value as a goodwill ambassador, one who could serve as a counterweight to unpopular White officials like American General Receiver Harry F. Worley. A consistent proponent of the American "program, for the rehabilitation of Liberia," Young was sent to Liberia in 1920 to help steady a keeling ship.[22]

Reunited with his friend Richard Bundy, who was still serving as U.S. chargé d'affaires in Monrovia, Young eagerly threw himself into the task of securing a preponderance of American influence in Liberia. At the request of the War Department, he submitted a general report on the political situation in the republic in which he noted widespread public disaffection with American officials in Liberia. Young attributed this sentiment in a large measure to the activities of British and French agents who, he charged, were spreading anti-American propaganda in an effort to undermine the U.S. reform plan. Young noted that certain U.S. officials, most notably General Receiver Worley, were unfit for the positions they held and their continued service was proving detrimental to American interests. Citing America's obligation to its "Negro population" and its commitments under the terms of the 1912 loan agreement, Young insisted that American creditability depended on putting into effect the reform measures outlined in the 1918 proposed loan. He remained as convinced in 1920 as he had been five years before, that the future independence and stability of Liberia depended on U.S. aid and assistance. The United States was there to cultivate "the prospects of trade" and promote principles of good government, and so Young saw no logical reason why Liberia should fear its outstretched arm of benevolence. "If the black world is not to be ashamed," he wrote Robert Russa Moton, "Liberia...can do better, should do better, and must do better."[23]

There were many observers in both the United States and Liberia who were far more skeptical of American motives than Young. The failure of the Wilson administration to recognize African claims for self-determination at the Paris Peace Conference and its acquiescence in turning over former German colonies to the British, French, and South Africans as mandates, seriously undermined U.S. anti-imperialist credentials. Critics of U.S. policy in Liberia charged that the West African republic was liable to face the same fate as Haiti, whose government had suffered a serious challenge to its sovereignty since the occupation of the island nation by U.S. Marines in 1915. In July 1920, the *Monrovia Weekly Review* reprinted an article from *The Crisis* titled "Haiti," which made just such a claim, and the editor urged his readers to study the article with "racial consciousness" to see how the Caribbean republic had "lost her independence and make your inference with a national vision."[24]

Comparisons between Liberia and Haiti placed Young in a very awkward situation, given his service as military attaché in both countries. The "Haiti" article posed a critical challenge to Young's previously unimpeachable creditability in Liberia. According to Young himself, "the man in the street" was now asking whether the American attaché was "a spy here drawing maps and plans for the U.S. to take us over as happened in Haiti." Young wrote to Du Bois that the "Haiti" article had made his work in the republic considerably more difficult, jeopardizing his ability "to be of future benefit to Liberia." In Monrovia the lesson of Haiti now became the centerpiece of the campaign to prevent the Liberian legislature from ratifying the proposed loan.[25]

Young was not deaf to these protestations; he simply did not think that they were warranted. He sincerely believed that the Liberian government had to sacrifice some of its sovereignty to the United States to maintain its status as an independent Black republic. In his mind, there was a significant distinction to be made between the United States and the European imperial powers. The latter represented the exclusive interests of the "white man," while U.S. involvement in Liberia was at least partly directed by African American officials on the ground such as himself, Bundy, and the officers of the LFF. As they had done during his first tour in Liberia, Young and Bundy once again joined forces to endeavor to cast a greater African American imprint on U.S. policy in Liberia. Their ultimate goal was to replace the corrupt and inefficient Americo-Liberian oligarchy with an "upstanding clean government wherein the native people will have a chance." Young exhorted his friends at home to recognize that the criticism of U.S. policy in Liberia aired with increasing frequency in the Black press was misplaced, and benefited only the entrenched elite in

Monrovia and the "foreign influences" that supported them. He defended Bundy against Black critics in the United States and urged Du Bois to push to have James Weldon Johnson, the widely respected NAACP secretary and former U.S. Consul in Venezuela and Nicaragua, sent to Liberia as U.S. minister "to discern the truth."[26]

Young's greatest concern was that the principle of Black self-government not be deemed a failure. With Africa "in the throes of the world's unrest" following the end of the war, a stable, prosperous Liberian republic could point the way to the continent's future. "As long as the African that does the work goes half-fed and half-clothed," the continent would "never be simple pickings for the white man alone." Young anticipated the rise of African nationalism that would gather momentum between the World Wars. Like many members of the Talented Tenth, he was both intrigued and leery of the plans of Marcus Garvey, the charismatic Jamaican whose Universal Negro Improvement Association (UNIA) was taking Harlem by storm in the early 1920s. Among Garvey's many grandiose schemes was a plan to make Liberia the seat of the UNIA's "Africa for the Africans" campaign. Although the Liberian government was suspicious of Garvey's motives and his self-appointed title of "Provisional President-General of Africa," Monrovia welcomed the UNIA's offer to float a $2 million Liberian construction loan to develop industry in the republic as a possible alternative to the proposal of the U.S. government. Young observed with interest as the Garvey movement stirred "race consciousness" all along the coast of West Africa in 1920, and he was convinced that "any all black proposition well financed...cannot fail of success in Africa" as long as it was "prepared to fight the machinations and commercial supremacy of the white man." The UNIA was neither well financed nor prepared for the machinations of the White governments of the United States, Britain, and France, all of which reacted to Garvey's meteoric rise with considerable alarm. In the fall of 1921 Young wrote his friend Billy Broad, "The Garvey Movement, from which the Liberians expected so much financially, has almost lost its last legs here."[27]

With charges of U.S. imperialism mounting in the Black press and the American loan held in abeyance by interminable negotiations, Young became increasingly frustrated and dispirited. "This Liberia muddle has taken much of the brightness out of my heart," he confessed in a letter to Du Bois. He was particularly frustrated with the political machinations of Liberian President C. D. B. King, that "Son of a Tinker," whom he held most responsible for holding up implementation of the loan. "I am damned fed up on Negroes and Negro Govts. [sic]," an exasperated Young wrote to Ada, and he vowed that once he had completed the monograph on Liberia and other materials required by the War Department he was going to quit the place for good. He was, however, still committed to linking "the blacks of the 2 continents together in sympathy and friendship during my life," and with this in mind he was determined to take advantage of his futile post in Liberia to continue his writings and research on Africa.[28]

In fact, Young spent much of his time during his second tour in Liberia cultivating his intellectual endeavors. He had finally completed work on the L'Ouverture drama and had contracted with New York actor Clarence Muse to make a motion picture version of the piece. Muse's billing of the production in fliers sent to prospective investors raised Young's ire, prompting him to complain to Ada "it hurts to hear my long work on the play called my 'story' and his dramatization." The completion of this project nonetheless inspired new undertakings. He now contemplated similar works on Montezuma and John Brown, and penned more than a hundred poems and song lyrics that he then forwarded to Ada in the hope that she might be able to secure a publisher in London. Young found inspiration in his dealings with other members of the international community in Monrovia, which he described as "a jolly bunch" even though "the country is getting overrun with missionaries." In particular, two Britons, writer-poet J. M. Stuart Young and colonial adventurer Sir Harry Johnston, served as critics of his work and sounding boards for his ideas.[29]

Young maintained a steady correspondence with friends and family and a voracious appetite for reading, storing his books in iron chests in his room to protect them from the tropical humidity. Liberia posed problems to even these small comforts, however. "I feel dreadful," he bewailed to Ada, after more than two hundred volumes of his best books had gone missing in New York en route to Liberia. With only a third of his collection left, he had to rely on Ada, Du Bois, and others to purchase volumes and subscriptions for him in the United States and mail them to Monrovia. He was particularly anxious to get a copy of Du Bois's new book, *Darkwater,* "whose good father," he wrote the author, "you remember I am." While Young's claim was somewhat tongue in cheek, his thinking on a range of issues, from the primacy of African civilization to the legacy of slavery, is clearly echoed in Du Bois's essays and social commentaries in this book. Although he eventually received an autographed copy from Du Bois, receiving mail on the West Coast of Africa was always an adventure. On one occasion Young had cause to lament U.S. postmen's poor knowledge of geography when he received a parcel of mail several months after it had left New York. His mail had gone first to Siberia, a corner of the world, Young noted with wry amusement, that could not have provided a greater environmental contrast to Liberia. "One is hot and harassing as 'ell and the other is as cold and uncomfortable as a mid-winter beach in Boston."[30]

The mail between Monrovia and Paris was more reliable, and Young received regular reports from his family there. Tonton and Kikik (Marie's nickname, meaning tomboy) were flourishing in school. Their parents were determined that they should learn as much as they could while they were in Europe, as they would have this chance only once. Both children were doing well in school, and Young took great pride in the fact that they could write to him in "good English and perfect French." Kikik's progress as a budding piano virtuoso was reported with regularity to her grandmother Arminta, who had taught both her and her father how to play. Young encouraged Ada to ensure that Kikik had every facility to pursue her music as he had little doubt that "her forte lies there." Tonton was working hard but was evidently missing the stature that came with being "Col. Young's son" back in Wilberforce. He desperately wanted to return to Youngsholm and questioned why his father could not return home. His father reassured him that Youngsholm would always be there for him, and that in the meantime he should exercise and remain focused on his studies.[31]

Ada, meanwhile, was not well, suffering periodic headaches and spending long periods confined to her bed. She continued to be plagued by anxiety on a range of issues, from personal finances to her husband's health, and in her most melancholy moments she confessed that she found little comfort in their marriage, given the miles that separated them. She pleaded with him to retire and concentrate on his verse and music. Young filled his letters with comforting assurances in an effort to set her "mind free," and promised that as soon as he was done in Liberia he would retire for good and "try to make up to you for some of my neglect of you and the kids." He also hoped that retirement would enable him to improve relations between his wife and mother, noting to Ada "we will not have her for long." He reported to her that Arminta was oblivious to the fact that she ever gave Ada trouble or cause to worry. As far as Young was concerned the chief cause of tension was Will Lowery, whom his mother had married several years earlier. He believed that Lowery was allowing his petty and selfish personal interests to supersede the common good of everyone else at Youngsholm. "I can not and will not have people around me," he wrote his mother, "who are trying to tear down what I am building."[32]

In addition to the strain of separation, the Youngs were experiencing some financial problems. The pressure of maintaining both the farm, with all its dependencies, and Ada and the children in Paris was beginning to tell on Young's resources. His return to Liberia was partly fueled by a desire to earn enough money to pay off his debts and retire, "making bad books, bad verse, and still worse songs," amid the bustle and activity of Youngsholm. In 1920, they took out a loan against their property in Oakland, and invited offers on the Dayton and Denver holdings, the latter valued at $3,000. Ada meanwhile, without first telling Charles, wrote to General Pershing, citing the strain of "maintaining three households on retired pay," to ask for his help in elevating Young to "a General's pay" and securing for him "a small post in Europe." Ada believed that her husband's service not only warranted such a reward, but that this might go some way toward healing the wound that his controversial retirement had opened up. She wrote to Pershing as someone who she believed had done much to help "your black brothers" and who was familiar with the hardships of service. However, there was one experience Ada noted that Pershing never had and that was "being a Negro officer" and, she added, "I thank God you have not." It was a burden that Young had carried for more than 30 years, and Ada felt its weight almost as much as her husband.[33]

With his personal problems mounting and the American loan plan no nearer to implementation than on the day he arrived, in June 1921 Young requested a leave of absence for four months so that he could go to Europe to adjust to "affairs of my family" and to have dental work done. He may also have been hoping to take up Du Bois's invitation to attend the second Pan-African Congress scheduled for Paris and London later that summer. Citing the "confused" state of Liberian affairs and the still uncertain status of the proposed loan, the State Department informed the Military Intelligence Division in July that "under the present circumstances the question of granting leave to Colonel Charles Young...be held in abeyance." The Youngs were left in limbo, waiting throughout the summer and fall for some positive news on the question of leave as the loan negotiations dragged on. In September Ada wrote to Arminta that she hoped to bring the colonel "home with me soon," but a month later Charles had still heard nothing from "Uncle Samuel." I "don't know why," he wrote Billy Broad, but "I suppose he does." Each passing month made Ada increasingly anxious that she might never see her husband again, "knowing how much longer he has to live." In November he put in a second request, and this time he was granted four months leave to begin on April 1, 1922, pending completion of the negotiations. In the meantime, he was ordered by the War Department to undertake "intelligence work in other sections of Africa."[34]

On November 15, 1921, Young boarded the Spanish steamer *Cataluna* bound for Nigeria. He stopped into the legation house that morning and, according to those who saw him, he was in excellent health and spirits, exhibiting only signs of a slight cold. Young's instructions were to travel to Lagos to "obtain certain information" on the political climate there and provide a report on issues such as the racial, ethnic, and cultural makeup of Nigeria. Young hoped to take advantage of this assignment to gather information for his work on African civilization and culture and "go to the sources in Africa where he believed he would find the truth about the black man." The journey down the coast involved stops on the island of Fernando Po and in the port city of Douala in the Cameroons. Young was in his element, taking detailed notes on the geography and culture of the areas he visited. It was such a "delightful trip" that not even being the victim of a robbery on his arrival in Lagos could temper his enthusiasm. By this point, though, the slight cold he had exhibited in Monrovia had become a serious flu-like ailment and he was confined to bed for several days. Young was not, however, about to pass this opportunity whiling away his time in bed. As soon as he felt marginally better, a week before Christmas, he left Lagos on a 500-mile round-trip journey into the Nigerian interior to visit the famous walled city and great symbol of African civilization, Kano.[35]

On the train journey back from Kano Young fell extremely ill, returning to Lagos on December 26 in "a state of collapse." He was taken directly from the train station to Grey's Hospital, suffering from complications brought on by chronic nephritis. Through the nuns who provided for his daily care Young managed to get off a cable to the Bank of British West Africa in Monrovia that he was "seriously ill" and required the immediate transfer of $100 to Lagos. News of his predicament soon reached the legation, and Harry Atwood caught the first steamer down to the coast. Atwood arrived in Lagos on January 6 and sat vigil by the bedside of the dying colonel for three days before Young "fell asleep upon the bosom of Africa." The following day Young's body was removed from Grey's Hospital in a casket draped with "Old Glory," the flag having been borrowed from a local Dutch firm, and carried to the European section of Ikoyi Cemetery in a procession led by the police band. Here, with the bishop of Nigeria officiating and an aid to the governor in attendance, he was laid to rest with full military honors. The bishop told the assembled dignitaries that Young's rise to prominence in a country renowned for its race prejudice was "proof positive of his ability and integrity." As the soil of Africa fell on his coffin, the Nigerian Regiment fired a volley over the gravesite and sounded the last post. In reporting the occasion, the British journal *West Africa* noted, "the case of Colonel Young should furnish an object lesson to the various European governments engaged in the development of Africa...that the watchword for white and black should...be cooperation."[36]

The news of Colonel Young's death was greeted with surprise, even by those closest to him who were aware of the fragility of his health. When she heard by cable on January 13 of the death and burial of her husband in Lagos, Ada hurried home from Europe with her grief-stricken children to be with her mother-in-law in Wilberforce. Initially unable to provide her with any further details, the War Department wrote that "Colonel Young's ability and devotion to his country were greatly appreciated...and it is a matter of extreme regret to us all that duty should have brought about his death in foreign land." Ada clearly was comforted by these words, but could not come to terms with the fact that her husband had been denied leave from duty in Liberia for the duration of the loan negotiation, which continued to drag on after his death. "It hurts," she wrote Colonel Heintzelman, her liaison at the General Staff, "I can tell you I almost believe the very fact of Charlie being sacrificed has kept that Loan in the air." In a final cruel irony, when Monrovia did finally agree to the terms of the American proposal, the U.S. Senate could see no justification for extending $5 million to Liberia under the terms of the Liberty Loan Act four years after the end of World War I. The measure died on the floor of the Senate on November 28, 1922, by a vote of 42–33, with many southern senators decrying it as little more that a "gift" to the "Negroes" of Liberia.[37]

The death of her husband began for Ada Young the "hardest of my battles." During the course of her marriage to Charles she had increasingly found comfort in her spiritual pursuits. Charles once noted that her Catholic faith made her "stronger and more contented" and she found "many consolations in that Church and much charity and democratic feeling and action." Later she had been drawn to various religious fads from the teachings of the Prophet Bahia to, after Charles's death, the Unity Movement. She noted in her diary that her husband's "work being completed here, he entered his new life, well fitted and like a beautiful dragon fly, his spirit often sweeps down to the earth in a helpful way, and I am benefited." Ada was greatly comforted by these communions and a year after her husband's death she declared "the Spirit of love will lead me when things get 'thick'." There were a great many earthly challenges ahead to test her spiritual resolve.[38]

Young's sudden death thousands of miles from home left his personal affairs in disarray and posed numerous problems for Ada, Arminta, and the children, who had always depended on him for income and support. Under the terms of the War Risk Insurance Act, Ada, as a veteran's widow with two dependents, was entitled to $42.50 a month from the government. This was substantially less than she was accustomed to live on. Between "paying off the incumbent on our home, the schooling of the children, [and] the farm not making itself pay," she was having difficulty making ends meet. To complicate matters, Young had been handling most of their financial affairs from Liberia, and vital documents pertaining to his estate remained locked in his desk in Monrovia. Ada spent months working with officers from the General Staff endeavoring to cut through red tape to secure the return of her husband's personal property. This included efforts to track down the former U.S. minister to Liberia, Joseph Johnson, to whom Young had entrusted money before leaving for Nigeria, and to recover a deposit made for Young by the U.S. legation in the Lagos branch of the Bank of British West Africa after he had been robbed shortly following his arrival in Nigeria. Within a year of Young's death, Ada's financial situation had spiraled into chaos. The Young's property holdings in Denver were being taken over by the city in lieu of back taxes, and the farm had ceased to pay for itself. In ailing health and at her wit's end, Ada appealed to Du Bois for help in securing a job or finding a guarantor for a loan. Du Bois's advice was brutally honest. He noted that she could no longer maintain the lifestyle she had become accustomed to, and recommended that she bring the children home from Europe, where they had returned to school, and "get rid of the parasites who live in your home and make that farm pay."[39]

Du Bois was nonetheless genuinely sympathetic to her plight and, motivated in equal measure by a desire to secure her financial future and to honor his friend, he spearheaded a campaign by the NAACP to have Congress secure a military pension for Mrs. Young. The Committee on Pensions eventually agreed to award Ada Young $58 per month on a colonel's pension, but balked at the NAACP protestation that her husband's "extraordinary and notable services," together with the circumstances surrounding his retirement, warranted the award of the $100 stipend given to retired brigadier generals. Du Bois took issue with those congressmen who claimed that Young's career had been in no way remarkable and that exception should not be made for him on account of his race. "I know of few officers," he wrote Representative Charles Brand of Ohio, "who deserve more of their country than Colonel Young."[40]

Outside Young's immediate family, few people were as deeply affected by news of his death as Du Bois. In the February issue of *The Crisis*, Du Bois penned a poignant memorial to "Charles Young, Soldier and Man and unswerving Friend." From the "Hell" of West Point through the "insult and intrigue" of 33 years in the army, Du Bois declared, Young had led a life that had been a "triumph of tragedy." He noted with bitterness that Young had been kept home from Europe during the war because "they could not stand a black American General. Therefore they sent him to the fever coast of Africa." Given the findings of the military doctors in 1917, this act, Du Bois concluded, amounted to sending him "there to die." Young went "quietly, ignoring appeal and protest" because "Duty to him, as to few modern men, was spelled in capitals." Du Bois concluded his emotive eulogy by emphasizing the importance of Young's achievements and career to African Americans and to the cause of racial equality. "The heart of the Great Black Race . . . rises and salutes his shining memory: Well Done!"[41]

This was not a call to action but a statement of fact. As Rayford Logan later observed, "many contemporary Negroes regarded him as a martyr on the altar of racial discrimination." Young's death received widespread publicity in the Black press and was reported in national publications such as the *New York Times*, which memorialized Young as a "noted U.S. Cavalry Commander" and a "picturesque and interesting figure in American Army Life." Letters of condolence poured into Youngsholm from all over the country expressing the collective opinions that he had died a hero in Africa and that "he belonged to the whole Negro race." In February, the Omega Psi Fraternity held a memorial service in Washington, D.C. A message from Secretary of War John Weeks was read at the service praising Young as "an outstanding character among the colored people of the world." Nathum Daniel Brascher, the editor in chief of the United Negro Press, with the cooperation of James Weldon Johnson, who saw the colonel's life as "the highest vindication of those who claim for the colored man all the opportunities which humanly and [under] the Constitution are his," organized a National Memorial Service for Young in Chicago on March 12. The centerpiece of this hugely successful event was the reading of a message from Ada thanking all those who had offered their sympathy and emphasizing Young's faith in "the highest possibilities for his people and their capability to attain this through" the work of the NAACP.[42]

The most ambitious plan to recognize the life and career of Charles Young involved exhuming his body and returning it to the United States for interment in Arlington Cemetery. In March, with the support of Du Bois and others who were willing to take a hand in the planning, Ada requested that the War Department return her husband's remains to the United States for burial with full military honors. According to Ada, Charles had always "wanted to occupy a soldier's grave at Arlington" after his death. The War Department agreed to comply with the widow's petition and to cover the expenses involved, and forwarded a request to the Department of State to arrange through the legation in Monrovia for the disinterment and shipping of Colonel Young's remains. The decision to comply with the request inspired conflicting opinions in the administration of the new Republican president, Warren Harding. Undersecretary of State William R. Castle warned against playing into the hands of those who wished "to make the return of the body a 'Nation Wide Affair'" and in the process "put a special emphasis upon the race" of the deceased officer. Assistant Secretary of the Navy Theodore Roosevelt, Jr., on the other hand, added the power of his name to the campaign to organize a major display on Young's behalf, and successfully intervened to overcome the army's objection to permitting services to be held in Arlington Amphitheatre. The Harding administration, recognizing the political value in honoring in death an officer it could never so honor in life, overrode the dissenting voices and agreed to comply with the ornate plans that were soon put in place for the funeral of an African America fallen hero.[43]

With Ada and Du Bois directing from behind the scenes, responsibility for handling Young's body on its return to New York and organizing the funeral in Washington, D.C., was placed in the hands of the newly named Charles Young Post of the American Legion in New York City. The bureaucratic difficulties involved in exhuming the body and returning it from a foreign territory, together with the increasingly elaborate arrangements being put in place for the ceremonies in the United States, postponed this final act in Charles Young's celebrated life until the spring of 1923. When all the details were finally in place, Carleton Wall, the clerk of the U.S.

legation in Monrovia, traveled to Lagos to oversee the exhumation. Young's body was disinterred and escorted from Ikoyi Cemetery by troops from the West African Frontier Force and a detachment of Nigerian sailors, before being placed aboard a waiting steamship to begin the journey home to America.[44]

On May 20, 1923, the *West Heseltine* docked in New York, where the body was handed into the care of veterans from the Charles Young Post. A week later a huge crowd gathered in the great hall of New York City College for a memorial service at which Du Bois, Joel Spingarn, Theodore Roosevelt, Jr., and West Point commandant Brigadier General Fred W. Sladen were the featured speakers. Following a solemn processional from the 139th St. Armory, the body was carried into the hall and the audience took their seats to hear Du Bois pay an emotional tribute to his friend. After highlighting Young's achievements and personal attributes, *The Crisis* editor launched into an explosive assault on the institution that had denied America's ranking Black officer the chance to wear a general's star and command troops on the western front. Du Bois charged that after years of racism and prejudice that had begun at West Point and continued through his army career, Young had suffered this final betrayal, which had hastened his death from a "broken heart." In what the *New York World* reported as a "clash over the body of [the] Negro officer," General Sladen departed from his notes to offer a rebuttal and defend West Point and the army against Du Bois's charges of discrimination. Sladen, a classmate of Young's at the military academy, later wrote an apology to Ada stating that he had been so "worked up" by Du Bois that he felt compelled to offer a rebuttal. Even in memory, the army's highest-ranking Black officer was a source of contention. Roosevelt, the last speaker to the podium, struck a conciliatory note and returned the focus of the proceedings to the legacy of Charles Young, who "by sheer force of character overcame prejudices that would have discouraged many a lesser man." The former president's son concluded by calling on all those who wished to honor Young, to emulate this man whose life was "a tribute of our ideal of equality of opportunity in citizenship."[45]

Colonel Young's body left New York for Washington by train the next day, stopping en route in Philadelphia where the Black citizenry of the City of Brotherly Love turned out in droves to pay their last respects. On the morning of June 1, the funeral train arrived at Union Station in the nation's capital, where it was met by a large gathering of Black veterans and citizens groups. The "colored schools" were closed for the day in honor of Black America's greatest military figure, and thousands of people lined the processional route, doffing their hats or bowing their heads as the flag-draped caisson moved slowly by on Pennsylvania Avenue. Dolly, one of Young's favorite mares, followed the casket with Young's boots turned backward in the stirrups of his saddle.[46]

It took more than an hour for the cortege to wind its way through the city before arriving at the Fort Myers gate of Arlington Cemetery. As the Third Cavalry band played a dirge, the body was removed from the caisson and, preceded by the Howard University choir, the clergy, and the family, was escorted into the amphitheatre and placed on the catafalque. Charles Young became only the fourth person to be honored with funeral services in the Arlington Amphitheatre, the others being two Confederate veterans buried in 1912 as a symbol of national union and the Unknown Soldier memorialized after the Great War. In addition to the numerous individual dignitaries and notables in attendance, the large crowd included delegations from the U.S. Army, the Grand Army of the Republic, the American Legion, the Army and Navy Union, United Spanish War Veterans, Wilberforce University, the NAACP, the State of Ohio, and the Y.M.C.A. They were joined by hundreds of ordinary citizens who came to honor "the hero of the entire colored race."[47]

Ada noted with pride that the chief of chaplains informed her that the ceremony for her husband was "quite as large a funeral as that for the unknown soldier." She recorded in her diary "one seeing will never forget the impression." Oscar Scott, United States Army chaplain, 10th Cavalry, Young's bunkmate from the Mexico campaign, delivered the obituary, and to the strains of "Deep River," the body was carried past the tomb of the Unknown Soldier to the gravesite. As the choir chanted the Lord's Prayer, the casket was lowered into the hallowed ground of Arlington Cemetery. A firing squad sounded the final salute over the grave and a lone bugler playing taps brought the ceremony to a poignant close. Charles Young was laid to rest surrounded by thousands of others who had served and fought for the United States; here there was no distinction made based on the color of his skin.[48]

For weeks and months after Charles Young's death tributes emanated from a variety of sources. There was an article penned by one of his classmates at West Point, a pamphlet written by a former president of Wilberforce, and interviews given by men who had served under him in the Spanish-American War and in Liberia. Like many notable figures, he received greater recognition in death than he had in life. This belated acknowledgment was hard to take for those who had known him most intimately. A month after the funeral at Arlington, Du Bois blasted what he deemed the insincerity of many of those Whites who had paid glowing tribute to his friend and the political exploitation of Young's funeral by the Harding administration. Throughout his career, Charles Young had been confined to the margins of military service despite his diligent service and his loyal adherence to the oath he took as an officer of the United States Army. Du Bois had every reason to question the sincerity and motives of the government and army, which for years had seen Young as an embarrassment, yet now so publicly recognized and honored him in death.[49]

There was no questioning the authenticity, however, of Black America's reverence for Charles Young. For those who organized his elaborate funeral, the ceremony was designed as much to recognize his efforts in the struggle for racial equality as it was to honor his service to the United States. To them, Young's life was a symbol of the struggle that he had euphemistically called "the cause"; a life that Du Bois so elegantly characterized as "the triumph of tragedy." Another prominent member of the Black intelligentsia in the 1920s offered perhaps the most poignant and prescient tribute to the military hero. Countee Cullen's 1925 poem "In Memory of Colonel Charles Young" captured the triumph and tragedy of his life and prophesized the lasting impact of his legacy:

> Along the shore the tall, thin grass
> That fringes that dark river,
> While sinuously soft feet pass,
> Begins to bleed and quiver.
> The great dark voice breaks with a sob,
> Across the womb of night;
> Above your grave the tom-toms throb,
> And the hills are weird with light.
> The great dark heart is like a well
> Drained bitter by the sky,
> And all the honeyed lies they tell
> Come here to thirst and die
> No lie is strong enough to kill
> The roots that work below;
> From your rich dust and slaughtered will
> A tree with tongues will grow.[50]

NOTES

1. Walter J. Stevens, *Chip on My Shoulder* (Boston, 1946), 178; *Cleveland Advocate,* 18 March 1917, 1; *Southwestern Christian Advocate,* 6 September 1917, clipping in Charles Young Papers National Afro-American Museum and Cultural Center, Wilberforce, Ohio [hereinafter Young Papers]; W. E. B. Du Bois, "The Curious Case of the Negro Soldier," unpublished 1917, W. E. B. Du Bois Papers, University of Massachusetts, Amherst, Mass. [hereinafter Du Bois Papers].

2. Charles Young to W. E. B. Du Bois, 25 April 1919, Du Bois Papers; Charles Young to W. E. B. Du Bois, 22 August 1919, Du Bois Papers; Gerald W. Patton, *War and Race: The Black Officer in the American Military* (Westport, Conn., 1981): 118–119; *Cleveland Advocate,* 10 January 1920, 1.

3. U.S. Department of War Memorandum for Chief, Personnel Branch, Operations Division, prepared by Brigadier General Marlborough Churchill, 21 October 1919, Military Information Division, General Correspondence, 1917–1941, Records of the Department of War, Record Group 165, National Archives, College Park, Md. [hereinafter MID].

4. Ada Young to John J. Pershing, 12 October 1921, John J. Pershing Papers, Library of Congress, Washington, D.C. [hereinafter Pershing Papers]; W. E. B.

Du Bois to Robert Lansing, 12 November 1919, Du Bois Papers; Robert L. Gill, *The Omega Psi Phi Fraternity and the Men Who Made Its History: A Concise History* (Washington, D.C., 1977), 13; John H. Purnell, "Colonel Charles Young, U.S.A.: Soldier, Diplomat, Philanthropist, Man of Culture," *The Oracle* (winter 1979): 8; Captain Harry Atwood, U.S.A., quoted in Wesley A. Brown, "Eleven Men of West Point," *Negro History Bulletin,* April 1956, 151.

5. Captain Harry Atwood, U.S.A., quoted in Brown, "Eleven Men of West Point," 152; Mary White Ovington to Charles Young, 9 January 1918, Coleman Collection, Akron, Ohio; Charles Young to Joel E. Spingarn, 3 July, 1916, Joel E. Spingarn Papers, Moorland Spingarn Research Collection, Howard University, Washington, D.C. [hereinafter Joel Spingarn Papers]; Charles Young to Joel E. Spingarn, 14 January 1918, Joel Spingarn Papers; Charles Young to W. E. B. Du Bois, 25 April 1919, Du Bois Papers; Charles Young to W. E. B. Du Bois, 22 August 1919, Du Bois Papers.

6. Florette Henri, *Black Migration: Movement North,* 1900–1920 (Garden City, N.Y., 1975), 318–22; W. E. B. Du Bois, "Returning Soldier," *The Crisis,* May 1919, reprinted in Henry Lee Moon, ed., *The Emerging Thought of W.E. B. Du Bois: Essays and Editorials from the Crisis* (New York, 1972), 259–61.

7. Charles Young to W. E. B. Du Bois, 22 August 1919, Du Bois Papers; Notes on a Speech, n.d. [1919], Coleman Collection; *Cleveland Advocate,* 11 November, 1919, 4.

8. "The Negro Officer," Letter to the Editor from Charles Young, *New York Evening Post,* 5 April 1919, editorial page.

9. Charles Young quoted in *Army and Navy Journal,* 20 December 1919; Charles Young to W. E. B. Du Bois, 22 August 1919, Du Bois Papers; John Whitelay Chambers II, *The Oxford Companion to American Military History* (New York, 1999), 29, 750; Moon, *Emerging Thought of W. E. B. Du Bois,* 316–317.

10. *Cleveland Advocate,* 11 November 1919, 4; Charles Young to W. E. B. Du Bois, 22 August 1919, Du Bois Papers; *Cleveland Advocate,* 10 January 1920, 1; Chisholm News Service, n.d. [1919], Coleman Collection.

11. *Cleveland Advocate,* 10 January 1920, 1; Charles Young Diary, Part I, Coleman Collection; Message from Ada Young read on the occasion of Memorial Services for Colonel Charles Young, New York, 12 March 1922, Du Bois Papers.

12. Charles Young Diary, Part I, Coleman Collection; Charles Young Diary, Part II, Coleman Collection.

13. Charles Young to Carter Woodson, 20 March 1919, Carter Woodson Papers, Library of Congress, Washington, D.C. [hereinafter Woodson Papers]; W.E.B. Du Bois, "Charles Young," *The Crisis* (February 1922); Bernice Young Mitchell Wells, "A Versatile Relative of Mine: Colonel Charles Young," in Herman Dreer, ed., *American Literature by Negro Authors* (New York, 1950), 183.

14. U.S. Department of War Memorandum for Chief, Personnel Branch, Operations Division, prepared by Brigadier General Marlborough Churchill, 21 October 1919, MID; Ada Young Diary, 1 January 1923, Coleman Collection; W. E. B. Du Bois, "Charles Young," *The Crisis* (February 1922).

15. George Lythcott, "Memorial to Charles Young," *Oracle* (spring 1922), cited in Robert L. Gill, *The Omega Psi Phi Fraternity and the Men Who Made Its History: A Concise History* (Washington, D.C., 1977), 13–14.

16. Stevens, *Chip on My Shoulder,* 178–9.

17. O. J. W. Scott, "Colonel Young—The Friend," Oration delivered on the occasion of funeral services for Charles Young, 1 June 1923, reprinted in Abraham

Chew, *A Biography of Colonel Charles Young* (Washington, D.C., 1923), 16–17; Charles Young Diary, Part I, Coleman Collection; Wells, "A Versatile Relative of Mine," 183–184.

18. William Scully to Robert Lansing, 2 January 1920, Records of the Department of State Relating to the Internal Affairs of Liberia, 1910–1929, Record Group 59, National Archives, College Park, MD [hereinafter RDSL]; Robert Lansing to American Legation, Monrovia, 3 January 1920, RDSL.

19. Binder Volume 3, Notes for a Monograph on Liberia, September 1920, Uncataloged Boxes, Charles Young Papers, National Afro-American Museum and Cultural Center, Wilberforce, Ohio [hereinafter Young Papers Uncataloged]; Charles Young to Director of Military Intelligence, 13 October 1920, MID; Charles Young to Ada Young, 6 December 1920, Coleman Collection; Charles Young to Ada Young, 4 January 1921, Coleman Collection; Charles Young to Director of Military Intelligence, 4 June 1921, MID.

20. David P. Kilroy, "Extending the American Sphere to West Africa: Dollar Diplomacy in Liberia, 1908–1926." (unpublished decision, University of Iowa), 1995, 137–40.

21. Ibid., 141–99; Joseph L. Johnson to Robert Lansing, 6 March 1920, RDSL.

22. Charles Young to Robert Scully, 19 February 1920, RDSL.

23. Charles Young to the Secretary of War, 30 June 1920, RDSL; Charles Young to Robert Russa Moton, 22 January 1921, Coleman Collection.

24. *Monrovia Weekly Review,* 17 July 1920, clipping in RDSL.

25. Charles Young to W. E. B. Du Bois, 20 July 1920, Du Bois Papers.

26. Charles Young to Charles Cuney, 15 May 1920, Woodson Papers; Charles Young to W. E. B., Du Bois, 14 January 1921, Du Bois Papers.

27. Charles Young to Charles Cuney, 15 May 1920, Woodson Papers; Charles Young to Ada Young, 13 June 1921, Coleman Collection; Charles Young to Ada Young, 31 July 1921, Coleman Collection; Charles Young to William Broad, 12 October 1921, Charles Young File, Moorland Spingarn Research Center, Howard University, Washington, D.C.

28. Charles Young to W. E. B., Du Bois, 14 January 1921, Du Bois Papers; Charles Young to Ada Young, 12 March 1921, Coleman Collection; Charles Young to Ada Young, 9 April 1921, Coleman Collection.

29. Charles Young to Ada Young, 1 November 1920, Coleman Collection; Charles Young to Ada Young, 6 December 1920, Coleman Collection; Charles Young to Ada Young, 9 April 1921, Coleman Collection; Charles Young to Ada Young, 8 March 1921, Coleman Collection.

30. Entry for 23 April 1950, Rayford Logan Diary Rayford Logan Papers, Library of Congress, Washington, D.C.; Charles Young to W. E. B., Du Bois, 20 July 1920, Du Bois Papers; Charles Young to Ada Young, 1 November 1920, Coleman Collection; Charles Young to Ada Young, 12 February 1921, Coleman Collection; W. E. B. Du Bois, *Darkwater: Voices from Within the Veil* (New York, 1920); David Levering Lewis, *W. E. B. Du Bois: The Fight for Equality and the American Century, 1919–1963* (New York, 2000), 11–23.

31. Ada Young to Arminta Young, 27 November 1920, Young Papers Uncataloged; Charles Young to Arminta Young, 26 August 1920, Coleman Collection; Charles Young to Ada Young, 18 December 1920, Coleman Collection; Ada Young to Arminta Young, 26 January 1921, Young Papers Uncataloged; Ada Young to

Arminta Young, 24 April 1920, Young Papers Uncatalogued, Ada Young to Charles Young, 20 November 1921, Coleman Collection; Charles Young to Charles Noel Young, 4 January 1921, Coleman Collection.

32. Ada Young to Arminta Young, 26 January 1921, Young Papers Uncatalogued; Ada Young to Charles Young, 12 1921, Coleman Collection; Charles Young to Ada Young, March 12, 1921, Coleman Collection; Ada Young to Charles Young, 20 November 1921, Coleman Collection; Charles Young to Ada Young, 18 March 1921, Coleman Collection; Charles Young to Ada Young, 9 April 1921, Coleman Collection; Charles Young to Ada Young, 18 December 1920, Coleman Collection; Charles Young to Ada Young, 10 February 1921, Coleman Collection; Charles Young to Arminta Young, 12 December 1918, Coleman Collection.

33. Charles Young to Arminta Young, 26 August 1920, Coleman Collection; Charles Young to Ada Young, 9 April 1921, Coleman Collection; Charles Young to Ada Young, 31 April 1921, Coleman Collection; Ellis Wood to Ada Young, 21 August 1920, Young Papers; William Hass to Ada Young, 22 October 1920, Young Papers; Charles Young to William Broad, 12 October 1921, Young File MSRC; Ada Young to John J. Pershing, 12 October 1921, Pershing Papers.

34. Charles Young to Adjutant General's Office, 4 June 1912, MID; W. E. B. Du Bois to Charles Young, 18 May 1921, Du Bois Papers; Charles Young to Ada Young, 31 July 1921, Coleman Collection; Colonel M.C. Buckley to Major W. A. Copthorne, 11 July 1921, MID; Ada Young to Arminta Young, 21 September 1921, Young Papers Uncatalogued; Charles Young to William Broad, 12 October 1921, Young File MSRC; Ada Young to John J. Pershing, 12 October 1921, Pershing Papers; Charles Young to Adjutant General's Office, 5 November 1912, MID; Colonel Marlborough Churchill to Charles Young, 17 December 1921, MID.

35. Binder, Volume 3, Nigeria, Political, 24 November 1919, Young Papers Uncatalogued; Colonel S. Heintzelman to Ada Young, 30 January 1922, MID; Joseph L. Johnson to the Secretary of State, 27 January 1922, MID; Joseph L. Johnson to Ada Young, 5 July 1922, MID; Captain Harry Atwood, U.S.A., quoted in Brown, "Eleven Men of West Point," 152; Josiah Massaquoi to Ada Young, 14 January 1922, Coleman Collection; Charles Young Diary, Part IV, Coleman Collection; Murray Sawyer to Ada Young, 22 August 1922, Coleman Collection; "Colonel Charles Young" West Africa (22 February 1922): 136.

36. Joseph L. Johnson to the Secretary of State, with attachments, 27 January 1922, MID; Charles Young to Bank of British West Africa, Monrovia, 26 December 1921, Coleman Collection; "The Desert and the Solitary Place," Notes on the life of Charles Young by Ada Young, 1922, Coleman Collection; "Colonel Charles Young," West Africa, (22 February 1922): 136.

37. Arminta Young to W. E. B. Du Bois, January 13 February 1922, Du Bois Papers; Ada Young to John Wilson, 22 February 1922, Coleman Collection; Memorandum for the Adjutant General's Office prepared by Colonel S. Heintzelman, General Staff, 13 January 1922, MID; Colonel S. Heintzelman to Ada Young, 17 January 1922, MID; Ada Young to Colonel S. Heintzelman, November [n.d.] 1922, MID; New York Times, 12 September 1922, 32, 34; New York Times, 13 September 1922, 20, 23.

38. Ada Young to John Wilson, 22 February 1922, Coleman Collection; Charles Young to Ada Young, 17 July 1916, Coleman Collection; Ada Young to Charles Young, 15 November 1921, Coleman Collection; Ada Young Diary, 1 January 1923, Coleman Collection.

39. Lieutenant Colonel E. S. Fries to Ada Young, 21 November 1922, MID; Ada Young to Colonel S. Heintzelman, 19 July 1922, MID; W. E. B. Du Bois to Ada Young, 12 April 1923, Du Bois Papers; Ada Young to W. E. B. Du Bois, 10 July 1924, Du Bois Papers; W. E. B. Du Bois to Ada Young, July 1924, Du Bois Papers.

40. W. E. B. Du Bois to James Weldon Johnson, 14 March 1924, Du Bois Papers; N.A.A.C.P. Press Release, 18 April 1924, Du Bois Papers; Walter White to Charles Brand, 21 April 1924, Du Bois Papers; Charles Brand to Walter White, 24 April 1924, Du Bois Papers; W. E. B. Du Bois to Charles Brand, 14 April 1924, Du Bois Papers.

41. W. E. B. Du Bois, "Colonel Young," *The Crisis* (February 1922).

42. Rayford W. Logan, *The Negro in the United States,* vol. I (New York, 1970), 73; *Cleveland Union,* 21 January 1922, 1; *New York Times,* 13 January 1922, 13; Pearl Shorter Smith to Ada Young, 15 February 1922, Coleman Collection; John W. Weeks to Melvin R. Davis, 10 February 1922, MID; Nathum Daniel Brascher to James Weldon Johnson, 6 February 1922, N.A.A.C.P. Papers, James Weldon Johnson to Nathum Daniel Brascher, 15 February 1922, N.A.A.C.P. Papers; Nathum Daniel Brascher to Ada Young, 1 April 1922, Du Bois Papers, Library of Congress, Washington, D.C. [hereinafter NAACP Papers]; Message from Ada Young to be read on the occasion of Memorial Services to Colonel Charles Young, 12 March 1922, Du Bois Papers.

43. H. J. Conner to Ada Young, 3 March 1922, Du Bois Papers; "The Desert and the Solitary Place," Notes on the life of Charles Young by Ada Young, 1922, Coleman Collection; U.S. Department of State Memorandum, prepared by William R. Castle for Colonel Marlborough Churchill, 1 April 1922, MID; Office of the Quartermaster General Memorandum, 3 May 1923, Charles Young File, Records of the Office of the Quartermaster General, Cemeterial Files 1915–1939, Record Group 92, National Archives II, College Park, Md. [hereinafter Burial File].

44. W. E. B. Du Bois to Ada Young, 26 June 1922, Du Bois Papers; Ada Young to W. A. Hamilton, n.d., 1923, Burial File; Solomon Porter Hood to Secretary of State, 18 June 1922, MID; Office of the Quartermaster General Memorandum, 17 July 1923, Burial File; Nancy G. Heinl, "Col. Charles Young: Pointman," *Army Magazine* 27 (March 1977): 34; H. J. Conner to Henry O. Lewis, 16 May 1923, Burial File.

45. *Cleveland Union,* 19 May 1923, 1; William Service Bell to James Weldon Johnson, 14 May 1923, N.A.A.C.P. Papers; *New York World,* May 28 1923, clipping in N.A.A.C.P. Papers; Fred E. Sladen to Ada Young, 21 June 1923, Coleman Collection; Text of Teddy Roosevelt, Jr., Address reprinted in Chew, *Biography of Charles Young,* 8–9.

46. *Washington Evening Star,* 1 June 1922, article reprinted in Chew, *Biography of Charles Young,* 11; *New York Times,* 2 June 1923, 11; E. H. Lawson, "One Out of Twelve Million: Unrevealed Facts in the Life Story of Col. Charles Young, West Pointer." *Washington Post,* May 26, 1929, 14.

47. *Washington Evening Star,* 1 June 1922, article reprinted in Chew, *Biography of Charles Young,* 11–12.

48. Ada Young Diary, n.d., summer 1923, Coleman Collection; *Washington Evening Star,* 1 June 1922, article reprinted in Chew, *Biography of Charles Young,* 12.

49. W. E. B. Du Bois, "Charles Young," *The Crisis* (July 1923).

50. Countee Cullen, *Color* (New York, 1925).

Epilogue

All his life Charles Young had struggled against those who judged him by the color of his skin; "this dusky son of America has done his damnedest to win out and show that he is worth while." His perseverance and determination in the face of adversity are at the core of his legacy. One of his oft-repeated personal mottos "what you got in your noggin no one can take from you" reflects his other great legacy, the promotion of education and intellectual pursuits as vital tools in the fight against prejudice. In addition to the material possessions he passed on to his children, Youngsholm for example was left in trust to them, Young instilled in Tonton and Kikik a passion for education and music. Like his father, Charles Noel had a gift for languages, eventually adding Russian to the French he had absorbed during eight years in Europe. Marie trained as a concert pianist, working with renowned instructors in Belgium and France. The death of their father when they were just 17 and 13, respectively, clearly took its toll on their young lives however. Tonton for one was extremely depressed for a long time thereafter.[1]

Charles Noel spent much of his early adulthood seeking direction in life. He earned a degree in agriculture from Ohio State University and briefly contemplated following his father's advice to pursue an agricultural career in Latin America. He opted instead to spend some time in the 1930s working as an agricultural advisor in the Soviet Union's collectivization program. Like many left-wing idealists who followed a similar path, his utopian vision of Soviet Russia soon evaporated and he returned with his Russian wife to the United States where he became a professor of languages, teaching French and Russian at Central State College in Wilberforce. Marie, too, struggled to find her niche, particularly after failing to gain admission to the Julliard School in 1930. After graduating from Wittenberg College she married and moved to the South, but it was an unhappy period and she returned to Wilberforce to teach music at the university her father had served for so many years.[2]

Ada, meanwhile, never quite adjusted to life without Charles and struggled financially for years after her husband's passing. She brought the children home from Europe to finish their education in the United States, and she and Charles's mother, Arminta, took on the management of the house and farm themselves. When Arminta fell seriously ill in 1927, Ada devoted most of her time to caring for her aged mother-in-law, and the farm became a "white elephant." She eventually took a job at Wilberforce University and, after Arminta's death in 1933 at the age of 94 and the children's graduation from college her financial situation gradually improved. She remained a widow, unable to "give up the memory of my kind husband for anyone else," until her death in 1953 when she was reunited with him in Arlington Cemetery 30 years after he was laid to rest.[3]

Many of those 30 years were spent honoring Charles Young's memory. With the help of Du Bois and the NAACP, Ada continued to campaign into the 1930s to have her husband's pension increased and to compel the government to acknowledge that Young had been "deprived of his rank of General." Despite a personal audience with President Harding following her husband's funeral, her efforts in this regard bore little fruit. She also worked with Harry Atwood and members of the Omega Psi Phi fraternity to raise money to erect a memorial headstone at Young's gravesite in Arlington. But her greatest efforts were reserved for the goal of having "Col. Young's life written and published . . . in order that justice be done to him." Her greatest hope in this regard was Du Bois, who promised to undertake the task. Although Du Bois worked with Ada to gather materials for the project, and even floated the proposal to the University of North Carolina Press in 1940 as one of relevance "not simply to American Negroes but to American whites," the proposed biography was never added to his enormous body of work. Howard University history professor Benjamin Brawley sought to include a work on Young in the Negro History Biography series, and Carter Woodson, the doyen of Negro history, at one point contemplated the task of treating the life of this "man who made history." For one reason or another none of these projects ever came to fruition, however, and the idea lived on only as a family pipe dream after Ada's death.[4]

Although the biography never made it into print, Young's legacy was preserved in other ways. Some of Young's Wilberforce students, such as Harry Atwood, forged successful careers in the officer corps of the United States Army; one of his most notable protégés, Benjamin O. Davis, Sr., achieved the coveted goal that had so cruelly eluded Young, becoming in

1941 the first Black general in America's history. In 1936 Davis's son, Benjamin, Jr., became the first African American to graduate from the United States Military Academy since Charles Young did so in 1889, a development that is inextricably linked to Young's role as mentor to his father. Many other Wilberforce students and NCOs in the army who were tutored, advised, and encouraged by Young sought to emulate him in the regular army or as volunteers in the Spanish-American War, the Philippine campaign, and World War I. In addition, there were countless young African American men who had never known or served with Young, but for whom his bravery and fortitude were nonetheless inspirational.

As late as 1948 annual services were being held throughout the United States to commemorate his birthday, and in 1964 the centennial of his birth was celebrated by a number of the 16 American Legion Posts across the country that bear his name. Only John F. Kennedy, after whom 15 posts are named, rivals Young for this honor. In 1944 a six-and-a-half-acre playground was opened in Harlem and named in his honor; a square and park in Cleveland, a street in Allensworth, California, and a number of elementary and grade schools in various parts of the country are also named after him. There are numerous organizations, from Buffalo Soldiers societies to the Omega Psi Phi fraternity, that continue to pay tribute in a variety of ways to Charles Young and his legacy. Some of the values that Young most emphasized in life—patriotism, duty, service, education, equality—are echoed in the function or goals of many of the institutions that carry his name. They represent just some of the branches of the "tree with tongues" that Countee Cullen predicted would spring from Young's memory.

NOTES

1. Charles Young Diary, Part II, Coleman Collection, Akron, Ohio; Charles Noel Young to Ada Young, 19 December 1923, Coleman Collection.

2. W. E. B. Du Bois to Theodore Roosevelt, Jr., 17 December 1929, Du Bois Papers, University of Massachusetts, Amherst, Mass. [hereinafter Du Bois Papers]; Charles Burroughs to Ada Young, 2 July 1931, Charles Young Papers National Afro-American Museum and Cultural Center, Wilberforce, Ohio [hereinafter Young Papers]; Marie Young to John Erskine, 8 February 1930, Arthur B. Spingarn Papers, Moorland Spingarn Research Center, Howard University, Washington, D.C.

3. Ada Young to W. E. B. Du Bois, 7 October 1924, Du Bois Papers, University of Massachusetts, Amherst, Mass.; Application for Reimbursement by Ada Young, n.d., January 1934, Pension Records for Gabriel Young, Old Military and Civil Records, National Archives, Washington, D.C.; Ada Young to Du Bois, 20 January 1928, Du Bois Papers; Ada Young to Arminta Young, 30 July 1921, Uncataloged Boxes, Charles Young Papers National Afro-American Museum and Cultural Center, Wilberforce, Ohio [hereinafter Young Papers uncatalogued]; Lt. Colonel D.C. Hughes to Charles Noel Young, 27 March 1956, Young Papers Uncatalogued.

4. W. E. B. Du Bois to Ada Young, 24 September 1924, Du Bois Papers; Ada Young Diary, n.d., summer 1923, Coleman Collection, Akron, Ohio; W. E. B. Du Bois to W. T. Couch, 30 September 1940, Du Bois Papers; Ada Young to Benjamin Brawley, 26 March 1933, Benjamin Brawley Papers, Moorland Spingarn Research Center, Howard University, Washington, D.C. [hereinafter Brawley Papers]; Carter Woodson to Benjamin Brawley, 27 August 1933, Brawley Papers.

Bibliography

MANUSCRIPT COLLECTIONS

Newton D. Baker Papers, Library of Congress, Washington, D.C.

Benjamin Brawley Papers, Moorland Spingarn Research Center, Howard University, Washington, D.C.

Asa A. Bushnell Papers, Ohio State Historical Society, Columbus, Ohio.

Benjamin O. Davis Papers, United States Military History Institute, Carlisle, Pa.

Caroline Bond Day Papers, Peabody Museum, Harvard University, Cambridge, Mass.

W. E. B. Du Bois Papers, University of Massachusetts, Amherst, Mass.

Marvin E. Fletcher Collection, United States Military History Institute, Carlisle, Pa.

T. Montgomery Gregory Papers, Moorland Spingarn Research Center, Howard University, Washington, D.C.

Rayford Logan Papers, Library of Congress, Washington, D.C.

George A. Myers Papers, Ohio State Historical Society, Columbus, Ohio.

National Association for the Advancement of Colored People Papers, Library of Congress, Washington, D.C.

John J. Pershing Papers, Library of Congress, Washington, D.C.

Charles Dudley Rhodes, "Diary Notes of a Soldier," United States Military Academy, West Point, N.Y.

William Sanders Scarborough Papers, Wilberforce University, Wilberforce, Ohio.

Spanish-American War, Philippine Insurrection, and Boxer Rebellion Veteran Research Project, United States Military History Institute, Carlisle, Pa.

Arthur B. Spingarn Papers, Moorland Spingarn Research Center, Howard University, Washington, D.C.

Joel E. Spingarn Papers, Moorland Spingarn Research Center, Howard University, Washington, D.C.

Oswald Garrison Villard Papers, Houghton Library, Harvard University, Cambridge, Mass.

Booker T. Washington Papers, Library of Congress, Washington, D.C.

Carter Woodson Papers, Library of Congress, Washington, D.C.

Charles Young File, Fort Huachaca Museum, Fort Huachaca, Ariz.

Charles Young File, Moorland Spingarn Research Center, Howard University, Washington, D.C.

Charles Young File, Private Collection of John H. Motley, Hartford, Conn.

Charles Young File, Ripley Museum, Ripley, Ohio.

Charles Young File, United States Military Academy, West Point, N.Y.

Charles Young File, Wilberforce University, Wilberforce, Ohio.

Charles Young Papers, Coleman Family Collection, Akron, Ohio.

Charles Young Papers, National Afro-American Museum and Cultural Center, Wilberforce, Ohio.

U.S. GOVERNMENT DOCUMENTS

U.S. Army, Letters received by the Appointment, Commission, and Personal Branch, Records of the Adjutant General's Office, Record Group 94, National Archives, Washington, D.C.

U.S. Army, Office of the Quartermaster General, Cemeterial Files 1915–1939, Record Group 92, National Archives II, College Park, Md.

U.S. Army, Post Returns, Records of the Adjutant General's Office, 1780–1917, Record Group 94, National Archives, Washington, D.C.

U.S. Army, Records of the U.S. Army Mobile Units, Record Group 391, National Archives, Washington, D.C.

U.S. Army, Regimental Book Records of the Ninth Ohio Battalion, Spanish-American War, Records of the Adjutant General's Office, Record Group 94, National Archives, Washington, D.C.

U.S. Department of State, Diplomatic Instructions of the Department of State, 1801–1906, Haiti and Santo Domingo, Record Group 59, National Archives II, College Park, Md.

U.S. Department of State, Dispatches from the Legation, Haiti, Record Group 84, National Archives II, College Park, Md.

U.S. Department of State, Dispatches from U.S. Ministers to Haiti, 1862–1906, Record Group 59, National Archives II, College Park, Md.

U.S. Department of State, Miscellaneous Letters from Legation, Haiti, Record Group 84, National Archives II, College Park, Md.

U.S. Department of State, Records of the Department of State Relating to the Internal Affairs of Liberia, 1910–1929, Record Group 59, National Archives II, College Park, Md.

U.S. Department of War, Military Information Division, General Correspondence, 1917–1941, National Archives II, College Park, Md.

U.S. Department of War, Military Information Division, General Correspondence, 1917–1941, Record Group 165, National Archives II, College Park, Md.

U.S. Department of War, Military Information Division, 1904–1906, Office of the General Staff, Army War College, Record Group 165, National Archives, Washington, D.C.

U.S. Department of War, Military Intelligence Branch, Correspondence regarding Negro troops, 1917–1924, Record Group 165, National Archives II, College Park, Md.

U.S. Department of War, War College Division, General Staff, General Correspondence, Record Group 164, National Archives, Washington, D.C.

U.S. National Park Service, Reports of the Acting Superintendent of Sequoia and General Grant National Parks, Sequoia and Kings Canyon Museum, Three Rivers, Calif.

U.S. GOVERNMENT PUBLICATIONS

U.S. Army, Office of the Chief of Military History, *American Military History: Army Historical Series* (Washington, D.C.: Government Printing Office, 1989).

U.S. Department of State, *Papers Relating to the Foreign Relations of the United States, 1908–1922* (Washington, D.C.: Government Printing Office).

U.S. Military Academy, *Fifty-Third Annual Report of the Association of Graduates of the United States Military Academy* (West Point, N.Y.: U.S. Military Academy, 1922).

U.S. Military Academy, *Official Register of the Officers and Cadets of the United States Military Academy*, (West Point, N.Y.: U.S. Military Academy, 1886).

U.S. National Park Service, *Civil War Soldier and Sailor System*, http:www.itd.nps.gov/cwss/

U.S. Senate, "Report of Affairs in Liberia," *U.S. Senate Document* 457, 61st Congress, 2nd Session (Washington, D.C.: Government Printing Office, 1910).

MEMOIRS AND AUTOBIOGRAPHIES

Flipper, Henry Osian. *The Colored Cadet: The Autobiography of Henry Osian Flipper, U.S.A.* Edited by Quintard Taylor, Jr. Lincoln, Neb.: University of Nebraska Press, 1998.

Parker, John B. *His Promised Land: The Autobiography of John B. Parker, Former Slave and Conductor on the Underground Railroad.* Edited by Stuart Seely Sprague. New York: Norton, 1996.

Rodney, George Brydges. *As a Cavalryman Remembers.* Caldwell, Idaho: Caxton Printers, 1944.

Schuyler, George S. *Black and Conservative: The Autobiography of George S. Schuyler.* New Rochelle, N.Y.: Arlington House Publishers, 1966.

Stevens, Walter J. *Chip on My Shoulder.* Boston: Meador Publishing Company, 1946.

Tompkins, Frank. *Chasing Villa: The Last Campaign of the U.S. Cavalry.* Harrisburg, Pa.: Military Service Publishing Company, 1934.

PUBLISHED DOCUMENTS

Harlan, Louis R., ed. *The Papers of Booker T. Washington,* 14 volumes. Champaign, Ill.: University of Illinois Press, 1975.

Link, Arthur S., ed. *The Papers of Woodrow Wilson,* 69 volumes. Princeton, N.J.: Princeton University Press, 1987.

MacGregor, Morris, and Bernard C. Nalty, eds. *Blacks in the United States Army: Basic Documents,* 13 volumes. Wilmington, Del.: Scholarly Resources, 1977.

Moon, Henry Lee, ed. *The Emerging Thought of W. E. B. Du Bois: Essays and Editorials from The Crisis.* New York: Simon and Schuster, 1972.

Morison, Elting E., ed. *The Letters of Theodore Roosevelt,* 8 volumes. Cambridge, Mass.: Harvard University Press, 1952.

Romero, Patricia W. *I Too Am an American: Documents from 1619 to the Present.* New York: Publishers Company, Inc. 1968.

Wilson, Woodrow. War and Peace: Presidential Messages, Addresses, and Public Papers (1917–1924). 2 volumes. Ed. Ray Stannard Baker and William E. Dodd. (New York: Harper and Brothers Publishers, 1970).

NEWSPAPERS AND PERIODICALS

The Army and Navy Journal.
The Chicago Defender.
The Cleveland Advocate.
The Cleveland Gazette.
The Union (Cleveland).
The Crisis.
The New York Evening Post.
The New York Times.
The New York Post-Gazette.
The Ohio Journal.
The Ripley Bee.
The Washington Post.
West Africa.

BOOKS

Ambrose, Stephen. *Duty Honor Country: A History of West Point.* Baltimore: Johns Hopkins University Press, 1966.

Barbeau, Arthur E. and Florette Henri. *The Unknown Soldiers: Black American Troops in World War I.* Philadelphia: Temple University Press, 1974.

Bidwell, Bruce W. *History of the Military Intelligence Division, Department of the Army General Staff: 1775–1941.* Lanham, Md.: University Press of America, 1986.

Buckley, Gail. *American Patriots: The Story of Blacks in the Military From Revolution to Desert Storm.* New York: Random House, 2001.

Broadstone, M. A., ed. *History of Greene County, Ohio: Its People Industries and Institutions,* II. Indianapolis: B. F. Bowen and Company, 1918.

Brown, Hallie Q. *Pen Pictures of Pioneers of Wilberforce.* Xenia: Aldin Publishing Company, 1937.

Carroll, John M., ed. *The Black Military Experience in the American West.* New York: Liveright, 1973.

Chambers, John Whitelaw II, ed. *The Oxford Companion to American Military History.* New York: Oxford University Press, 1999.

Chew, Abraham. *A Biography of Colonel Charles Young.* Washington, D.C.: R. L. Pendleton, 1923.

Clendenen, Clarence C. *Blood on the Border: The United States Army and the Mexican Irregulars.* New York: MacMillan, 1969.

Coffman, Edward M. *The Old Army: A Portrait of the American Army in Peacetime, 1784–1898.* New York: Oxford University Press 1986.

Cullen, Countee. *Color.* New York: Harper and Brothers, Publishers, 1925.

Cuney-Hare, Maud. *Negro Musicians and Their Music.* Washington, D.C.: Associated Publishers, 1936.

Dilsaver, Larry M., and William C. Tweed. *Challenge of the Big Trees of Sequoia and Kings Canyon National Parks.* Three Rivers, Calif.: Sequoia Natural History Association, 1990.

Downing, Henry F. *The American Cavalryman: A Liberian Romance.* College Park, Md.: McGrath Publishing Company, 1969.

Du Bois, W. E. B. *Darkwater: Voices from Within the Veil.* New York: Harcourt, Brace and Howe, 1920.

Du Bois, W. E. B. *Dusk of Dawn: An Essay Towards an Autobiography of a Race Concept.* New York: Harcourt, Brace and World, Inc., 1940.

Dreer, Herman. *American Literature by Negro Authors.* New York: MacMillan, 1950.

Fletcher, Marvin E. *America's First Black General: Benjamin O. Davis Sr., 1880–1970.* Lawrence, Kans.: University Press of Kansas, 1989.

Fletcher, Marvin E. *The Negro Soldier and Officer in the United States Army. 1891–1917.* Columbia, Mo.: University of Missouri Press, 1974.

Foner, Eric. *Reconstruction: America's Unfinished Revolution, 1863–1877.* New York: Harper and Row, 1988.

Forman, Sidney. *West Point: A History of the United States Military Academy.* New York: Columbia University Press, 1950.

Gatewood, Willard B. Jr. *Aristocrats of Color: The Black Elite, 1880- 1920.* Fayetteville, Ark.: University of Arkansas Press, 2000.

Gatewood, Willard B. Jr. *"Smoked Yankees," and the Struggle for Empire: Letters from Negro Soldiers, 1898–1902.* Urbana, Ill.: University of Illinois Press, 1971.

Gill, Robert L. *The Omega Psi Phi Fraternity and the Men Who Made Its History: A Concise History.* Washington, D.C.: Omega Psi Phi, 1977.

Glatthaar, Joseph T. *Forged in Battle: The Civil War Alliance of Black Soldiers and White Officers.* New York: Meridian, 1990.

Greene, Robert E. *Black Defenders of America, 1775–1973.* Chicago: Johnson Publications, 1974.

Greene, Robert E. *Colonel Charles Young: Soldier and Diplomat.* Washington, D.C.: Robert E. Greene, 1985.

Greene, Robert E. *The Early Life of Colonel Charles Young, 1864–1889.* Washington, D.C.: Student Publication Series, Howard University, 1973.

Haley, Edward P. *Revolution and Intervention: The Diplomacy of Taft and Wilson in Mexico, 1910–1917.* Cambridge, Mass.: MIT Press, 1970.

Hart, Herbert M. *Old Forts of the Far West.* Seattle: Superior Publishing Company, 1965.

Heinl, Robert Debs, and Nancy Gordon Heinl. *Written in Blood: The Story of the Haitian People, 1492–1995.* Lanham, Md.: University Press of America, 1996.

Henri, Florette. *Black Migration: Movement North, 1900–1920.* Garden City, N.Y.: Anchor Press/Doubleday, 1975.

Jordan, William G. *Black Newspapers and America's War for Democracy, 1914–1920.* Chapel Hill, N.C.: University of North Carolina Press, 2001

Kenner, Charles L. *Buffalo Soldiers and Officers of the Ninth Cavalry, 1867–1898: Black and White Together.* Norman, Okla.: University of Oklahoma Press, 1995.

Leckie, William H. *The Buffalo Soldiers: A Narrative of the Negro Cavalry in the West.* Norman, Okla.: University of Oklahoma Press, 1967.

Lewis, David Levering. *W. E. B. Du Bois: Biography of a Race, 1868- 1919.* New York: Henry Holt, 1993.

Lewis, David Levering. *W. E. B. Du Bois: The Fight for Equality and the American Century, 1919–1963.* New York: Henry Holt, 2000.

Link, Arthur S. *Wilson: Confusions and Crises, 1915–1916.* Princeton, N.J.: Princeton University Press, 1964.

Logan, Rayford W. *The Negro in the United States,* vol. I. New York: Van Nostrand Reinhold Company, 1970.

Logan, Rayford W., and Michael R. Winston, eds. *Dictionary of American Negro Biography.* New York: Norton, 1985.

Marszalek, John F. *Assault at West Point: The Court-Martial of Johnson Whittaker.* New York: Collier Books, 1994.

Miller, Nathan. *Theodore Roosevelt: A Life.* New York: William Morrow, 1992.

Miller, Stuart Creighton. *"Benevolent Assimilation": The American Conquest of the Philippines, 1899–1903.* New Haven, Conn.: Yale University Press, 1982.

Nalty, Bernard. *Strength for the Fight: A History of Black Americans in the Military.* New York: The Free Press, 1986.

Pappas, George S. *To the Point: The United States Military Academy, 1802–1902.* Westport, Conn., 1993.

Patton, Gerald W. *War and Race: The Black Officer in the American Military, 1915–1941.* Westport, Conn.: Greenwood Press, 1981.

Pusateri, Samuel J., and John R. White. *Sequoia and Kings Canyon National Parks.* Palo Alto, Calif.: Stanford University Press, 1952.

Schubert, Frank N. *Buffalo Soldiers, Braves and the Brass: The Story of Fort Robinson, Nebraska.* Shippensburg, Pa.: White Mane Publishing Company, 1993.

Schubert, Frank N., ed. *On the Trail of the Buffalo Soldier: Biographies of African Americans in the U.S. Army, 1866–1917.* Wilmington, Del.: Scholarly Resources, 1995.

Scott, Emmett J. *Scott's Official History of the Negro in the World War.* Chicago: Homewood Press, 1919.

Spradling, Mary Mace. *In Black and White: A Guide to Magazine Articles, Newspaper Articles, and Books Concerning More than 15,000 Black Individuals and Groups,* 3rd ed., II. Detroit: Gale Research Company, 1980.

Steward, T. G. *The Colored Regulars in the United States Army.* New York: Arno Press, 1969.

Stivers, Eliese Bambach. *Ripley, Ohio: Its History and Families.* Ripley: Ripley Historical Committee, 1965.

Vagts, Alfred. *The Military Attaché.* Princeton, N.J.: Princeton University Press, 1967.

Young, Charles. *The Military Morale of Nations and Races.* Kansas City: Franklin Hudson Publishing Company, 1912.

ARTICLES

Bethel, Elizabeth, "The Military Intelligence Division: Origin of the Intelligence Division." *Military Affairs* 11 (spring 1947): 17–24.

Bowles, Emma Castleman. "Concerning the Origin of Wilberforce." *Journal of Negro History* 8 (July 1923): 335–37.

Brown, Wesley. "Eleven Men of West Point." *Negro History Bulletin,* (April 1956) 147–57.

"A Chronicle of Race Relations." *Phylon* 2 (winter 1941): 76–90.

Clegg, Claude. "'A Splendid Type of Colored American': Charles Young and the Reorganization of the Liberian Frontier Force." *International Journal of African Historical Studies* 29 (winter 1996): 47–70.

Coleman, Ronald. "The Buffalo Soldiers: Guardians of the Utah Frontier, 1886–1901." *Utah Historical Quarterly* 47 (fall 1979): 420–39.

Du Bois, W. E. B. "The Future of Wilberforce University." *Journal of Negro Education* 9 (October 1940): 553–70.

Fletcher, Marvin. "The Black Volunteers in the Spanish American War." *Military Affairs* 38 (April 1974): 48–53.

Foster, Robert. "Buffalo Soldiers in the Utah Territory." *Wild West* 12 (February 2000): 1–7.

Gatewood, Willard B. Jr. "Black Americans and the Quest For Empire, 1898–1903." *Journal of Southern History* 38 (November 1972): 545–66.

Gatewood, Willard B. Jr. "John Hanks Alexander of Arkansas: Second Black Graduate of West Point." *Arkansas Historical Quarterly* 41 (summer 1982): 103–28.

Gatewood, Willard B. Jr. "Ohio's Negro Battalion in the Spanish American War." *Northeast Ohio Quarterly* 45 (1973): 55–66.

Giffen, William W. "Mobilization of Black Militiamen in World War I: Ohio's Ninth Battalion." *Historian* 40 (fall 1978): 686–703.

Heinl, Nancy G. "Col. Charles Young: Pointman." *Army Magazine* 27 (March 1977): 30–34.

Howard, Victor B. "The Civil War in Kentucky: The Slave Claims His Freedom." *Journal of Negro History* 67 (autumn 1982): 245–56.

Hustlar, Donald A., and David A. Simmons. "Taking the Waters: Xenia Springs in 1853." *Timeline* (November/December 1999): 36–39.

Katz, Friedrich. "Pancho Villa and the Attack on Columbus, New Mexico." *American Historical Review* 83 (February 1978): 101–30.

Killian, Lewis G. "Generals, The Talented Tenth, and Affirmative Action." *Society* 36 (September/October 1999): 32–40.

Lawson, E. H. "One Out of Twelve Million: Unrevealed Facts in the Life Story of Col. Charles Young, West Pointer." *Washington Post,* May 26, 1929, 11, 14.

Ngozi-Brown, Scott. "African-American Soldiers and Filipinos: Racial Imperialism, Jim Crow and Social Relations." *Journal of Negro History* 82 (winter 1997) 42–54.

Norvell, Stanley B., and William M. Tuttle, Jr. "Views of the Negro During the 'Red Summer' of 1919." *Journal of Negro History* 51 (July 1966): 209–18.

Pierce, Lucy France. "Shoulder Straps for Colored Men." *Leslie's Illustrated Weekly Newspaper* 125 (October 13, 1917): 512–14.

Purnell, John H. "Colonel Charles Young, U.S.A.: Soldier, Diplomat, Philanthropist, Man of Culture." *Oracle* (winter 1979): 5–8.

Reddick, L. D. "The Negro Policy of the United States Army, 1775–1945." *Journal of Negro History* 34 (January 1949): 9–29.

Robinson, Michael C., and Frank N. Schubert. "David Fagen: An Afro-American Rebel in the Philippines, 1899–1901." *Pacific Historical Review* 44, no. 1 (1975): 68–81.

Smith, Gene. "A Fighting Man." *American Legacy* (spring 1998): 12–14.

Spivey, Mary Elizabeth. "Colonel Charles Young." *Negro History Bulletin* (May 1942): 185–86.

Sprague, Stuart Seely. "More African-Americans Speak: The New Mother Lode." *Journal of Negro History* 78 (autumn 1993): 258–65.

Suggs, Henry Lewis. "The Response of the African-American Press to the United States Occupation of Haiti, 1915–1934." *Journal of Negro History* 73 (spring/fall 1988): 33–45.

Tweed, William C. "Captain Charles Young: Military Superintendent of Sequoia National Park, 1903." www.nps.gov/seki/young.htm.

Young, Paul. "John Parker: Ripley's Black Abolitionist." *Ohio Southland* (winter 1990): 4–12.

UNPUBLISHED MATERIALS

Kilroy, David P. "Extending the American Sphere to West Africa: Dollar Diplomacy in Liberia, 1908–1926." Ph.D. Dissertation, University of Iowa, 1995.

Shellum, Brian. "Captain Charles Young in Hispaniola, 1904–1907: Point Man for an Invasion." Paper presented at U.S. Army History Conference, Washington, D.C., summer 1998.

Shellum, Brian. "Charles Young in Liberia, 1912–1915: Man With Two Missions." Paper presented at Annual Meeting of the Society for Military History, Pennsylvania State University, April 15–18, 1999.

Index

About the Author

DAVID P. KILROY is Associate Professor of History at Wheeling Jesuit University. He holds a Ph.D. from the University of Iowa and an M.A. from University College Dublin. This is his first book.